Christopher J. Fagan

Everyman, I will go with thee, and be thy guide,
In thy most need to go by thy side.

This is No. 953 of Everyman's Library. A
list of authors and their works in this series
will be found at the end of this volume. The
publishers will be pleased to send freely to all
applicants a separate, annotated list of the
Library.

J. M. DENT & SONS LIMITED
10–13 BEDFORD STREET LONDON W.C.2

E. P. DUTTON & CO. INC.
286–302 FOURTH AVENUE
NEW YORK

EVERYMAN'S LIBRARY
EDITED BY ERNEST RHYS

PHILOSOPHY & THEOLOGY

THOMAS AQUINAS
SELECTED WRITINGS EDITED BY
THE REV. FATHER M. C. D'ARCY

THOMAS AQUINAS, born 1225 of noble parents at Roccasecca near Naples. Joined the Dominican Order and became university lecturer at Naples and Cologne. Repeatedly refused high ecclesiastical honours. Died in 1274.

THOMAS AQUINAS

SELECTED WRITINGS

LONDON: J. M. DENT & SONS LTD
NEW YORK: E. P. DUTTON & CO. INC.

PREFACE

To Dante Aristotle was *il maestro di color che sanno*, 'the master of those that know,' but Thomas Aquinas was *fiamma benedetta*, a flame of heavenly wisdom, wiser even than Aristotle. In his very lifetime S. Thomas was known as the Angelic Doctor, and he has held pride of place among Christian thinkers ever since. Born in 1225 he entered the new Order of the Dominicans, was taught by a genius, Albert the Great, went to the University of Paris, the intellectual centre of the world at the time, and captured it by the freshness and wisdom of the views he taught. He died at the early age of forty-nine in the year 1274, and his writings have been accepted ever since without break as the classic expression in philosophy and theology of the Christian faith. The period in which he lived was one which asked for an architectural genius who could co-ordinate the multitudinous ideas, ancient and new, which were stirring men's minds. Christian leaders were settling down to remake a world which had fallen in ruins during the barbarian invasions. A new culture was coming into being; its inspiration was Christian, and its material was provided by Jew and Greek and Roman and Moor. It was now that art and architecture, city and village life, philosophic and theological speculation found their complete expression. The universities received their permanent charters and statutes, common law and jurisprudence took shape in England and France, Chartres and Salisbury Cathedrals were built, S. Francis of Assisi and S. Dominic created the Friars, and S. Louis of France set the pattern of moral kingship. The reflection of this time, and perhaps of all time, is seen in S. Thomas Aquinas. He is the figure chosen out by Dante in the *Paradiso* to sing the glories of truth which stretched from God in His heaven to the abyss, and his fame as a thinker has grown with the ages and is as fresh to-day as it was in his lifetime. The Thomist philosophy flourishes to-day and from all sides its views are

sought out as containing what may be the answer to
the questions of justice, freedom, personality, war, the
sovereignty of the State, and other problems which vex the
modern world.   Other philosophers have made great con-
tributions to the stock of human wisdom, but S. Thomas
with a quiet originality gathered up, at a time when the
tradition still existed and the manuscripts were available,
the wisdom of ancient Greece and Rome and Judaism, and
subsumed it under a Christian philosophy which gave a
pattern to the diverse activities of nature and man.

It is for these reasons that everyman should be
acquainted with Aquinas.   The editor, however, of a
volume in this series has to face special difficulties.   S.
Thomas was a prolific writer.   Though he died at the age
of forty-eight or forty-nine his writings fill thirty-two
volumes of quarto size in double columns of the Vivès
edition.   That would not be an obstacle if there existed
some one book amongst the many he wrote which could
serve to illustrate the essence of his teaching, and at a
length suitable for reproduction in a small volume.   S.
Augustine was an equally prolific writer, but his *Confessions* are the testimony to his genius, and are among the
treasures of literature.   But S. Thomas was not a literary
genius and he wrote no work to correspond with the *Confessions*.   His smaller works deal usually with some knotty
philosophic problem, and would be too dry and incomprehensible for general reading.   His best-known work, the
Summa Theologica, extends to over ten volumes, and it is
impossible to give an idea of the range and depth of it by
extracting any one section of the treatise.   I must warn
readers, also, at this place, not to expect any personal
element in the writings of S. Thomas nor, again, to hope for
brilliant suggestions and persuasive rhetoric.   He has a dry
style, a quiet quasi-mathematical precision suitable to the
method he usually follows, namely, a series of objections
against the view he intends to hold, an exposition of that
view, and then the answer to the objections which have
been raised.

Since no one book can do S. Thomas justice, I have been
forced to pick and choose out of his works a series of
passages which will be sufficiently long and interconnected

to convey the main theme of his philosophy. In the selection made there are examples of his method of argument and the way he arrives at his favourite conclusions. S. Thomas held that there was a sphere of natural reason and, above this, a region known by faith through revelation. Faith, however, is not opposed to reason; its content fulfils the highest of human hopes while surpassing them, and the latter part of this book shows how S. Thomas applied his philosophic principles to the interpretation of Christian doctrine. I cannot claim that this is the best way to introduce S. Thomas to readers, nor that the excerpts chosen are the best possible. Thomist scholars are rightly sensitive for the honour of their master, and therefore I have not relied merely on my own judgment, but sought counsel from those qualified to give it. I owe a special debt of gratitude to the Prior of Blackfriars, Fr Hilary Carpenter, O.P., and the Dominicans of Oxford, and to Heythrop College, Chipping Norton, for their generous co-operation in the composition of this book. The responsibility for it is mine, but, in fact, the scheme adopted was worked out with the help of Fr Gervase Mathew, O.P. Part of the works of S. Thomas have already been translated by the Dominican Fathers, and where it was possible I have used this standard translation by the kind permission of the Very Rev. Bernard Delaney, the Provincial of the Dominicans, and the publishers, Burns, Oates & Washbourne. A few changes have been made in the text to make the sense more easy for those who are not acquainted with technical philosophical language and its difficulties. For the passages from the *De Ente et Essentia*, Sheed & Ward have kindly allowed me the use of Clare C. Riedl's translation first issued by the Thomist school at Toronto. The Office of Corpus Christi is taken from the Marquis of Bute's translation of the Roman Breviary by permission of the executors. A number of passages have been translated for the first time into English, and for the labour involved in this, and for its successful accomplishment, I have to thank the Revs. Gervase Mathew, O.P., and Peter Whitestone, O.P., and the Revs. T. Crehan, S.J., F. Copleston, S.J., A. Stephenson, S.J., and A. Doyle, S.J. I also wish to thank Sir Humphrey Milford and the Oxford University Press for permission to reproduce the bibliography from my book *St. Thomas Aquinas*.

In the scheme adopted the reader ought to be able to follow the main lines of the Thomist philosophy and thus to understand the scope and magnitude of the task he set himself. Both as a philosopher and a Christian thinker S. Thomas is probably unrivalled in the size of his canvas; and as it is the desire of every one to have a complete picture of the meaning of human life, to see its origin and powers and destiny, I have purposely chosen passages which bring out the characteristic features of S. Thomas's map. To make this study of a thinker who rarely unbends a little more easy, I have put at the beginning three of his sermons. The first, for the Feast of S. Martin of Tours, describes the virtues of a saint, and with but little alteration it gives a description of S. Thomas himself. The second sermon, preached on the Feast of All Saints, sums up the ideal always present before S. Thomas in his writings, the ideal of wisdom and of being assimilated to God through knowledge and love. The third sermon is for the Feast of Corpus Christi. S. Thomas wrote, also, the Office for that feast. So well known is the beauty of the *Lauda Sion* and other hymns and prayers in that Office that I have included it in this book. The philosophical writings give no inkling of the poetic genius these hymns reveal. Evidently the Eucharist was a breviary of all his beliefs, and in the sermon, too, the usually cold style takes fire.

After these sermons the subject-matter proper begins with a passage on the true aim of philosophy and the function of the wise man. His object is to see all that is in nature and life co-ordinated and made intelligible by ultimate principles. All that exists or may exist can be graded into ranks which reach up from the bare negation of nothingness to consummate being, and it can be shown that this consummate being must be God, the beginning and end of all. His law directs nature and living things according to their own intrinsic structures, which science investigates, and in rational living beings this direction is made manifest in the moral law. Duty and virtue are the steps and stages in man's perfection, and this perfection is ultimately realized when he is made like to God in wisdom and goodness.

Reason in man provides him with the power of judging himself, being free and knowing reality in truth, and since God is pre-eminently real He cannot be completely unknowable. Since, however, man's knowledge is limited by his nature and finds what is congenial to it in sensible things, it is necessary to inquire into the extent and conditions of our knowledge of the supersensible and of God. A series of passages show how S. Thomas advanced on all previous thinkers in the working out of this problem. The limitations of human thinking explain, too, how S. Thomas is able to pass without a complete break from the realm of natural knowledge to that of faith. The Christian Revelation tells us something new; its mysteries are above reason but do not contradict reason; they can even supplement the weakness inherent in human speculation about 'immortal things.' According to S. Thomas our longing for wisdom and supreme love is carried up higher by the gift of Christ, who has initiated a new life of union with God to be perfected in bliss, in the loving contemplation of God as He is in Himself. The way to this union is by the imitation of Christ and the reception of his grace and life in the Sacraments of the Church. I have tried to give a glimpse of this in the closing selections and ended with what S. Thomas has to say on the greatest Christian virtue, charity.

Such, then, is the scheme of this work. Some of the passages chosen may appear very dry and metaphysical, but I could not omit them, because a profound philosophy is bound to be metaphysical. Some philosophers lead us into a wonderland of their own where everything seems topsy-turvy. The thought of S. Thomas is not like this, and if the reader perseveres he will find that much that he says may sound like enlightened common sense.

M. C. D'ARCY

BIBLIOGRAPHY

Opera Omnia, 25 vols., Parmae, 1862–75; *Opera Omnia*, 34 vols., Paris, ed. Vivès, 1871–80; *Opera Omnia*, Romae, Leonine ed.

LIVES. De Tocco; Toceron, 1737; Bareille, 1846; Joyau, 1886. R. Vaughan, *Life and Labours of St Thomas of Aquino*, 2 vols.; abridged ed., 1 vol. Conway, *St Thomas Aquinas*.

TRANSLATIONS. *Summa Theologica*, translated by members of the Dominican Order, with Introduction; *Summa contra Gentiles*, translated by members of the Dominican Order, with Introduction; *Summa contra Gentiles* translated by J. Rickaby, with notes.

GENERAL WORKS OF REFERENCE. *Acta Hebdomadae Thomisticae*, Rome, 1924. Bäumke, *Beiträge zur Geschichte der Mittelalterlichen Philosophie*. Carra de Vaux, *Avicenne*. De Bruyne, *S. Thomas d'Aquin*, 1928. Descoqs, *Essai critique sur l'hylémorphisme*, 1924. De Wulf, *Histoire de la philosophie médiévale* (trans. 1909); *Scholasticism, Old and New*, 1907. Duhem, *Le Système du monde*, tome v. Durantel, *Le Retour à Dieu par l'intelligence et la volonté dans la philosophie de S. Thomas*. Ehrle, *Der Augustinismus und der Aristotelismus in der Scholastik gegen Ende des XIII Jhdt*. Garrigou-Lagrange, *Le Sens commun*, 1909; *Dieu, son existence et sa nature*, 1915. Gemelli in *S. Tommaso d' Aquino, pubblicazione commemorativa del sesto centenario della canonizzazione*. Gilson, *Le Thomisme; La Philosophie au moyen âge; La Philosophie de S. Bonaventure*. Grabmann, *Die Geschichte der Scholastiken Methode; Thomas Aquinas*, Longmans, 1928. Hauréau, *Histoire de la philosophie scolastique*. Hugon, *Les Vingt-quatre Thèses thomistes*, 1922. Jarrett, Bede, *The English Dominicans*. Kennedy, article 'Thomas Aquinas' in *Catholic Encyclopaedia*. Mandonnet, *Siger de Brabant*. Mandonnet et Destrey, *Bibliographie thomiste*. Maréchal, *Le Point de départ de la métaphysique*, vol. v, 'Le Thomisme.' Maritain, *Réflexions sur l'intelligence; Éléments de philosophie; Mélanges thomistes*. Mercier, *Logique*. Noël, *Notes d'épistémologie thomiste*. Olgiate-Zybura, *The Key to the Study of St Thomas*. Pègues, *Introduction à la philosophie thomiste*. Picavet, *Esquisse d'une histoire générale et comparée des philosophies médiévales*. Poole, *Medieval Thought and Learning*. Rashdall, *Universities of Europe in the Middle Ages*. Reade, *Cambridge Medieval History*, vol. v, chap. xxiii. Rimaud, *Thomisme et méthode*, 1925. Rougier, *Le Scolastique et le thomisme*. Rousselot, *L'Intellectualisme de St Thomas*. Sertillanges, *St Thomas d'Aquin*, 1910; *La Philosophie morale de St Thomas*, 1916; *Les Grandes Thèses de la philosophie thomiste*, 1928. Sheen; *God and Intelligence*. Webb, *Problems in the Relation of God and Man; God and Personality*. Whitacre, article 'Thomism' in Hastings's *Dictionary of Religion and Ethics*. Wicksteed, *Reaction between Dogma and Philosophy*. *Xenia Thomistica*, Rome, 1925. Zybura, *Present-day Thinkers and the New Scholasticism*.

CONTENTS

NOTE

The present selection differs in arrangement from the Dominican edition (Burns, Oates & Washbourne) in one important particular: all references have been removed from the body of the text to the footnotes. Many of these footnotes refer to matter which is not included in the selection. It has been considered advisable, however, to retain them for the convenience of the student who may make reference to the Dominican edition.

AUTHORITIES QUOTED

The version of the Holy Scriptures used is the Douay. The titles of works quoted by S. Thomas are generally abbreviated.

A list of their authors and titles is here appended.

AMBROSE: *De Officiis Ministrorum* (*De Offic.*).

ARISTOTLE: *Ars Rhetorica* (*Rhet.*); *De Anima*; *De Caelo*; *De Generatione et Corruptione* (*De Gen. et Corr.*); *De Partibus Animalium* (*De Part. Anim.*); *Ethica Nicomachea* (*Eth. Nic.*); *Physica* (*Phys.*); *Politica* (*Polit.*); *Sophistici Elenchi* (*De Soph. Elench.*); *Topica* (*Top.*).

AUGUSTINE: *Contra Faustum Manichaeum* (*Contra Faust.*); *Confessiones* (*Conf.*); *Contra Parmenianum* (*Contra Parmen.*); *De Civitate Dei* (*De Civ. Dei*); *De Doctrina Christi* (*De Doct. Christ.*); *De Libero Arbitrio* (*De Lib. Arb.*); *Quaestionum Evangeliorum* (*De Qu. Evang.*); *De Spiritu et Anima*; *De Trinitate* (*De Trin.*); *De Vera Religione* (*De Vera Relig.*); *De Genesi ad Litteram* (*Gen. ad Lit.*); *In Joannis Evangelium Tractatus* (*In. Ioan. Tract.*); *Soliloquia* (*Soliloq.*).

AVERROES: *In De Anima* (*In De An.*).

AVICENNA: *Metaphysica* (*Met.*).

BERNARD: *De Consideratione* (*De Consid.*).

BOETHIUS: *De Hebdomadibus* (*De Hebd.*).

CHRYSOSTOM: *Homilia* (*Hom.*).

DAMASCENE: *De Fide Orthodoxa* (*De Fide Orth.*).

DIONYSIUS: *Ad Caium Monachum* (*Ad Caium Monach.*); *De Caelesti Hierarchia* (*Cael. Hier.*); *De Ecclesiastica Hierarchia* (*Eccl. Hier.*).

GREGORY THE GREAT: *Dialogorum Libri IV* (*Dial.*); *Homiliarum in Evangelia* (*Hom. in Evang.*); *Homiliarum in Ezechielem Prophetam* (*Hom. in Ezech.*); *Expositio in Librum Job sive Moralium* (*Moral.*).

HILARY: *De Trinitate* (*De Trin.*).

HUGH OF S. VICTOR: *Allegoriae in Novum Testamentum* (*Alleg. in N. T.*).

ISIDORE: *De Summo Bono; Differentiae, sive de Proprietate Sermonum; Etymologiae* (*Etym.*).

JEROME: *De Interpretatione Nominum Hebraicorum. Liber de Situ et Nominibus Locorum Hebraicorum* (*De Nom. Hebr.*).

MIGNE: *Patrologia Latina* (*P.L.*).

ORIGEN: *Commentarium in Joannem* (*In Ioan.*).

REMIGIUS: *Catena Aurea.*

RICHARD OF S. VICTOR: *De Gratia Contemplationis* (*De Grat. Contempl.*).

VULGATE (*Vulg.*).

SERMON FOR THE FEAST OF S. MARTIN

Blessed is the man whose help is from Thee.   In his heart he hath disposed to ascend by steps, in the vale of tears, in the place which he hath set.—Ps. lxxxiii. 6.

WITH sufficient clearness the text chosen shows that S. Martin attained to the heights of heaven by the aid of God.   This aid lies ready to every one, and just as S. Martin needed this divine aid in order to reach the pre-eminence of glory, so, too, we stand in need of it to reach to glory.   Let us, then, at the advice of the apostle, *go therefore with confidence to the throne of His grace, that we may obtain mercy and find grace in seasonable aid.*[1]

Blessed is the man whose help is from Thee.   It is one among the customs of men that when a man is advanced to some high position or great dignity, he and his kinsfolk keep the anniversary of such promotion.   To-day, S. Martin was advanced to the highest dignity and lordship, to the kingdom of heaven, and so the Church keeps the anniversary of his blessedness.   Now concerning blessedness there arise three things to be considered from the words of the text.   We can consider the cause, the working out, and the end of that blessedness.   Its cause or origin was the divine aid, which is noted in the words, *whose aid is from Thee.*   Its working out is in the ascent by steps, that is, in progress from virtue to

[1] Heb. iv. 16.

virtue, according to the words, *In his heart He hath disposed to ascend by steps.* The end of this blessedness is the gaining of eternal bliss, which is expressed by *the place which He hath set.* Why is this so? The Psalmist adds at once in explanation: *The lawgiver shall give a blessing,* that is the divine aid: *they shall go from virtue to virtue,* there is the ascent by steps: *the God of gods shall be seen in Sion,* that is the *place which He hath set.*

First, then, I say that the cause or reason of a man's arrival at such eminence is the divine aid. We find by natural reasoning that among created things if a thing has some natural property, it is the cause of that same property in other things that have it not naturally; as fire being naturally hot is the cause of heat in things that are not hot naturally. Now God is naturally blessed, and is the cause of blessedness in others. Hence the apostle says: *He who is the Blessed and only Mighty, the King of kings and Lord of lords.*[1] No one, then, can come to blessedness but by the divine aid.

Let us see what is the aid which God provides for a man to come to blessedness. I say that it is threefold; first He corrects a man, then He schools him, and finally takes him up to Himself. That God's correction is the way to blessedness follows from Job: *Blessed is the man whom God correcteth.*[2] This correction is a part of God's call. A man is not corrected unless for sin; now the call is to those who are far off, and sin sets a man far from God; *Your sins* (says Isaias) *have set division between you and your God.*[3] The benefit of this calling is shown by the apostle when he says: *Whom He predestinated, them He also called.*[4] S. Martin was called by God and corrected, that is, he was cleansed from original

<hr />

[1] I Tim. vi. 15.   [2] v. 17.   [3] lix. 2.   [4] Rom. viii. 30.

sin and kept from actual sin; and *Who hath raised up the just one from the East, hath called him to follow Him?*[1] They who are raised from sin are raised up by God, but some are raised up 'in the East,' that is, are converted in childhood, as S. Martin, who, when ten years old, became a catechumen against the will of his parents, and when he was twelve made plans to go as a solitary into the desert. See now the aid which God gives a man by His correction, how necessary it is, that you may know that however much you may be corrected by men, if the grace of God is not present and calling within you, that correction is worthless. *Consider the works of God, that no man can correct whom He hath despised.*[2] Thus that a man be corrected by prelates or by others is of no worth unless God work in him by His grace, but if God correct a man, it is a sign of His love, *for whom the Lord loveth, He chastiseth.*[3]

God has three ways of correcting, and the first is by instilling fear, *for he that is without fear cannot be justified,*[4] and the *beginning of wisdom is the fear of the Lord.*[5] We must, therefore, seek to have fear, for that is our first step towards blessedness. Secondly, God corrects a man by forgiving his sins, and it is only God who can forgive sins: *Blessed are they whose iniquities are forgiven.*[6] Thirdly, God corrects a man by withdrawing him from sins, for is not that also a divine benefit that God should keep a man from sins, just as He forgives his past sins? S. Augustine in his *Confessions* says: *I put it down to Your grace and mercy that You melted the ice of my sins; I put down to Your grace also all the sins that I did not, that I could not, commit.*[7] This blessedness is touched

---

[1] Isa. xli. 2. [2] Eccles. vii. 14. [3] Prov. iii. 12. [4] Ecclus. i. 28.
[5] Prov. i. 7. [6] Ps. xxxi. [7] *Conf.* ii. 7.

upon in Psalm i: *Blessed is the man who hath not walked in the counsel of the ungodly.* S. Martin had no need of the grace of forgiveness of sins, for it is not recorded that he committed any, but in this did God correct him that He kept him from sin.

God's second manner of giving aid to a man is His schooling. *Blessed is the man whom Thou shalt instruct, Lord: and shalt teach him out of Thy law.*[1] This is not a schooling which enlightens the mind only; it also warms the heart. Orators have the art of exciting the sentiments of the judge, and if human skill can do this, divine skill can do more. Hence it is that *every one that hath heard of the Father and hath learned cometh to Me.*[2] A man hears from the Father when the good inspiration comes, he fails to learn when he rejects the inspiration. Isaias did not do this, for he says: *The Lord God hath opened my ear, and I do not resist: I have not gone back.*[3] I will listen to Him as to a master. The learner is he who bends his will to the divine inspiration, and that is a part of justification, for *whom He called, them He also justified.*[4]

There are three stages in God's schooling; the first is the enlightening of the intellect by faith, and this is the most excellent lesson. It is a greater thing that a man have a modicum of faith than that he should know everything that all the philosophers have discovered about the universe, *for this is your understanding and wisdom in the sight of the nations,*[5] and *Blessed are they that have not seen and have believed.*[6] The second stage is the raising of the mind by hope, for when the mind believes by faith, then is it raised up by hope, and this

---

[1] Ps. xciii. 12.   [2] John vi. 45.   [3] Isa. i. 5.
[4] Rom. viii. 30.   [5] Deut. iv. 6.   [6] John xx. 29.

is the second step to blessedness; *Blessed is the man whose trust is in the name of the Lord: and who hath not had regard to vanities and lying follies.*[1] Some put their trust not in God but in vanities; and what are these vanities? They are temporal goods, riches, honour, and the like, *and indeed all things are vanity, every man living.*[2] You must not then trust to them. Others, and this is worse, put their trust in foolishness; they give heed to auguries and divinations and the superstitions of necromancers. The third stage of this schooling is the moving of the sentiments by love, for *Blessed are all they that love Thee.*[3] S. Martin, whose father and mother were pagans, kept in his heart none but holy sentiments, and made such progress in this schooling that he wrote a book on the Blessed Trinity.

God's third aid to a man is when He taketh him up; *Blessed is he whom Thou hast chosen and taken to Thee; he shall dwell in Thy courts.*[4] This taking up belongs to God's third blessing, to His glorification, for *those whom He justified, them He also glorified.*[5] How then did God glorify S. Martin? Clearly in three ways, and firstly by sanctifying his works. If we read the life of S. Martin and see his great courage and restraint and his purity, we shall find him to be a great man. It is of this greatness that Genesis says: *Isaac went on prospering and increasing till he became exceeding great.*[6] S. Martin grew great in the observance of the Commandments, for *Blessed are they that search His testimonies, that seek Him with their whole heart.*[7] S. Martin was also great for the wonder of his miracles; he raised three men from the dead, and his garments and the letters he sent

---

[1] Ps. xxxix. 5. [2] Ps. xxxviii. 6. [3] Tobit xiii. 17. [4] Ps. lxiv. 5.
[5] Rom. viii. 30. [6] Gen. xxvi. 13. [7] Ps. cxviii. 2.

brought healing to the sick. It is of this greatness that
we read in Ecclesiasticus: *He magnified him in the fear
of his enemies* (i.e. the pagans) *and with his words he made
prodigies to cease,* for there was once a tree broken
through and he put his body against the tree and it
fell to the other side. Again, he went without weapons
among the ranks of the enemy, and then, indeed, made
prodigies to cease, for the enemy sent envoys for peace.
For such miracles is S. Martin to be magnified. It was
the Blessed Virgin who said: *He hath done great things to
me,* meaning the greatest of miracles that in her womb
God should became man, and that she, a virgin, should
bear a child; in a similar way S. Martin had great things
done to him, and for these is he to be magnified by all.

The third stage in the glorification of S. Martin is the
spreading of his renown upon earth. What land or
what city is there in which the name and fame of
S. Martin is not proclaimed? *Thou hast magnified Thy
holy name above all.*[1] Though the Gloss explains this
text of Christ, it can be applied also to S. Martin. Think
of the miracles which he wrought. Many kings and
emperors have striven to make for themselves a name
upon earth. They have set up their triumphal arches,
they have built palaces and forts, and yet their memory
has perished with a noise. Few there are who can say
who Trajan was, or who Octavian, but S. Martin, who
was lowly upon earth, is become great. *The ear that
heard me blessed me.*[2] All that hear of S. Martin bless
him.

We have made clear now the beginning of S. Martin's
blessedness, which is the divine aid, and how God
corrects a man and schools him and takes him up.

---

[1] Ps. cxxxvii. 2. [2] Job xxix. 11.

Next comes S. Martin's progress to blessedness, according to the text: *He hath disposed to ascend by steps.* If a man would come to some exalted estate, he must ascend by little and little. To come, then, to the high estate of blessedness from his depth of misery S. Martin prepared to ascend by steps, and of these we can consider three, of which the first is his sacramental regeneration, the second his rise in status, the third his growth in merit.

I say, then, that S. Martin disposed to ascend by the sacrament of regeneration, and whoever receives the benefit of being born again in Christ takes no small step upwards. It is not a little thing to be clothed upon with Christ and to be conformed to Him: *As many of you as have been baptized in Christ have put on Christ.*[1] It is this ascent that is mentioned in the Canticle: *Thy teeth as flocks of sheep that are shorn.*[2] The clippings are sins, and the shorn sheep *coming up from the washing* are they who, by baptism, are cleansed from sin, and these, indeed, ascend; this too is the significance of Christ's coming up from the water when he was baptized. S. Martin gave much thought to the task of attaining to this blessing, and afterwards strove carefully to keep himself from sin.

The second ascent is in change of status. *God said to Moses, 'Come up to the Lord, thou, and seventy of the Ancients of Israel, to the mountain.'*[3] God bade the rest to stay behind and Moses alone to ascend; the people did not ascend, for they are not to come to this place of eminence, the Ancients went up a little way, but only Moses went up into the mount. Now if we consider the status of S. Martin, he changed it for a higher three

[1] Gal. iii. 27.   [2] Cant. iv. 2.   [3] Exod. xxiv. 1.

times, going from the military state to the clerical, from
the clerical to the religious, and from the religious to
the pontifical. I say, then, that S. Martin ascended
from the military state to the clerical, for the army of
the Church is higher in status than the army of the
world; its warfare is a higher one, and its soldiers fight
against spiritual enemies, but the soldiers of the world
against enemies in the flesh. *For the weapons of our
warfare are not carnal*,[1] but spiritual, set by God unto
the destruction of error, vice, and sin. This is the
ascent of which Isaias speaks: *Come and let us go up to the
mountain of the Lord and to the house of the God of Jacob:
and He will teach us His ways and we will walk in His paths.*[2]
The clerical state is like a mountain, and we have to go
up to the house of the Lord and do service there, and be
instructed in the teachings of the Church. God will
teach us His way, and the downward path we must
not follow; *let it not so much as be named among you*,[3]
says the apostle, and we must walk in the path of the
Lord. He who ascends to the mount of the Lord is
chosen to receive the portion of the Lord. S. Martin
ascended therefore when he was instructed by S. Hilary
and was by him made a cleric.

S. Martin ascended again from the clerical state to
the religious, for he became a monk in Italy. *Every one
that striveth for the mastery refraineth himself from all
things*, and the more a man keeps himself from those
things that hinder his undertaking, the more legitimate
is his warfare. The secular clergy have temporal goods,
but religious have them not, that they be not impeded.
This ascent is described in Genesis: *Arise and let us go
up to Bethel*,[4] and, *let us stay there*, abiding and in no

---

[1] 2 Cor. x. 4.   [2] ii. 3.   [3] Eph. v. 3.   [4] Gen. xxxv. 3.

wise going forth; for religious must abide in their calling and not go forth unless it be for the good of souls.

S. Martin's third ascent was from the religious to the pontifical state, and this ascent was direct. What did he here ascend to? Surely to the ministry of the altar and the conferring of the sacraments of the Church. Of this ascent we are told in Ecclesiasticus: *When he went up to the holy altar, he honoured the vesture of holiness.*[1] And did the Lord magnify S. Martin even here? Most assuredly, for a ball of fire was seen above his head while he celebrated the sacrifice of the altar. This ascent was for the salvation of his people. *In the joy of the just there is great glory: when the wicked reign, men are ruined.*[2] One evil bishop is certainly the ruin of many men. It is written in the prophecy of Abdias: *Saviours shall come up into Mount Sion,*[3] that is, prelates must rise up for the salvation of souls; but the Lord makes complaint in Ezechiel: *You have not gone up to face the enemy, nor have you set up a wall for the house of Israel,*[4] against the heretics and against all evils. This, then, was the triple ascent of S. Martin in status.

It would be of no advantage to ascend in status if a man did not also grow in merit, and hence Pope S. Symmachus says: *Most cheaply is he to be accounted that excels in dignity if he be not outstanding in knowledge and holiness. A small thing it is to be a cleric if he pass not the layman's virtue, and equally is it of small account for a man to be a religious or a prelate if he be not above the rest in holiness of life.* It is necessary, then, for one who ascends in status to grow also in merit. This ascent is described in the Canticle: *Who is she that goeth up by the desert, as a pillar of smoke of aromatic spices,*

[1] Ecclus. i. 12.   [2] Prov. xxviii. 12.   [3] Abdias, 21.   [4] xiii. 5.

*of myrrh and frankincense, and of all the powders of the
perfumer ?*[1] The ascent is, as it were, of a pillar of smoke,
but of fragrant smoke, not of that which is pungent.
And whence this smoke? Surely from the spices of
myrrh, from the mortification of the flesh, and from the
incense of prayer, and from the powder of every virtue.
In every state a man must strive for progress. Let us
see then how S. Martin strove. As a soldier he strove
to advance in kindness and meekness, and with reason,
for soldiers are rapacious, and he wished to keep himself
free from that charge during his service, and therefore
aimed at kindness and meekness. Soldiers are told in
the gospel : *Do violence to no man, neither calumniate
any man.*[2] Again in the clerical state he strove to be
obedient, and was, in fact, most obedient, following all
the directions of S. Hilary, and showing himself fitted
for the word of Ecclesiasticus: *The sons of wisdom are
the church of the just.*[3] In religion, too, he made progress in poverty and austerity of life. In the episcopal
state he grew in humility, and maintained the same
humility that he had shown when a religious, according
to the saying: *The greater thou art, the more do thou
humble thyself in all things. Have they made thee ruler ?
Be not lifted up, be among them as one of them.*[4]

See now the manner of S. Martin's ascent. I tell you
that he went up with prudence, with humility, and with
earnestness. And first I say that he was prudent in his
changing from the military state to the clerical, since
warfare requires planning, and this change of state was
wisely planned. Yet he was not anxious to ascend too
high, for when S. Hilary would have made him a deacon,
he was unwilling and remained an acolyte. Again, the

[1] iii. 6.   [2] Luke iii. 4.   [3] iii. 1.   [4] Ecclus. iii. 20 and xxxii. 1.

ascent from clerical to religious state was wisely planned in his heart, whereas the ascent to the episcopal state was not planned in his heart at all, for he was promoted against his own will.   I say this because the episcopal state, for all its greatness, is not to be sought out.   If a man says: 'I want to be a learned man, that afterwards I may be the wise ruler of a great church,' his plan is not good.   Augustine says: *It is not fitting for a man to aspire to that high place which is needed for the governance of the people, even though he may occupy it fittingly. . . . If no man put upon you the burden of this charge, give your time to the search for, and the gathering of, truth.*[1]

S. Martin made this ascent with humility also, for our text speaks of the *vale of tears*, and *every one that humbleth himself shall be exalted*;[2] he made it earnestly, too, for the text mentions tears.   In the greatness of his longing he would have shed tears, and could say: *As the hart panteth after the fountains of water, . . . my tears have been my bread day and night.*[3]   And since this saint wisely planned his ascent in working towards blessedness, he therefore came to the goal of blessedness which is heavenly glory; to which may He lead us Who with the Father and the Holy Spirit reigneth . . . Amen.

[1] *De Civ. Dei*, xix. 19.   [2] Luke xiv. 11.   [3] Ps. xli. 2.

2

SERMON FOR THE FEAST OF ALL SAINTS

Blessed is the nation whose God is the Lord; the people whom He hath chosen for his inheritance—Ps. xxxii. 12.

IN many ways does Holy Mother Church strive to incite sons to the desire of heavenly things, and if you examine the matter aright it appears that all her efforts are directed to leading us to despise earthly things and desire those of heaven. This is made clear by our Saviour, the founder of the Church, who said in the fervour of His preaching and doctrine *Do penance*,[1] that He might separate us from earthly things, and *the kingdom of heaven is at hand*, that He might entice us to the desire of heavenly things.

Among other ways of calling up this heavenly desire, the Church reveres and implants in our hearts to-day the glory of the saints, after which we strive. With your permission, we will first ask God to grant me that I may say something fitting and worthy of such great renown, that may be to His honour and that of all the saints, and for the salvation of our souls.

Blessed is the nation, etc. There is implanted in the souls of men that by which they rejoice to hear the praises of their country and of their parents: the praises of their country, that they may hasten to return to it; the praises of their parents, that by imitating them they may be not unworthy of them.

[1] Matt. iii. 2.

But what is our country? The country to which we are going is a heavenly country. Whence the apostle says: *We have not here a lasting city, but we seek one that is to come.*[1] Our parents are spiritual men, who have taught us, instructed us, and shown us by example how to live the good life. They are the saints in our country whose festival we celebrate to-day, and therefore we ought to dwell with delight upon their praises. Hence we read in Ecclesiasticus: *Let us now praise men of renown, and our fathers in their generation.*[2]

See how the Holy Spirit, through the mouth of David, commends this college of the saints to us in four ways: first for their merit, second for their ruler, third for their array, fourth for their being chosen; he commends the assembling of the saints for their merit by the words *Blessed is the nation*, for their ruler by the words *whose God is the Lord*; from their array he names them people when he says *the people*, and from their being chosen when he says *whom the Lord hath chosen, etc.*

First, I say, David commends this college of the saints for their merit, in the words *Blessed is the nation*. He alludes to the merit of this assembly because they have reached that goal towards which we are striving. Again, they possess whatever we desire. So, too, they are set above what we can understand. First, then, the merit of the saints is considered, because they have reached that goal towards which we are striving. Blessedness is the end of all our actions. Hence the apostle says to the Romans: *You have your fruit unto sanctification, and the end life everlasting.*[3] So, too, Augustine says in the *De Civitate Dei*: *What is the end of our desires, but to come to the kingdom where there is no end?* Now

[1] Heb. xiii. 14.   [2] xliv. 1.   [3] vi. 22.

the end of man is compared in sacred Scripture to three things. First it is compared to a crown. Hence the apostle says: *As to the rest, there is laid up for me a crown of justice.*[1] Sometimes it is compared to a prize. Hence the apostle says to the Philippians: *I press towards the mark, to the prize of the supernal vocation.*[2] In the same way it is sometimes compared to a reward. Hence we read in the Gospel of S. Matthew: *Be glad and rejoice, for your reward is very great in heaven.*[3]

With good cause did the Son of Man compare it to these three, for all our activities are comprised in three types. The actions of some consist in striving for a crown—I refer to those who follow the active life. Hence we read in Job: *The life of man upon earth is a warfare,*[4] and to those who have striven lawfully the crown is due, for we read in 2 Tim.: *He is not crowned, except he strive lawfully.*[5] Others, as the contemplatives, are runners, and they have nothing which keeps them back, but they run swiftly. Of them says the Scripture: *I have run the way of Thy commandments.*[6] But to those who strive is due the prize. The apostle says: *All run indeed, but one receiveth the prize.*[7] There are others who toil and labour, as for instance, prelates, who perform the works of salvation among the people, and to them is due the reward. Hence, the apostle says: *Every man shall receive his own reward, according to his own labour.*[8]

But what is the glory of the saints in their country? I say that they have obtained the crown like those who have striven well. They have gained the prize like runners, and have obtained the reward like good workmen. Men in the world labour to gain a crown, but that

---

[1] 2 Tim. iv. 8.   [2] iii. 14.   [3] v. 12.   [4] vii. 1.
[5] ii. 5.   [6] Ps. cxviii. 32.   [7] 1 Cor. ix. 24.   [8] 1 Cor. iii. 8.

is a corruptible crown, the crown of the saints is incorruptible. Hence the apostle says: *They indeed that they may receive a corruptible crown: but we an incorruptible one.*[1] It is, therefore, the merit of the saints that they have reached that goal towards which we are striving.

So, too, they have whatever we desire and still more. *To the just their desire shall be given.*[2] Think of whatever you can want in pleasures and delights, and the saints have all that I speak of spiritual delights, not of worldly and unclean ones. *At thy right hand are delights.*[3] If you desire riches, the saints are the most wealthy, for nothing is lacking to those who fear God; *they shall enjoy abundance.*[4] So, too, if you desire honours, the saints enjoy the highest honours: *Thy friends, O God, are made exceedingly honourable.*[5] If you seek knowledge, the saints have it in perfection, for they drink knowledge at the very fount of wisdom. The saints possess most fully everything that a man here could seek whether by sinning or by not sinning. Thus the merit of the saints stands revealed to us in their having reached the goal towards which we are striving, and in their possessing whatever we can desire.

In the same way they are set high above anything that we can understand, because the blessedness of the blessed is above what we can understand. Isaias says: *The eye hath not seen, O God, besides Thee, what things Thou hast prepared for them that wait for Thee.*[6] Why is it that the saints are set high above what we can understand? No doubt because the saints in their home in heaven have their desires fulfilled in every respect. And how can they be filled with all good unless they come to the

---

[1] 1 Cor. ix. 25.   [2] Prov. x. 24.   [3] Ps. vx. 11.
[4] Prov. i. 33.   [5] Ps. cxxxviii. 17.   [6] xliv. 4.

fount of all good? If a tree is laden with fruit, and you come to one branch only, you cannot take all its fruit; so too if you go to another branch; but if a man cut it down at the root, he would carry off all its fruit. So, too, you cannot enjoy all good unless you come to the fount of all good, which in the words of the Psalm *satisfieth thy desire with good things*.[1] Hence the Lord said to Moses: *I will show thee all good*,[2] that is, Myself, in Whom is all good; and because God is great and above all understanding, the saints who enjoy God are raised to that unto which none can attain. So we read in Isaias: *I will lift thee up above the high places of the earth*,[3] that is, above every height that earthly man can understand: *I will feed thee with the inheritance of thy father*, says the Psalmist, *this glory is to all His saints*.[4] It is clear, then, that the merit and glory of the saints in their home in heaven is that they have reached that goal towards which we are striving, that they possess whatever we can desire, and that they are set on high above what we can understand.

Let us consider their ruler. The whole merit of the saints depends on their ruler. It is a wretched and degrading and dreadful thing for a man to be subjected to one who is beneath him or base, and the Lord issues threats through His prophet, saying: *I will deliver Egypt into the hands of cruel lords*. He who serves one who is worthy, is blessed, and we read in Ecclesiasticus: *Blessed is he that hath not served such as are unworthy of him*.[5] The devils are unworthy, for we are the sons of God. It is unworthy that sons should serve their father's enemy; blessed are they who serve God; as we

---

[1] cii. 5.   [2] Exod. xxxiii. 19.   [3] lviii. 14.
[4] Ps. cxlix. 9.   [5] xxv. 11.

read in the third book of Kings: *Blessed are Thy servants.*[1] It is just that we should be subject to God. The highest perfection of a thing is that it should be subject to that which perfects it. Matter is not perfect unless it be subjected to form, and the atmosphere is not beautiful save when it is transfigured by sunlight, and the soul is not perfect except it be subject to God. In this, then, consists our blessedness, that we be subject to God.

You may say, *Are we not subject to God?* It is true that we are, but only indirectly. That is, by means of the angels, prelates, and pedagogues, who keep us in the way we ought to come to blessedness, whereas the saints in their home in heaven are not subject to pedagogues. Hence the apostle says: *Afterwards the end, when Christ shall have delivered up the kingdom of God to the Father, when He shall have brought to naught all principality.*[2] So our text says: *Blessed is the nation whose God is the Lord.*

Notice, too, that there were and are some who have said that happiness and blessedness consist in earthly things, and their opinion is set forth in Ps. cxliii. 13: *Their storehouses full, flowing out of this into that. Their sheep fruitful in young*, and the rest that he says there. The Psalmist goes on: *They have called the people happy, that hath these things.* So speak the common herd, and their opinion is false, because all things pass away like a shadow. Further, they are not satisfying, for *the covetous man shall not be filled with money.* Find among earthly things that which will remain, that which will satisfy desire, and I will admit to you that blessedness is there; but it cannot be found. Wrongly, therefore,

[1] x. 8.   [2] 1 Cor. xv. 24.

do they think that blessedness is in earthly things. When, then, is blessedness? The Psalmist answers and says: *Happy is that people whose God is the Lord.*[1]

Likewise there are, or were, others, as the Stoics, who said that blessedness and happiness lay in interior goods. They said that to have virtues and knowledge was the highest good, and their opinion is condemned in Jeremias: *Let not the wise man glory in his wisdom, and let not the strong man glory in his strength.*[2] Why? Because whatever is within you is subject to your nature, but that which makes you blessed ought to be above you, not subject to you, and so the text goes on: *But let him that glorieth glory in this, that he understandeth and knoweth me.*

There are others who say that blessedness lies in these things which are near to us. Such people have trusted in man, and against them the Psalmist speaks: *Put not your trust in princes.*[3] Nor are we to put our trust even in the angels (for some have said that our end is to see the angels), but our mind is made for the vision of the highest cause. In the words of Anselm: *We are not blessed by seeing the angels, but by seeing that mighty power by which we love the angels.*

Blessed is the nation whose God is the Lord. And how is God theirs? I say that God is theirs to know, to possess, and to enjoy. First, I say, God is theirs to know. The perfect blessedness of the saints in their country lies in this, that they know God. Hence Augustine says, in the Book of the *Confessions*: *Hapless the man who knows all those things, but knows not Thee: blessed is he who knows Thee, even if he knows not those things. He, however, who knows both Thee and them, is not the more*

---

[1] Ps. cxliii. 15.   [2] ix. 23.   [3] Ps. cxlv. 2.

blessed on account of those things, but is blessed on account of Thee alone. Blessedness is that we should know God, or that we should possess God so as to know Him. But do the saints in their home in heaven know God? Most certainly, and therefore we read in Jeremias: *And they shall teach no more every man his neighbour, and every man his brother, saying: Know the Lord: for all shall know Me from the least of them even to the greatest.*[1]

How then do the saints possess God so as to know Him? I say that two things accompany that knowledge: clear and open vision, and a perfect likening to God. First, I say, clear and open vision accompanies that knowledge. For now we see God from afar through the likeness of creatures and in riddles; as we read in Job: *All men see Him, every one beholdeth afar off,*[2] and in Romans: *For the invisible things of Him, from the creation of the world, are clearly seen, being understood by the things that are made,*[3] but in their home in heaven the saints see God clearly, not in a glass and in a riddle. Now in order that we may see God clearly, we must have eyes undimmed. If our eyes are misty or turbid, they are unable to see the brightness of the sun. Similarly if in your soul there is the fire of concupiscence, the fire of anger, or the fire of evil desires, you are hindered from the vision of God. The Psalmist says: *Fire* (that is, the fire of concupiscence) *hath fallen on them, and they shall not see the sun,*[4] that is, God. Therefore clear and open vision accompanies that knowledge.

There also accompanies this knowledge a perfect likening to God, for knowledge only comes through the likening of the one knowing to the thing known as Aristotle maintains, and the saints enjoy this perfect

[1] xxxi. 34. [2] xxxvi. 25. [3] i. 20. [4] lvii. 9.

likeness to God. St John therefore says: *When He shall appear, we shall be like to Him: because we shall see Him as He is.*[1] If you wish to attain to this likening to God in our heavenly country, you must take pains to be likened to Him in good works here on earth. Christ came to send peace upon earth. *He is our peace, Who hath made both one.*[2] Do not sow quarrels, then, but heal dissension, if you wish here to be likened to Christ. *Blessed are the peacemakers: for they shall be called the children of God.*[3] The Son has this perfect likeness to the Father, and therefore in our heavenly country we shall have God to know and to see. Augustine says: *The end that is set for all our actions is this contemplation.*[4] It is written in Deuteronomy that the sons of Levi had no part with their brethren, because the Lord was their possession.[5] The saints have God as their possession, and He is sufficient for them. We read: *The lines are fallen unto me in goodly places: for my inheritance is goodly to me. The Lord is the portion of my inheritance and of my cup, etc.*[6]

How then do the saints possess God? I say that they are blessed in possessing God because of the words *blessed is he who hath feared Him.* And in what way do they come to the possession of Him? By love I say, and so we read: *He that abideth in charity, abideth in God, and God in him,*[7] and *blessed are all they that love Thee.*[8] What, then, do you possess in possessing God? I say that in possessing God you possess what is in God. And what is in God? Glory and riches. *Glory and wealth shall be in his house.*[9] The saints in their

---

[1] I John iii. 2.   [2] Ephes. ii. 14.   [3] Matt. v. 9.
[4] On Ps. cxviii.   [5] x. 9.   [6] Ps. xv. 6, 5.
[7] I John iv. 16.   [8] Tobias xiii. 8.   [9] Ps. cxi. 3.

home in heaven have glory and honour. They are all kings: in the words of the Apocalypse: *Thou hast made us kings*; we are *to our God a kingdom*.[1] That glory is promised to the humble, for we read in Job: *He that hath been humbled, shall be in glory*,[2] and in the Gospel of S. Matthew: *Blessed are the poor in spirit: for theirs is the kingdom of heaven*.[3] In the same way the saints have infinite riches, for they have whatsoever man can desire.

Now to whom is given this possession? Is it given to the contentious? Certainly not. In this world a man sometimes obtains earthly goods by contentiousness and deceit, but heavenly riches are obtained by meekness, according to the words of the canonical epistle of S. James, *with meekness receive the ingrafted word*,[4] and those of the Gospel of S. Matthew: *Blessed are the meek: for they shall possess the land*.[5] The saints, then, have God as theirs by knowing Him and possessing Him. Again, the saints have God as theirs by enjoying and delighting in Him, according to the words of Job: *Then shalt thou abound in delights in the Almighty*.[6] The saints in their country delight not in temporal things, but in God the fount of all good, and hence the Lord says: *That you may eat and drink at My table, in My kingdom*.[7] What is it to eat at the table of God? It is to delight and to be refreshed with that by which God is refreshed. And what is that by which God is refreshed? It is His goodness. When you are refreshed by the goodness of God, then you are eating at the table of God, and that is the blessedness of the saints. Hence the words spoken: *Blessed is he that shall eat bread in the kingdom of God*.[8]

[1] v. 10. [2] xxii. 29. [3] v. 3. [4] i. 21.
[5] v. 4. [6] xxii. 26. [7] Luke xxii. 30. [8] Luke xiv. 15.

See, too, how this delight has three qualities: for the joy is a consoling joy. Through it man parts with all sadness, so that we read in Isaias: *The former distresses are forgotten . . . and the former things shall not be in remembrance, and they shall not come upon the heart. But you shall be glad and rejoice for ever in these things, which I create.*[1] Augustine says [2] that the highly educated and learned man forgets his sorrow in one way, the man who has known it by experience and has suffered, in another way. The educated and learned man forgets his sorrow when he grows heedless of it; the man who has experienced it and suffered, when he passes over to joy. And the saints forget all their sorrows for joy, so that their joy is a consoling joy. So also it is full. Why full? Because it is joy of the Creator, and from among all creatures nothing will occur to the mind that will not make you rejoice. They will go in to the contemplation of the divinity, and will go out to the contemplation of creatures, and everywhere will find refreshment in God and creatures. It is, therefore, a joy which is full, and hence we read in John: *Ask, and you shall receive: that your joy may be full,*[3] and in Augustine: *To that fullness no one can attain save by hungering after justice,* and in the Gospel of S. Matthew: *Blessed are they that hunger and thirst after justice: for they shall have their fill.*[4]

That joy is also pure, and not mingled with grief and apprehension like the joy of the world, of which it is said: *Laughter shall be mingled with sorrow.*[5] We read: *They shall obtain joy and gladness, and sorrow and mourning shall flee away,*[6] and *he shall enjoy abundance, without*

---

[1] lxv. 16–18. [2] *De Civ. Dei*, xxii. 30. [3] xvi. 24.
[4] v. 6. [5] Prov. xiv. 13. [6] Isaias xxxv. 10.

fear of evils.[1] The merciful shall have that joy, according to those words: *Blessed are the merciful: for they shall obtain mercy.*[2] Augustine says: *He is our end whom we shall see without end, love without distaste, and praise without growing weary: but what shall there be in that end? We shall have leisure without end, in our leisure we shall see, in seeing we shall love, by loving we shall praise.* Blessed is he who shall have reached that end, for the Psalmist says: *Blessed are they who dwell in Thy house, O Lord.*[3]

To that blessedness may He bring us who with the Father and the Son and the Holy Ghost liveth and reigneth, etc.

[1] Prov. i. 33.   [2] Matt. v. 7.   [3] Ps. lxxxiii. 5.

3

SERMON ON THE BODY OF THE LORD

NOTE.—*This sermon, according to the fourteenth-century MS. of the library of Troyes in which it is preserved, was preached on the Thursday in Holy Week, in the presence of Pope Urban IV and the Cardinals. This must have been at Orvieto, as Urban never went to Rome, and probably in 1264, as it was in the autumn of this year, the last of his brief pontificate, that he published the decrees setting up the feast of Corpus Christi, the liturgical offices for which were composed by S. Thomas.*

THE joyful memory, very reverend father, of the feast we keep to-day reminds us that it is our duty and our privilege ever to find our gladness in praising the most sacred Body of Christ. Is there any employment, indeed, more congenial to Christian men than eulogizing the abyss of divine charity? Could there be for the panegyrist a more attractive theme than this love? It overflows, and it is like a furnace, this love of God, Who, in the banquet of regenerating grace gives unceasingly, through the ministry of His priests, His own flesh to be eaten and His own precious blood to be drunk by them who are His own sons and the heirs of the kingdom He has promised to them that love Him.

Thine is this august work, O Christ, Thine Whose power is without limits and Who art faithful and kind. It is Thou Who, recalling the memory of former marvels, hast, in this sacred food and supersubstantial bread, wonderfully found means and the way whereby, in the eating of the Lamb without spot or stain, they may be healed who, through the eating of the forbidden tree, had been made sick, and had lost the unfading and imperishable crown of everlasting glory.

Wonderful, indeed, in our regard, and most worthy of all praise, is the goodness of God, bounteous and unweariedly loving, who, to meet and greet His children, in the sacrament which is the term and final realization of all sacrifices everywhere, dwells without end till the world's end. He gives us men for our refreshment the bread of angels, and for our drink (ours, who are but children of adoption) strong wine, the Blood of His Son, though we are not of His blood. Lowliness, we know, is pleasing to God and it was extolled by Christ; and surely in this sacrament He preaches by the example of an unrivalled lowliness, which disdains no dwelling, but consents to come as a guest to any, even a defiled, heart.

O purity clean as the sun's ray, near which no tainted thing should come, which no sullied thing has power to stain, which casts out all earthly lusts from the heart it enters! O food, truly, of the blessed spirits, Thou who every day unfailingly dost nourish us, and who in Thyself dost never fail! In the breaking of the bread Thou art not broken, nor art Thou divided. Thou art eaten, but, like the burning bush, Thou art not consumed. Nay, Thou continuest whole and entire, even as that meal and oil of old which lasted miraculously without diminution or waste.

O marvellous sacrament in which God lies concealed, and our Jesus, like another Moses, cloaks His face under the creatures He has made! May all generations praise Him! Wonderful is this sacrament in which, in virtue of the words of institution, charged with the Divine power, the symbolic species are changed into flesh and blood; in which accidents subsist without a subject;

and in which, without violation of nature's law, by consecration the single and whole Christ self-identically exists in different places—as a voice is heard and exists in many places—continuing unchanged, remaining inviolable when partaken, nor suffering any diminution; nay, He is whole and entire and perfect in each and every fragment of the host, as visual appearances are multiplied in a hundred mirrors.

Christ is fittingly offered by the faithful under the twofold species (though He truly exists whole under either) to signify that the salvation He brings to men affects both their constituent parts, soul and body, and to remind them that His bitter passion was likewise twofold. O unspeakable efficacy of this sacrament, which sets the affections ablaze with the fire of charity, and sprinkles our home's lintel, on either doorpost, with the blood of the immaculate Lamb! What wholesome journey-provision have we in this food for our precarious sojourning! What strengthening manna here regales the traveller! It restores vigour to the weak, health to the sick; it gives increase of virtue, makes grace to abound, purges away vices, refreshes the soul, renews the life of the ailing, knits together all the faithful in the union of charity! This Sacrament of Faith also inspires hope and increases charity. It is the central pillar of the Church, the consolation of the dead, and the completion of Christ's Mystical Body.

By these sacred species we recognize the tree of life. Here, Lord Jesus, art Thou both shepherd and green pasture, priest and victim, meat and drink of the elect, living bread, a food for spirits, a remedy for daily falls, the fare of the twice-born. O sacrifice of praise and righteousness, holocaust of the New Covenant, heavenly repast, not of beeves and fatlings, but of strong meats full of marrow and of wine purified from the lees, at which Thy friends on earth renew their strength and in heaven the blessed are made drunk with Thy love!

O table of the infinite God! The many marvels of this Feast amaze the mind: it is luscious beyond all dainties, delicious beyond the rarest delicacies, more fragrant than any odour, more pleasing than any form of grace, more desirable than every other food. This is the banquet to which Christ entertained those who on earth were His companions, sitting with Him at table. It is the supper to which the householder invited his son on his return from the feast of the prefiguring lamb. O cleansing waters foreshown in earlier springs! This pasch in which Christ is immolated requires that virtue supersede vice; it makes free those who are Hebrews after the spirit. This is the food that appeases the hunger of the devoted heart. Faith is its seasoning, and devotion and fraternal charity its relish. The teeth of the body may break this food, but only an unfaltering faith can savour it. What a ration for the march is this, which brings the traveller even to the mountain of virtues! O living Bread, begotten in heaven, barmed in the womb of the Virgin, baked in the furnace of the Cross, brought forth to the altar under the disguise of the wafer: strengthen my heart unto good, make it steadfast on the path through life, make glad my mind, make my thoughts pure!

This is the true Bread which is eaten and not consumed, eaten and not dissolved, which conveys, without losing, energy. It has power to save, and it completes the work. It is the source of life and the fount of grace. It forgives sin and weakens concupiscence. The faithful find here their repast, and souls a food which enlightens the intelligence, inflames the affections, purges away defects, elevates the desires. O chalice of sweetness which devout souls drain! O fiery cup, which sealed in Christ's blood His covenant: purge out the old leaven, make full the spirit of our minds, that we may be a new paste, feasting with the unleavened bread of sincerity and truth! O dish of Solomon, cenacle of consolation, sovereign remedy of life's disease, sweet nourishment, nurse of virtues, seal of sanctity, bread that fosters harmony and is a pledge of eternal felicity!

We are reminded by the smallness of the host to be humble, by its roundness to be obedient, to be thrifty by its little substance, by its whiteness to be pure, by its lacking leaven to be patient and kind, by its being baked to be charitable, by its inscription to be discreet, by its sensible appearances to be solid and enduring, by its circularity to round off a life of holiness. O rich unleavened bread! O hiding-place of most high power! What the eye sees is small; yet what is therein contained is wonderful and excellent. O body and soul of the Divinity, and divine substance inseparable from both!

This sublime sacrament, good Jesus, declares to the believing soul Thy wonderful works. For after the consecration the accidents subsist alone; that which is eaten is not changed nor lessened; though it is received wholly by all, there is no increase; a thousand receive as much as one, and one as much as a thousand. The whole Christ is present on many altars, and on each in many fragments of the host. Thy flesh, O Christ, is eaten indeed and Thy blood is truly drunk. And Thou art priest and victim; and there are present the holy angels there, praising Thy greatness and Thy incomparable majesty. This is the work of Thy power, Lord, Who dost do great and wonderful works of Thyself, Who dost transcend sense and intellect, human conception and reason and fancy. Thou it was Who didst institute this sacrament and commit it to Thy disciples.

Let none, then, approach this awful Table without reverent devotion and fervent love, without true penitence, or without recalling his redemption. For it is the Lamb without spot, without taint or smirch of sin, that is eaten in the unleavened bread. Approach not before the cleansing waters have poured over thy soul; approach not without firm faith, burning charity, the vinegar of suffering, and the proving of trial. So approach, child of faith, the Supper of the Lord, the table of plenitude and holiness, that at the last thou mayest attain to the wedding feast of the Lamb: there we shall be inebriated with the plenty of the house of God; then we shall see the King of Glory and the Lord of Hosts in His beauty, and shall taste bread in the kingdom of our Father; and our host shall be our Lord Jesus Christ, Whose power and empire are without end for ever. Amen.

4

FEAST OF CORPUS CHRISTI

Chapter and Prayer from Lauds

First Antiphon. Christ the Lord, being made an High Priest for ever after the order of Melchisedec, hath offered bread and wine.[1]

Second Antiphon. He hath made His wonderful works to be remembered; the Lord is [gracious and] full of compassion. He hath given meat unto them that fear him.

Third Antiphon. I will take the cup of salvation, and offer the sacrifice of thanskgiving.

Psalm cxv

I believed, therefore have I spoken, etc.

Fourth Antiphon. Let the children of the Church be like olive-plants round about the table of the Lord.

Psalm cxxvii

Blessed be every one, etc.

Fifth Antiphon. The Lord, that maketh peace in the borders of the Church, filleth her with the finest of wheat.

[1] Heb. vi. 20; Gen. xiv. 18.

Psalm cxlvii

Praise the Lord, O Jerusalem, etc.

Hymn

Of the glorious Body telling,
  O my tongue, Its mystery sing;
And the Blood, all price excelling,
  Which for this world's ransoming
In a noble womb once dwelling
  He shed forth, the Gentiles' King.

Given for us, for us descending
  Of a Virgin to proceed,
Man with man in converse blending
  Scattered He the Gospel seed:
Till His sojourn drew to ending
  Which He closed in wondrous deed.

At the Last Great Supper seated,
  Circled by His brethren's band,
All the Law required, completed,
  In the Feast its statutes planned,
To the twelve Himself He meted
  For their Food, with His own Hand.

Word made Flesh, by word He maketh
  Very bread His Flesh to be;
Man for wine Christ's Blood partaketh;
  And if senses fail to see,
Faith alone the true heart waketh
  To behold the Mystery.

Therefore, we, before It bending,
  This great Sacrament adore;
Types and shadows have their ending
  In the new rite evermore;
Faith, our outward sense amending,
  Maketh good defects before.

Honour, laud, and praise addressing
  To the Father and the Son,
Might ascribe we, virtue, blessing,
  And eternal benison;
Holy Ghost, from Both progressing,
  Equal laud to Thee be done.   Amen.[1]

Verse. Thou didst send them from heaven.[2] [Alleluia.]

Answer. Bread able to content every man's delight. [Alleluia.]

Antiphon at the Song of the Blessed Virgin. O Lord, how kindly is Thy Spirit! even Thine, Whose sustenance declared Thy sweetness unto Thy children when Thou didst send them from heaven bread tempering itself to every man's liking, O Thou, Who hast filled the hungry with good things, and the rich, that are proud in the imagination of their hearts, Thou hast sent empty away.[3]

MATTINS

Invitatory. O come, and let us worship Christ,
    Of all the nations Lord,
  Who doth, to them that feed on Him,
    The Bread of Life afford.

[1] Translation by the late Dr Neale (two words altered, 'noble' for 'generous,' as a translation of 'generosi' in the 1st, and 'for' for 'in' in the 4th).
[2] Wisd. of Sol. xvi. 20.   [3] Ibid. xii. 1; xvi. 21.

Hymn

Let old things pass away;
   Let all be fresh and bright;
And welcome we with hearts renewed
   This Feast of new delight.

Upon this hallowed eve,
   Christ with his brethren ate,
Obedient to the olden Law,
   The Pasch before Him set.

Which done,—Himself entire,
   The True Incarnate God,
Alike on each, alike on all,
   His sacred Hands bestowed.

He gave His Flesh; He gave
   His Precious Blood; and said,
'Receive and drink ye all of This
   For your salvation shed.'

Thus did the Lord appoint
   This sacrifice sublime,
And made His Priests the ministers
   Through all the bounds of time.

Farewell to types! henceforth
   We feed on Angels' Food;
The slave—O, wonder!—eats the Flesh
   Of his Incarnate God!

O Blessed Three in One!
Visit our hearts, we pray,
And lead us on through Thine own paths
To Thy eternal day.   Amen.[1]

FIRST NOCTURN

First Antiphon. The Lord brought forth His fruit in the season of His death, even that fruit whereof if any man eat, he shall live for ever.[2]

Psalm i

Blessed is the man, etc.

Second Antiphon. His faithful ones which are increased by the fruit of His corn and His wine do lay them down in peace and sleep in Christ.

Psalm iv

When I called, etc.

Third Antiphon. Us, being many, hath the Lord made one body, for we are all partakers of that one cup, which is not the communion of the blood of bulls, but of God Himself.[3]

Psalm xv

Preserve me, O Lord, etc.
Verse. He gave them of the bread of heaven.[4]
[Alleluia.]
Answer. Man did eat Angels' bread.   [Alleluia.]

---

[1] Translation by the Rev. E. Caswall.   [2] John vi. 51.
[3] 1 Cor. x. 17; Heb. ix. 13, 14.   [4] Ps. lxxvii. 24, 25.

First Lesson

The Lesson is taken from the First Epistle of the
Blessed Apostle Paul to the Corinthians.[1]

When ye come together, therefore, into one place, this
is not to eat the Lord's Supper. For every one taketh
before his own supper to eat, and one is hungry, and
another is drunken. What! have ye not houses to eat
and to drink in? or despise ye the Church of God, and
shame them that have not? What shall I say to you?
Do I praise you? In this I praise you not.

First Responsory

The whole assembly of the children of Israël shall kill
the lamb toward the evening of the Passover. And they
shall eat the flesh, and unleavened bread.[2]

Verse. Even Christ our Passover is sacrificed for us;
therefore let us keep the feast with the unleavened bread
of sincerity and truth.[3]

Answer. And they shall eat the flesh, and unleavened
bread.

Second Lesson

For I have received of the Lord that which also I
delivered unto you, That the Lord Jesus, the same night
in which He was betrayed, took bread; and, when He
had given thanks, He brake it, and said: Take, eat: This
is My Body, Which shall be given for you; this do in
remembrance of Me. After the same manner also He
took the cup, when He had supped, saying: This Cup
is the New Testament in My Blood. This do ye, as oft
as ye drink it, in remembrance of Me. For as often as

[1] xi. 20.   [2] Exod. xii. 6, 8.   [3] I Cor. v. 7, 8.

ye eat this Bread, and drink this Cup, ye do show the
Lord's death till He come.

Second Responsory

Ye shall eat flesh, and shall be filled with bread. This
is the bread which the Lord hath given you to eat.[1]

Verse. Moses gave you not that Bread from heaven,
but My Father giveth you the true Bread from heaven.[2]

Answer. This is the bread which the Lord hath given
you to eat.

Third Lesson

Wherefore, whosoever shall eat this Bread, or drink
the Cup of the Lord, unworthily, shall be guilty of the
Body and Blood of the Lord. But let a man examine
himself, and so let him eat of that Bread, and drink of
that Cup. For that he eateth and drinketh unworthily,
eateth and drinketh damnation to himself, not discern-
ing the Lord's Body. For this cause many are weak
and sickly among you, and many sleep. For if we would
judge ourselves, we should not be judged. But when
we are judged, we are chastened of the Lord, that we
should not be condemned with the world.

Third Responsory

Elijah looked, and, behold, there was a cake baken on
the coals at his head, and he arose, and did eat and drink;
and went in the strength of that meat [forty days and
forty nights] unto the mount of God.[3]

Verse. If any man eat of this Bread, he shall live for
ever.[4]

---

[1] Exod. xvi. 12, 15.   [2] John vi. 32.
[3] 3 (1) Kings xix. 6, 8.   [4] John vi. 51.

Answer. And went in the strength of that meat [forty days and forty nights] unto the mount of God.

Verse. Glory be to the Father, and to the Son, and to the Holy Ghost.

Answer. And went in the strength of that meat [forty days and forty nights] unto the mount of God.

SECOND NOCTURN

First Antiphon. The Lord remember our offering, and accept our burnt-sacrifice.

Psalm xix

The Lord hear thee, etc.

Second Antiphon. The Lord prepareth His Table before us in the presence of our enemies.

Psalm xxii

The Lord is my Shepherd, etc.

Third Antiphon. Let them that keep holiday around the table of the Lord make the voice of joy and praise to be heard [in the house of God].

Psalm xli

As the hart panteth, etc.

Verse. He fed them with the finest of the wheat.[1] [Alleluia.]

Answer. And with honey out of the Rock did He satisfy them.   [Alleluia.]

Ps. lxxx. 17.

Fourth Lesson

The Lesson is taken from the Sermons of St Thomas of
Aquino.[1]

The immeasurable benefits, which the goodness of
God hath bestowed on Christian people, have conferred
on them also a dignity beyond all price. 'For what
nation is there so great, who hath gods so nigh unto
them, as the Lord, our God, is' unto us? [2] The Only-
begotten Son of God, being pleased to make us 'partakers of the Divine nature,' [3] took our nature upon Him
being Himself made Man that He might make men gods.
And all, as much of ours as He took, He applied to our
salvation. On the Altar of the Cross He offered up His
Body to God the Father as a sacrifice for our reconcilia-
tion; He shed His Blood as the price whereby He re-
deemeth us from wretchedness and bondage, and the
washing whereby He cleanseth us from all sin. And for
a noble and abiding memorial of that so great work of
His goodness, He hath left unto His faithful ones the
Same His very Body for Meat, and the Same His very
Blood for Drink, to be fed upon under the appearance
of bread and wine.

Fourth Responsory

As they were eating, Jesus took bread, and blest it,
and brake it, and gave it to the disciples, and said:
Take, eat; this is My Body.[4]

Verse. The men of my tabernacle said: O that we had
of his flesh! we cannot be satisfied.[5]

Answer. Take, eat; this is My Body.

[1] 7 March. (*17th or 57th of his Opuscula, or Lesser Works.*)
[2] Deut. iv. 7.   [3] 2 Pet. i. 4.
[4] Matt. xxvi. 26.   [5] Job xxxi. 31.

Fifth Lesson

O how precious a thing then, how marvellous, how health-giving, how furnished with all dainties, is the Supper [of the Lord]! Than His Supper can anything be more precious? Therein there is put before us for meat, not, as of old time, the flesh of bulls and of goats, but Christ Himself, our very God. Than this Sacrament can anything be more marvellous? Therein it cometh to pass that bread and wine are bread and wine no more, but in the stead thereof there is the Body and there is the Blood of Christ;[1] that is to say, Christ Himself, Perfect God and Perfect Man, Christ Himself is there, under the appearance of a little bread and wine. His faithful ones eat Him, but He is not mangled; nay, when [the veil which shroudeth Him in] this Sacrament is broken, in each broken piece thereof remaineth whole Christ Himself, Perfect God and Perfect Man. All that the senses can reach in this Sacrament, [look, taste, feel, smell, and the like, all these] abide of bread and wine, but the Thing is not bread and wine. And thus room is left for faith; Christ Who hath a Form That can be seen, is here taken and received not only unseen, but seeming to be bread and wine, and the senses, which judge by the wonted look, are warranted against error.

Fifth Responsory

Jesus took the cup, after supper, saying: This cup is the New Testament in My Blood. This do in remembrance of Me.[2]

[1] Panis et vinum in Christi Corpus et Sanguinem substantialiter convertuntur.
[2] Luke xxii. 20, 19.

Verse. My soul hath them [1] still in remembrance, and is humbled in me.

Answer. This do in remembrance of Me.

Sixth Lesson

Than this Sacrament can anything be more health-giving? Thereby are sins purged away, strength renewed, and the soul fed upon the fatness of spiritual gifts. This Supper is offered up in the Church both for the quick and dead; it was ordained to the health of all, all get the good of it. Than this Sacrament can anything be more furnished with dainties? The glorious sweetness thereof is of a truth such that no man can fully tell it. Therein ghostly comfort is sucked from its very well-head. Therein a memorial is made of that exceeding great love which Christ showed in time of His sufferings. It was in order that the boundless goodness of that His great love might be driven home into the hearts of His faithful ones, that when He had celebrated the Passover with His disciples, and the last Supper was ended, the Lord 'Jesus, knowing that His hour was come that He should depart out of this world, unto the Father, having loved His own which were in the world, He loved them unto the end,' [2]—and instituted this Sacrament, —— this Sacrament, the everlasting forth-'showing of His death until He come' again,[3] —— this Sacrament, the embodied fulfilment of all the ancient types and figures, —— this Sacrament, the greatest miracle which He ever wrought, and the one mighty joy of them that

---

[1] Viz. the affliction and the misery, the wormwood and the gall. See context in Lam. iii. 20.
[2] John xiii. 1.   [3] 1 Cor. xi. 26.

now have sorrow, till He shall come again, and their
heart shall rejoice, and their joy no man take from
them.[1]

Sixth Responsory

I am that Bread of Life.   Your fathers did eat manna
in the wilderness, and are dead.   This is the Bread Which
cometh down from heaven, that a man may eat thereof
and not die.[2]

Verse. I am the living Bread Which came down from
heaven; if any man eat of this Bread, he shall live for
ever.

Answer. This is the Bread Which cometh down from
heaven, that a man may eat thereof, and not die.

Verse. Glory be to the Father, and to the Son, and
to the Holy Ghost.

Answer. This is the Bread Which cometh down from
heaven, that a man may eat thereof, and not die.

THIRD NOCTURN

First Antiphon. I will go unto the Altar of God;
I will feed on Christ, Which is the Renewer of my youth.

Psalm xlii

Judge me, O God, etc.

Second Antiphon. The Lord hath fed us with the
finest wheat, and with honey out of the Rock [3] hath He
satisfied us.

[1] John xvi. 22.　　[2] John vi. 48–51.　　[3] I Cor. x. 4.

Psalm lxxx

Sing aloud unto God, etc.

Third Antiphon. It is at Thine Altar, O Lord, that we do feed on Christ, for Whom our heart and our flesh crieth out.

Psalm lxxxiii

How lovely are Thy tabernacles, etc.

Verse. Thou bringest forth food out of the earth.[1] [Alleluia.]

Answer. And wine that maketh glad the heart of man.   [Alleluia.]

Seventh Lesson

The Lesson is taken from the Holy Gospel according to John.[2]

At that time: Jesus said unto the multitudes of the Jews: My Flesh is meat indeed, and My Blood is drink indeed.   And so on.

Homily by St Augustine, Bishop [of Hippo]. [3]

By use of meat and drink men would fain that 'they shall hunger no more, neither thirst any more,'[4] and yet there is but one Meat and one Drink, Which doth work in them that feed thereon that 'this corruptible must put on incorruption, and this mortal put on immortality'[5] —namely, communion with that general assembly[6] and Church of God's holy children, who are 'kept in perfect peace,'[7] and are 'all one,'[8] fully and utterly.

---

[1] Ps. ciii. 15.   [2] vi. 56.
[3] 26th Tract on John.   [4] Apoc. vii. 16.
[5] 1 Cor. xv. 53.   [6] Heb. xii. 23.
[7] Isa. xxvi. 3.   [8] John xvii. 11.

And therefore it is, as men of God before our time have taken it, that our Lord Jesus Christ hath set before us His Body and His Blood in the likeness of things which, from being many, are reduced into one. In one loaf are many grains of corn, and in one cup of wine the juice of many grapes. And now He giveth us to know how that which He spake cometh to pass, and how indeed 'this Man can give us His Flesh to eat,' and His Blood to drink.

Seventh Responsory

He that eateth My Flesh and drinketh My Blood, dwelleth in Me, and I in him.[1]

Verse. What nation is there so great, who hath gods so nigh unto them, as the Lord our God is to us? [2]

Answer. Dwelleth in Me, and I in him.

Eighth Lesson

'He that eateth My Flesh and drinketh My Blood, dwelleth in Me, and I in him.' To dwell in Christ, therefore, and to have Him dwelling in us, is to 'eat of that Bread and drink of that Cup,' [3] and he which dwelleth not in Christ, and in whom Christ dwelleth not, without all doubt doth not spiritually eat His Flesh nor drink His Blood, although he do carnally and visibly press the Sacrament with his teeth; but, contrariwise, he 'eateth and drinketh damnation to himself,' because he dareth to draw nigh filthy to that secret and holy thing of Christ, whereunto none draweth nigh worthily, save he which is pure, even he which is of them concerning whom it is said:—'Blessed are the pure in heart, for they shall see God.' [4]

[1] John vi. 56.　　　[2] Deut. iv. 7.
[3] I Cor. xi. 28.　　[4] Matt. v. 8.

Eighth Responsory

As the living Father hath sent Me, and I live by the Father, so he that eateth Me, even he shall live by Me.[1]

Verse. With the bread of life and understanding hath the Lord fed him.[2]

Answer. So he that eateth Me, even he shall live by Me.

Verse. Glory be to the Father, and to the Son, and to the Holy Ghost.

Answer. So he that eateth Me, even he shall live by Me.

Ninth Lesson

'As the living Father hath sent Me, and I live by the Father, so he that eateth Me, even he shall live by Me.' This is as though He said:—The Father hath sent Me into the world [3] and I have emptied Myself [and taken upon Me the form of a servant, and being found in fashion as a man],[4] I have My life from the Father, as One That is greater than I.[5] He that eateth Me, even he, by thereby taking part in Me, shall live by Me. It is as having humbled Myself [6] that I live by the Father, but he that eateth Me, him will I raise up,[7] and so he shall live by Me. It is said:—'I will live by the Father'; that is to say, He is of the Father, not the Father of Him, and yet not so, but that the Father and the Son are co-equal together. Also it is said:—'So he that eateth Me, even he shall live by Me,' whereby He showeth the gracious work toward His people of Him

[1] John vi. 67.   [2] Ecclus. xv. 3.   [3] John x. 36.   [4] Phil. ii. 7, 8.
[5] John xiv. 28.   [6] Phil. ii. 8.   [7] John vi. 54.

Who is the 'one Mediator between God and man,' [1] and not that He Which is eaten and he which eateth Him are co-equal together.

The hymn, 'We praise Thee, O God,' etc., is said.

LAUDS

First Antiphon. Wisdom hath builded her house, she hath mingled her wine, she hath also furnished her table.[2] [Alleluia.]

Second Antiphon. Thou feddest Thine Own people with Angels' food, and didst send them bread from heaven.[3] [Alleluia.]

Third Antiphon. Out of Christ His bread shall be fat, and He shall yield royal dainties.[4] [Alleluia.]

Fourth Antiphon. The Priests shall be holy; for the offerings [of the Lord] made by fire, and the bread of their God, they do offer, [therefore they shall be holy].[5] [Alleluia.]

Fifth Antiphon. To him that overcometh will I give of the hidden manna, and will give him a new name.[6] [Alleluia.]

Chapter

Brethren, I have received of the Lord that which also I delivered unto you, That the Lord Jesus, the same night in which He was betrayed, took bread, and, when He had given thanks, He brake it, and said: Take, eat; this is My Body, Which shall be given for you: this do in remembrance of Me.[7]

[1] 1 Tim. ii. 5.   [2] Prov. ix. 1, 2.
[3] Wisd. of Sol. xvi. 30.
[4] Adapted from Jacob's blessing on Asher.   Gen. xlix. 20.
[5] Lev. xxi. 6.   [6] Apoc. ii. 17.
[7] 1 Cor. xi. 23.

Hymn

The Word of God proceeding forth,
    Yet leaving not the Father's side,
And going to His work on earth,
    Had reached at length life's eventide.

By a disciple to be given
    To rivals for His Blood athirst;
Himself, the very Bread of Heaven,
    He gave to His disciples first.

He gave Himself in either kind;
    His precious Flesh; His Precious Blood;
Of flesh and blood is man combined,
    And He of man would be the Food.

In Birth, man's Fellow-man was He;
    His Meat, while sitting at the Board;
He died, his Ransomer to be:
    He reigns, to be his Great Reward.

O Saving Victim, slain to bless!
    Who openest heaven's bright gates to all;
The attacks of many a foe oppress;
    Give strength in strife, and help in fall.

To God, the Three in One, ascend
    All thanks and praise for evermore;
He grant the life that shall not end,
    Upon the heavenly country's shore.
                                        Amen.[1]

[1] Translation extracted from *The Hymnal Noted*.

Verse. He maketh peace in thy borders. [Alleluia.]

Answer. And filleth thee with the finest of wheat. [Alleluia.]

Antiphon at the Song of Zacharias. I am the living Bread Which came down from heaven: if any man eat of this Bread he shall live for ever.[1] [Alleluia.]

Prayer throughout the Office

O God, Who under a wonderful Sacrament hast left unto us whereby to show forth thy Suffering Death, grant unto us, we beseech Thee, so reverently to handle the Sacred Mysteries of Thy Body and Thy Blood that we may always feel within ourselves the fruit of Thy Redeeming Work. Who livest and reignest with God the Father, in the unity of the Holy Ghost, one God, world without end. *Amen.*

Antiphon. Wisdom, etc. (*First Antiphon at Lauds.*) *The Psalms are liii and the two first parts of cxviii.*

In the Short Responsory, instead of 'Thou That sittest,' etc., *is said:*

Verse. Thou That wast born of the Virgin Mary.

Chapter at the end

Whosoever shall eat this Bread, or drink this Cup of the Lord unworthily, shall be guilty of the Body and Blood of the Lord.[2]

[1] John vi. 51.　　　　[2] 1 Cor. xi. 27.

TERCE

Antiphon. Thou feddest, etc. (*Second Antiphon at Lauds.*)

Chapter from Lauds.

Short Responsory

He gave them of the bread of heaven. [Alleluia, Alleluia.]

Answer. He gave them of the bread of heaven. [Alleluia, Alleluia.]

Verse. Man did eat Angels' bread.

Answer. [Alleluia, Alleluia.]

In the Votive Office out of Paschal time: 'The bread of heaven.'

Verse. Glory be to the Father, and to the Son, and to the Holy Ghost.

Answer. He gave them of the bread of heaven. [Alleluia, Alleluia.]

Verse. He fed them with the finest of the wheat. [Alleluia.]

Answer. And with honey out of the rock did He satisfy them.   [Alleluia.]

SEXT

Antiphon. Out of Christ, etc. (*Third Antiphon at Lauds.*)

Chapter

For as often as ye eat this Bread, and drink this Cup, ye do show the Lord's death till He come.[1]

[1] 1 Cor. xi. 26.

Short Responsory

He fed them with the finest of the wheat. [Alleluia, Alleluia.]

Answer. He fed them with the finest of the wheat. [Alleluia, Alleluia.]

Verse. And with honey out of the rock did He satisfy them.

Answer. [Alleluia, Alleluia.]

In the Votive Office out of Paschal-time: 'The finest of the wheat.'

Verse. Glory be to the Father, and to the Son, and to the Holy Ghost.

Answer. He fed them with the finest of the wheat. [Alleluia, Alleluia.]

Verse. Thou bringest forth food out of the earth. [Alleluia.]

Answer. And wine that maketh glad the heart of man. [Alleluia.]

NONE

Antiphon. To him that overcometh, etc. (*Fifth Antiphon at Lauds.*)

Chapter as at the end of Prime.

Short Responsory

Thou bringest forth food out of the earth. [Alleluia, Alleluia.]

Answer. Thou bringest forth food out of the earth. [Alleluia, Alleluia.]

Verse. And wine that maketh glad the heart of man.

Answer. [Alleluia, Alleluia.]

In the Votive Office out of Paschal-time: 'Out of the earth.'

Verse. Glory be to the Father, and to the Son, and to the Holy Ghost.

Answer. Thou bringest forth food out of the earth. [Alleluia, Alleluia.]

Verse. He maketh peace in thy borders. [Alleluia.]

Answer. And filleth thee with the finest of the wheat. [Alleluia.]

SECOND VESPERS

All as the First, except the following :

Antiphon at the Song of the Blessed Virgin. Holy exceedingly is the Supper of the Lord, wherein we do feed on Christ, do show His death till He come,[1] do get grace abundantly to our souls, and do take pledge of the glory which shall hereafter be revealed in us.[2] [Alleluia.]

[1] Ibid.　　　　　1 Rom. viii. 18.

5

I. IN WHAT CONSISTS THE OFFICE OF A WISE MAN

My mouth shall meditate truth, and my lips shall hate wicked-ness.—Prov. vii. 7.

THE general use which, in Aristotle's [1] opinion, should be followed in naming things, has resulted in those men being called *wise* who direct things themselves and govern them well. Wherefore among other things which men conceive of the wise man, Aristotle reckons that *it belongs to the wise man to direct things.*[2] Now the rule of all things directed to the end of government and order must needs be taken from their end: for then is a thing best disposed when it is fittingly directed to its end, since the end of everything is its good. Wherefore in the arts we observe that the art which governs and rules another is the one to which the latter's end belongs; thus the medical art rules and directs the art of the druggist, because health which is the object of medicine is the end of all drugs which are made up by the drug-gist's art. The same may be observed in the art of sailing in relation to the art of ship-building, and in the military art in relation to the equestrian art and all warlike appliances. These arts which govern others are called *master-arts* (*architectonicae*), that is *principal arts*, for which reason their craftsmen, who are called *master-craftsmen* (*architectores*), are awarded the name of wise men. Since, however, these same craftsmen, through being occupied with the ends of certain singular things, do not

[1] 2 *Top.* i. 5. [2] 1 *Metaph.* ii. 3.

attain to the universal end of all things they are called wise
about this or that, in which sense it is said: *As a wise archi-*
tect, I have laid the foundation,[1] whereas the name of being
wise simply is reserved to him alone whose consideration is
about the end of the universe, which end is also the beginning of the universe: wherefore, according to Aristotle,[2] it
belongs to the wise man to consider the *highest causes*.

Now the last end of each thing is that which is intended by the first author or mover of that thing; and
the first author and mover of the universe is an intellect,
as we shall prove further on.[3] Consequently the last
end of the universe must be the good of the intellect: and
this is truth. Therefore truth must be the last end of
the whole universe; and the consideration thereof must
be the chief occupation of wisdom. And for this reason
divine Wisdom, clothed in flesh, declares that He came
into the world to make known the truth, saying: *For*
this was I born, and for this cause came I into the world,
that I should give testimony to the truth.[4] Moreover
Aristotle defines the First Philosophy as being the
knowledge of truth,[5] not of any truth, but of that truth
which is the source of all truth, of that, namely, which
relates to the first principle of being of all things; wherefore its truth is the principle of all truth, since the disposition of things is the same in truth as in being.

Now it belongs to the same thing to pursue one
contrary and to remove the other: thus medicine which
effects health, removes sickness. Hence, just as it
belongs to a wise man to meditate and disseminate
truth, especially about the first principle, so does it
belong to him to refute contrary falsehood.

---

[1] 1 Cor. iii. 10.   [2] 1 *Metaph.* i. 12; ii. 7.   [3] I. xliv; II. xxiv.
[4] John xviii. 37.   [5] 1a *Metaph.* i. 4, 5.

Wherefore the twofold office of the wise man is fittingly declared from the mouth of Wisdom, in the words above quoted; namely, to meditate and publish the divine truth, which antonomastically is *the* truth, as signified by the words, *My mouth shall meditate truth*; and to refute the error contrary to truth, as signified by the words, *and my lips shall hate wickedness*, by which is denoted falsehood opposed to divine truth, which falsehood is contrary to religion that is also called *godliness*, wherefore the falsehood that is contrary thereto receives the name of *ungodliness*.

6

II. THE AUTHOR'S INTENTION IN THIS WORK

Now of all human pursuits, that of wisdom is the most perfect, the most sublime, the most profitable, the most delightful. It is the most perfect, since in proportion as a man devotes himself to the pursuit of wisdom, so much does he already share in true happiness: wherefore the wise man says: *Blessed is the man that shall continue in wisdom.*[1] It is the most sublime because thereby especially does man approach to a likeness to God, Who *made all things in wisdom*;[2] wherefore since likeness is the cause of love, the pursuit of wisdom especially unites man to God by friendship: hence it is said that *wisdom is an infinite treasure to men; which they that use become the friends of God.*[3] It is the most profitable, because by wisdom itself man is brought to the kingdom of immortality, for *the desire of wisdom bringeth to the everlasting kingdom.*[4] And it is the most delightful

---

[1] Ecclus. xiv. 22.
[2] Ps. ciii. 24.
[3] Wisd. of Sol. vii. 14.
[4] Ibid. vi. 21.

because *her conversation hath no bitterness, nor her company any tediousness, but joy and gladness.*[1]

Wherefore, taking heart from God's loving kindness to assume the office of a wise man, although it surpasses our own powers, the purpose we have in view is, in our own weak way, to declare the truth which the Catholic faith professes, while weeding out contrary errors; for, in the words of Hilary, *I acknowledge that I owe my life's chief occupation to God, so that every word and every thought of mine may speak of Him.*[2] But it is difficult to refute the errors of each individual, for two reasons. First, because the sacrilegious assertions of each erring individual are not so well known to us, that we are able from what they say to find arguments to refute their errors. For the doctors of old used this method in order to confute the errors of the heathens, whose opinions they were able to know, since either they had been heathens themselves, or had lived among heathens and were conversant with their teachings. Secondly, because some of them, like the Mohammedans and pagans, do not agree with us as to the authority of any Scripture whereby they may be convinced, in the same way as we are able to dispute with the Jews by means of the Old Testament, and with heretics by means of the New, whereas the former accept neither. Wherefore it is necessary to have recourse to natural reason, to which all are compelled to assent. And yet this is deficient in the things of God.

And while we are occupied in the inquiry about a particular truth, we shall show what errors are excluded thereby, and how demonstrable truth is in agreement with the faith of the Christian religion.

I. i. ii.

[1] Wisd. of Sol. viii. 16.   *De Trin.* i. 37.

7

COMMENTARY ON ARISTOTLE'S 'DE ANIMA'

I. When studying any particular class of things, the first thing to do, as Aristotle indicates,[1] is to study separately those qualities which are held in common by all the members of that class, and afterwards to study special qualities of each individual in it. And this is the method which Aristotle follows in First Philosophy; for in the *Metaphysics* he begins by bringing to light, and contemplating, those qualities which belong to being as such, and afterwards devotes his attention to the characteristics of individual beings, his reason for following this order being, that he would otherwise often repeat himself.

Now since there is one class of things under which all living beings can be included, it follows that the best way to study beings endowed with life, is to consider their common qualities first, and their special ones afterwards.

The soul is common to all the living creation, for all living things alike possess it; and so in order to impart knowledge about them the convenient procedure is to deal first with the soul which is possessed by all of them. Aristotle, therefore, wishing to hand on the fruits of his researches amongst animals, discussed the soul first, and considered individual characteristics of particular animals later, in the following books.

[1] *De Part. Anim.* 645 b. 10–22.

In his treatise *On the Soul*, which we have here in front of us, he commences by setting out an introduction, wherein he incorporates the three elements necessary in any preface to a work—for whoever writes an introduction has three tasks to perform, namely, to dispose his pupil in his favour, to make him eager to learn, and to make him attentive. Such a one disposes his disciple favourably by showing the value of the knowledge to be acquired; makes him eager to learn by showing him the plan and divisions of the treatise; and makes him attentive by pointing out the difficulty of the matter in hand.

Aristotle does all three in his introduction to this work, first showing the dignity of the science; secondly, where he says: *We seek to ponder upon and to know the nature and substance of the soul, and afterwards all things which are adventitious to it*, showing its order—what it is, in other words, and how the inquiry about the soul should be prosecuted; and thirdly making clear its difficulty, where he says: *It is altogether, and in every way, a most difficult task to obtain any certainty about it.*

As regards the first of these, he makes two points: one showing the dignity of the science, and the other, where he says: *It would seem that knowledge about it (the soul) is of great worth to the study of total truth*, manifesting its utility.

For the right understanding of the first, it should be noted that all knowledge is good, indeed, not merely good, but even worthy of honour—though it is true that one science can be greater than another in this respect.

That all knowledge is good is self-evident, because that is considered good for a thing which makes it perfect, and this because all things seek and desire perfection. And since knowledge perfects man, according to his very nature, it follows that knowledge is good for man.

But amongst things which are good some are merely praised, namely such as are useful for the accomplishing of some desire—we praise a good horse because it runs well—whereas others, those which are sought for their own sake, are worthy even of honour, for we are accustomed to honour such things. Now in the realms of knowledge, some sciences are practical, whilst others are speculative, and the difference between them is, that the practical sciences are related to a work to be performed, whereas the speculative are self-sufficient. Of the two, then, the speculative are both good and honourable, but the practical are merely praiseworthy.

Thus far, then, it has been shown that all speculative knowledge is both good and honourable, yet there are to be found grades of goodness and nobility even in this kind of knowledge. Every science is praiseworthy only in so far as it is actual, and everything which is actual derives its worth from two sources, from its subject-matter, and from its type or kind, as instanced by the fact that it is better to construct a building than to make up a bed, because the object made by building is superior to a bed. But even in the same category, and in respect of the same thing, the type of the thing can constitute a grade of perfection, as instanced again by the fact that the more perfect is the kind of building, so much the more perfect is the building itself. If therefore a science, or its act, be examined from the point of view of its subject-matter, then that science will be greater which attains to knowledge of more perfect and more noble objects. On the other hand, if it be considered from the point of view of its type, that science which is more certain will be more perfect.

And so it has been proved that some sciences are more perfect than others, either because the knowledge they give is of more perfect and nobler things, or because they give greater certainty. Yet here again is room for difference where some kinds of knowledge are in question, because some are more certain than others, although their subject-matter is inferior, whilst others contemplate more beautiful and more honourable objects, yet the certainty they yield is weaker. None the less it remains true that those sciences are better which deal with better and more worthy objects, since, as Aristotle points out,[1] we prefer to know little about more perfect and more exalted things, even though we only hold that little knowledge by conjecture and in probable matter, than to know a great deal, and certainly, about inferior things. And this is because the first type is noble in itself, of its very nature, but the other kind is only good according to its degree.

The knowledge about the soul, however, is to be honoured on both accounts, because it is certain, as any one may know from his own experience, that man is endowed with a soul, and that his soul gives life, and it is more honourable than other sciences in that the soul is of the noblest among the lower creatures. And this is what Aristotle has in mind when he says: *We esteem knowledge,* that is speculative knowledge, as *being good*—that is to say one of the multitude of good things—*and noble.* But one kind of knowledge can be more perfect than another in two ways; either because

---

[1] *De Part. Anim.* 644 b. 23–35.

more certain, as has already been proved, and hence he says, *according to the certainty it gives*, or because it is knowledge of nobler objects, that is to say knowledge of things which are in their very nature good, *and of more marvellous things*, that is, of things whose cause is unknown; *for both these reasons*, that is on account of the two foregoing reasons, *we think that the history of the soul is to be accounted amongst the first sciences*. And he says *history* because in a summary way he discusses the soul without, in this tractate, coming to any final conclusion about all the properties pertaining to it. And this is the nature of a history. Again, if *amongst the first* be taken as applying to the whole of Natural Philosophy, it refers to superiority, and not to priority in order. If, on the other hand, it be predicated only of the science of living things, then it refers to order.

And when he says that *it would seem that knowledge about the soul is of great value in the study of total truth*, he puts his disciple into a frame of mind favourable to the inquiry, by saying that the study of the soul is exceedingly useful for the study of all the truth embodied in other sciences. For indeed it gives great scope to the other parts of philosophy. Consider First Philosophy; we cannot acquire knowledge of the most divine and ultimate causes of things, unless through the medium of the possible intellect; and if the nature of the possible intellect were unknown to us, we could not understand the hierarchy of the separated substances, as Avicenna showed when discussing the eleventh book of the *Metaphysica*. Again, if we consider Moral Philosophy, we cannot arrive at a perfect knowledge of moral philosophy, if we do not understand the powers of the soul; indeed, it was consequent on this knowledge that Aristotle ascribed certain virtues to the various powers of the soul.[1] Again, it is of value to the natural philosopher, because a great part of the physical universe is composed of beings endowed with souls, and the soul is the starting point of all motion in things which live. The soul *is indeed, as it were, a life-giving principle in animate things, 'as it were'* being understood, not as expressing similitude, but as being descriptive.

And when he says: *We seek to ponder upon, and to know, the nature and substance of the soul, and afterwards all things adventitious to it,* he shows the plan of the treatise by saying that we intend to *ponder*—upon the manifest data, that is—and to *know*—namely by demonstrative proof—what the soul is, or what its nature and substance, *and afterwards all things adventitious to it,* in other words, its conditions. And in this matter there is room for discussion, since some of them seem to be conditions of the soul alone, as understanding and speculation, whilst others seem to be caused by the soul, in animals generally, such as delight, sadness, perception, and imagination.

And consequently, when he says: *It is altogether and in every way a most difficult task to obtain any certainty about it,* he shows the complexity of this discussion, and this for two reasons, the first being the difficulty of knowing the substance of the soul, and the second being the difficulty of knowing its various conditions—as he says: *There is some doubt as to whether the attributes of the soul are all common to the compound of soul and body, or whether any of them are proper to the soul itself.*[2] But then he shows that there is a double complication over the first of these, on the question of its definition,

[1] *Eth. Nic.* 1139 a 1.   [2] *Lect.* ii.

and again on the elements which go to make up that definition. Where he says: *No doubt the first thing is to decide upon the category into which the soul is to be placed, and also what is the soul.* What he says, in other words, is that, although the inquiry about the soul is valuable, yet it is very difficult, and this is a difficulty in any inquiry, for to determine the nature and substance of a thing is a question common to the process of learning about the soul as well as many other things.

And the first difficulty arises because we do not know what approach to adopt when constructing a definition of the soul; some say the method should be negative by pointing to the cause, others say that it should be by dichotomy or by comparison. Aristotle prefers the comparative method.

The second difficulty arises from the component parts of the definition. For a definition denotes the nature of a thing, and this cannot be known unless the elements from which the thing is derived are also known; but it is a matter of great difficulty to discover the elements from which things are derived, because different things have different elements.

And thus the obstacles which make the task of those who propose and search for a definition, an arduous one, can be reduced to three; of which the first is the one of knowing the substance of the soul; the second is concerned with the parts of the soul; and the third has regard to the assistance which the non-essential attributes of the soul render in defining it.

Now there is question as to the category of the substance of the soul, for when composing a definition, the first thing we want to know is the genus of the thing to be defined. And so we ask the question, What is the category which includes the soul; is it substance, quantity, or quality? And to determine only its more general category is not sufficient, it must also be located in its particular class; we do not, for instance, define man merely as a substance, but also as an animal. Then, every category can be viewed from two points of view, either as being a class of things actually existent, or a class of things yet only possible, and so if the soul should be found to be a substance, there will still have to be an inquiry as to whether it is an actual or only a possible one. Also it will have to be decided whether the soul is simple or composite, since substances may be either simple or compound, and again whether it is divisible or indivisible. Again, there is the discussion about the species of the soul: are all souls specifically one or not, and if it can be shown that they do not all belong to one species, then do they differ generically or not? Then there remains uncertainty as to the things which are covered by the definition, for some things are defined by their generic category, but others by their species; and so there is uncertainty as to whether the soul should be defined according to genus, or according to *infima species*. And this uncertainty had its origin in that some people, studying the soul, seemed to confine their attention to the human soul. But amongst the ancients there were two opinions about this matter. The Platonists, who held that universals could exist in an independent state, as forms and ideas which caused knowledge and existence in individual things, said that there was a universal soul, the cause and idea of all particular souls, and that all the properties of individual souls were derived from it. But the natural philosophers maintained that there were no universal

substances at all, only individual ones, and that universals had no real existence in the external world.   And
so because of these opinions there is another question
to solve, namely whether we are to seek only one common
soul, or whether we are to study the nature of this and
that soul, as, for example, the nature of the soul of the
horse, or the nature of the human soul, or the soul of
a god.   And he says *of a god* because the philosophers
of his day believed that the heavenly bodies were gods,
and taught that they were alive.   But Aristotle wished
to discover both the nature of the common soul, and of
the souls existing in particular species.   But when on
this point he says that the *animal as universal is either
non-existent or is posterior*, it should be noticed that we
can speak of the universal animal in two ways, either
precisely as universal, that is to say, one nature verified
in many individuals, or predicable of many individuals,
or as animals; and if in the latter way, then we can consider it either as existent in the real world, or as existing
only in the mind.   Plato considered that it had real
external existence, and said that the universal animal
does really exist, and is, moreover, prior to the individual.
And this was his opinion because, as has already been
shown, he thought that universals and ideas really
exist.   Aristotle, on the other hand, taught that the
universal is not to be found in the world, and that if
it is anything real at all, it is posterior to the individual.
But if we are to think of the nature of animal not precisely as being universal, then it is something real; and
in the same sense that a thing which can possibly exist,
is prior to the thing which actually does exist, so is
the nature of animal prior to the individual animal.

And when he says: *Given that there are not several souls,*

but only parts in the same soul, there is question whether we should first inquire into the nature of the whole soul, or part by part, he puts his finger on the difficulties which arise about the faculties of the soul. For in the soul are potential parts, namely the vegetative, sensitive, and intellective parts. And, because of this, there will be an inquiry as to whether these are different souls, as the Platonists held and firmly maintained, or whether they are only potential parts. And if the latter, we shall ask first whether we ought first to seek the faculties before seeking their acts, or whether we should first seek the acts and then the faculties of which they are acts, as, for example, to seek first understanding before the intellect, or perception before the sense-faculty— feeling being the act of sensation, and the sense faculty its potency—and so also the other with faculties and their acts. Again, if the acts are to be studied before their potencies, there will still remain the question as to whether the objects attained by these acts ought to be studied before the faculties, as, for example, ought we to study the perceived object before the sense faculty, or the thing understood before the intellect which knows it?

And when he says: *It seems that not only is it valuable to know what a substance is in order to know what are its attributes—as, for instance, in mathematics it is useful to know the meaning of straight and curved, line and surface, in order to know that the angles of a triangle are equal to (two) right angles—but conversely, it is useful to know the nature of a thing's attributes in order better to know the nature of the thing,* he expresses the problems which have their source in those non-essential elements which assist in the compounding of a definition of the soul.

And this is because a definition ought to include not only the essential constituents of the nature, but also all accessory ones, and if the essentials were rightly defined, and could be known, then the accessory elements would not be required in the definition. But since it is a fact that we do not know the essences of things, we need to use accidental differences in defining natures; to have two feet is not essential for any being, and yet in defining things, *two-footed* is included in the definition. And it is through these adventitious circumstances that we arrive at knowledge of things, and that is where the problem lies; because we ought to know the nature of the soul before we can know what are its attributes, just as in mathematics it is useful for the student to know what is meant by straight, curved, and plane surface in order the better to know that the angles of a triangle are equal to (two) right angles. But on the other hand, as already shown, to know the attributes of a thing, before knowing its nature, is of great assistance in discovering the nature.

And so if any one were to propose a definition which did not include the attributes of the thing defined, such a definition would not be real, but merely abstract and theoretical. But a definition by which the accidents are expressed, is a true definition, and is formed from the characteristic and natural properties of the thing to be defined.

II. And now that Aristotle has shown the problem which is concerned with the nature and substance of the soul, he next shows the difficulty to be met when treating of its conditions and attributes. And in investigating this question he makes two stages, first proposing, and solving, a question about the attributes of the soul, and secondly, showing, in the light of this solution, that the inquiry is the task of the natural philosopher or physicist, and this is where he says: *For this reason, therefore, it immediately becomes the work of the natural philosopher to perform this research on the soul, either in its entirety, or at least in the particular aspect described.*

What he means, in the first place, is that there is a difficulty about deciding whether the attributes and operations of the soul belong to it alone, independently of its association with the body, as Plato thought, or whether all of them belong either to the body, or the compound of body and soul, and none of them to the soul alone.

Then when he says: *This is a question which must be settled, though it is not an easy one,* he again makes two stages in his argument, first showing that questions of this kind are not easy, and secondly, where he says: *If, therefore, any operation or attribute of the soul belongs to it alone, then it will be possible for the soul to be separated from the body,* showing their necessity. Thus what he has said is, first that we must make certain whether the attributes and operations of the soul belong to it alone, or whether they are common to soul and body, and that this is no easy matter, but rather, on the contrary, exceedingly difficult. And that it is problematical, he makes clear by saying that the problem consists in that, on manifest evidence, it seems clear that many attributes are enjoyed by soul and body together, and that the soul cannot be acted upon unless through the body, as is, indeed, the case in such affections as anger, and perception, and other things of like nature in which there is no action upon the soul except through the body.

But if any operation of the soul were proper to it,

then it would seem to be intellectual operation, for understanding, which is especially intellectual operation, seems to belong only to the soul. Yet, on the other hand, if one think further on the matter, understanding does not seem to be the peculiar province of the soul. Understanding is either identical with imagination, as the Platonists maintained, or else it does not take place without the assistance of imagination (there were certain sages, such as the natural philosophers of former days, who said that the intellect in no way differed from the sense-faculties, and if this were indeed the case, it would follow that intellect and imagination were identical, and so the Platonists were led to assert that the intellect was the imagination). But, they said, since the imagination is dependent upon the body, then the understanding is not a property of the soul, but of soul and body combined. And so, even if it be granted that the intellect is not identical with the imagination, yet there can be no process of knowledge without it. And hence the conclusion is that understanding cannot belong to the soul alone, since it is dependent upon the body. There can, therefore, be no understanding without the body.

Although Aristotle deals with this difficulty, expounding its solution with great clarity in the third section of this work, none the less we will say something about it here. Understanding, viewed from one aspect, is proper to the soul, but seen from another point of view, it is an operation of soul and body combined. And therefore it should be noted that there are attributes and operations of the soul which are dependent upon material things, both instrumentally, and for the provision of their object. Sight, for instance, needs a material thing for its object, for colour, which is its object, is to be found in corporeal substance; yet also, though sight is an operation of the soul, yet it can only take place by means of the organ of sight—the pupil of the eye—which serves it as an instrument; hence sight is not only an operation of the soul, but also of a corporeal organ.   But there is another function which is dependent upon the body, but only for its object, since it does not act through a material instrument; the act of knowledge does not take place through a material instrument, though it requires corporeal substance for its object.   As Aristotle shows in the third part of this work, sense-imagery is related to the intellect, in the same way that colours are related to the faculty of sight, that is to say, the images are the objects of the intellect.   And since one cannot have sense-imagery without corporeal substance, it seems clear that there can be no intellectual operation without matter; but only the object is material, and not the organ.

Two consequences follow from this.   One is that the process of knowledge is the peculiar operation of the soul—and as already said, does not need a material organ, but only a material object—whereas sight and other such operations do not pertain only to the soul, but to body and soul combined; and the other consequence is, that a thing having an independent operation has also independent subsistence and existence, and things which have not independent operations, have no independent existence.   And this is what gave rise to the difficulty in a question of this kind, namely that all the operations and attributes of the soul seemed, at first sight, to belong to the compound being.

And when he says: *If, therefore, any operation or attribute belongs to the soul alone, then it will be possible for the soul to be separated from the body*, he shows why this treatise is necessary, because valuable information is to be gained from it on a point about the soul which every one wishes to know, namely whether it is possible, or not, for it to be separated from the body; and he says that if the soul can have any operation or attribute independently of the body, then it can be separated from it; and this because, as proved already, a thing which is independent in operation, is independent in subsistence and existence. But if there were no proper operation or attribute of the soul, it would be in the same state as the straight line. Many things can affect a line, as such; for instance a line can touch a brass sphere at a given point, but this can only take place in a material way, since a straight line cannot touch a brazen sphere at any point except through matter. And so if the soul has no distinctive operation many things may affect it, but they will only be able to do so by reason of their material conditions.

Hence, when he says that *it appears that all the attributes of the soul affect it through the body*, he shows that all the attributes of the soul belong to the composite whole, and not merely to the soul as he had presupposed above. He proves this by one argument which has two parts. And this is the process of the argument. Every action in which the body participates, is not performed merely by the soul, but also by the body; but the body participates in all such affections of the soul as anger, meekness, fear, confidence, and other like dispositions; and so it seems that all attributes of the soul pertain also to the body. And that the body participates in all affections of the soul, he proves by two arguments. First in this way: Because we notice that sometimes severe and manifest trials come upon a man, and yet he is not angry or frightened; but at other times he is moved by very small and light matters, if the cause be his excitability (i.e. something physical), and he then behaves as if really angry. His second proof is as follows: *It is still more evident* that the body participates in affections of this kind, for we see that sometimes, even when no danger is present, some people suffer from affections similar to the dispositions of the soul. Melancholy folk, for instance, from physical causes are often unnecessarily timid. Therefore, since this is the case, since bodily disposition affects the passions in this way, it is clear that such affections are *forms existing in matter*, that is to say, they exist in a corporeal way. And for this reason *their boundaries*, that is, the definitions of these dispositions, must not be constructed without including matter; so that if anger were to be defined, it would be described as a motion *of a certain body*, say, the heart, or *of some part or faculty of such a body*. This he said in reference to the material cause (of anger); but when he said: *Caused by such and such agent*, he was describing its efficient cause; *and for such and such purpose* had reference to its final cause.

And when he says: *It is for this reason that the physicist should study the soul*, he concludes from what has gone before, that to speculate about the soul is the work of the natural philosopher. And he reaches this conclusion from the way in which the soul is defined, making two points. First he proves the proposition which he has enunciated. Secondly, he follows up the discussion about definitions, where he says: *The physicist and the logician would define every such attribute in a different way*. And this is his manner of proving the proposition. Operations and attributes of the soul are attributes and operations of the body also, as shown above. But whenever an attribute is defined, the thing of which it is an attribute should be included in its definition, for the subject always enters into the definition of an attribute. If, therefore, such attributes do not belong to the soul alone, but to the body also, it follows necessarily that matter enters into their definition; but everything into which corporeal substance or matter enters, is in the province of the natural philosopher; therefore attributes of this nature are to be studied by the natural philosopher. But further, it is his task, whose function it is to consider the attributes, to consider their subject as well. And hence it is the duty of the physicist to study the soul, either simply *in its entirety, or in this particular respect,* namely as being the partner of the body. This he says, because he leaves it uncertain, whether or not the intellect is a faculty joined to the body.

And so when he says: *The physicist and the logician would define every such attribute in a different way,* he resumes the consideration of the definitions, because he indicates that amongst definitions of the attributes of the soul, some include matter and corporeal substance, whereas others do not; and some, again, do not include matter at all, but only form—and definitions of this latter type, he says, are not sufficient. And he makes inquiries about this matter, investigating the differences to be found amongst these various descriptions. For sometimes a definition will be given, in which there is no description of the material element, such as that anger is the desire for revenge; at other times, though, a definition will be given in which the material is expressed, as for instance, that anger is a rush of blood to the heart.

The first is merely a logical description, but the second is physical, since the material enters in, and therefore it comes under the consideration of the natural philosopher. For this latter, namely the physicist, determines the matter when he says that it is a rush of blood to the heart. But the former, the logician namely, determines the species and form of anger, for to say that anger is the desire for revenge, is to express only its form. That the first definition is inadequate, is quite clear. For unless matter be included in the definition of a form which has its existence in the matter which it determines, such a definition is inadequate; but this form in question, *desire for revenge*, is a form having existence in matter which it determines; whence, since its matter is not included in its definition, it is evident that its definition is inadequate. So it is necessary, that in every definition, the form should be shown as existing in such and such matter, that is, matter determined in a particular way. And so we have three kinds of definition. One describes the species and nature of the species, a house might be defined as a shelter warding off wind, rain, and heat—and such a description is merely formal. Another one denotes the matter, defining a house as a shelter made of stones, bricks, and planks. But another type expresses, that is, includes in the definition, *both*—matter and form, saying that a house is a certain kind of shelter, made of certain materials, and made for a definite purpose, namely to keep out the wind, and so on. And so Aristotle says that another type of definition has three elements which are: *in these* planks and stones, denoting the material element; *species*, which constitutes the formal part; and *for this purpose*, which is the final cause. And so he postulates

matter when he says *in these*, form when he says *species*,
and final cause when he says *for this purpose*, and these
are the three requirements for the perfect definition.
And if it be asked which of these descriptions is the
physical one, we reply that the one which has reference
to the form only, is not physical, but rather logical.
But that which includes matter to the exclusion of form,
pertains to no other branch of science than natural
philosophy. For only the natural philosopher studies
matter. None the less, the definition including both
matter and form is the more accurate one even in
natural philosophy. Both of them pertain to this
science, but the one denoting the matter alone is imperfect, whilst the one expressing both is perfect; there
is no one, apart from the physicist, who considers the
attributes which are inseparable from matter. But since
philosophers study material attributes in different ways,
he shows who these philosophers are, and explains their
method of study. There are, he says, three types.
There are students who consider attributes realized in
matter, but they differ from the natural philosopher in
their starting point; these are craftsmen, who, although
they contemplate a form encased in matter, differ from
the natural philosophers in that their starting point is
a craft, whereas the latter have their origin in nature.
Another class of students considers forms which exist
in matter, but which do not include matter in their
definition; such forms as straight, curved, and so on,
which exist in matter and belong to the category of
inseparable attributes in their mode of existence; yet
the mathematician does not take any account of them
as existent in corporeal substance. And the reason for
this is that there are some substances which are objects

of experience through the qualities which they possess; but quantity is prior to quality, and so the mathematician is able to take account of their independent quantity, without determining this or that particular material substance. Again, a third class of students study beings whose existence is not altogether immersed in matter, or which can even exist entirely independently of it; and these are the first philosophers. It should be noticed, too, that the whole justification for the classification of the philosophical sciences derives from definition, and the ways of defining them; because the origin of all demonstration is to be found in the definitions of things, since things are always described by their essential characteristics. Hence different definitions express different essential notes, and it is thus that one science is distinguished from another.

And when he says: *But we must return to the starting point of the discussion*, he recalls himself to the question under discussion, since he seems to have digressed somewhat in inquiring about definitions, and says that we must return to the point from which the digression arose, namely, to the discussion as to whether such affections of the soul as anger, fear, and the like are inseparable from the physical matter of animals, in so far as their existence is of this kind—that is, in so far as they are attributes dependent upon corporeal matter; or whether they are like lines and planes or surfaces, which can be separated from their connatural matter by the mind. If this is, indeed, the case, to study them as well as the soul is the task of the natural philosopher. *As regards this latter*, the soul, it is necessary for the purpose of the present inquiry to study the assertions of the ancients, no matter who they were, or what their opinions about the soul. And to do this will be useful in two ways: first, because what they have maintained with truth will be helpful to us; secondly, because what they have taught in error, we will be careful to avoid.

De Anima, 1 and 2.

8

QUESTION: OF THE ESSENCE OF LAW

WE have now to consider the extrinsic principles of acts. Now the extrinsic principle inclining to evil is the devil, of whose temptations we have spoken.[1] But the extrinsic principle moving to good is God, Who both instructs us by means of His law, and assists us by His grace: wherefore in the first place we must speak of law; in the second place, of grace.

Concerning law, we must consider: (1) law itself in general; (2) its parts. Concerning law in general three points offer themselves for our consideration: (1) its essence; (2) the different kinds of law; (3) the effects of law.

Under the first head there are four points of inquiry: (1) whether law is something pertaining to reason? (2) concerning the end of law; (3) its cause; (4) the promulgation of law.

FIRST ARTICLE

WHETHER LAW IS SOMETHING PERTAINING TO REASON?

We proceed thus to the First Article.

Objection 1. It would seem that law is not something pertaining to reason. For the apostle says, *I see another law in my members*,[2] etc. But nothing pertaining to

---

[1] I. Q. cxiv.　　　　[2] Rom. vii. 23.

reason is in the members; since the reason does not make use of a bodily organ. Therefore law is not something pertaining to reason.

Obj. 2. Further, in the reason there is nothing else but power, habit, and act. But law is not the power itself of reason. In like manner, neither is it a habit of reason: because the habits of reason are the intellectual virtues of which we have spoken above.[1] Nor, again, is it an act of reason: because then law would cease, when the act of reason ceases, for instance, while we are asleep. Therefore law is nothing pertaining to reason.

Obj. 3. Further, the law moves those who are subject to it to act aright. But it belongs properly to the will to move to act, as is evident from what has been said above.[2] Therefore law pertains, not to the reason, but to the will; according to the words of the jurist: *Whatsoever pleaseth the sovereign, has force of law.*[3]

On the contrary, it belongs to the law to command and to forbid. But it belongs to reason to command, as stated above.[4] Therefore law is something pertaining to reason.

I answer that law is a rule and measure of acts whereby man is induced to act or is restrained from acting: for *lex* (law) is derived from *ligare* (to bind), because it binds one to act. Now the rule and measure of human acts is the reason, which is the first principle of human acts, as is evident from what has been stated above,[5] since it belongs to the reason to direct to the end, which is the first principle in all matters of action, according to Aristotle.[6] Now that which is the principle in any genus, is the rule and measure of that genus: for instance,

[1] Q. lvii.
[2] Q. ix. a. 1.
[3] I ff., *De Const. Prin.* leg. i.
[4] Q. xvii. a. 1.
[5] Q. i. a. 1, r. obj. 3.
[6] *Phys.* ii.

unity in the genus of numbers, and the first movement in the genus of movements. Consequently it follows that law is something pertaining to reason.

Reply Obj. 1. Since law is a kind of rule and measure, it may be in something in two ways. First, as in that which measures and rules: and since this is proper to reason, it follows that, in this way, law is in the reason alone. Secondly, as in that which is measured and ruled. In this way, law is in all those things that are inclined to something by reason of some law: so that any inclination arising from a law may be called a law, not essentially but by participation as it were. And thus the inclination of the members to concupiscence is called *the law of the members*.

Reply Obj. 2. Just as, in external action, we may consider the work and the work done, for instance the work of building and the house built; so in the acts of reason, we may consider the act itself of reason, i.e. to understand and to reason, and something produced by this act. With regard to the speculative reason, this is first of all the definition; secondly, the proposition; thirdly, the syllogism or argument. And since also the practical reason makes use of a syllogism in respect of the work to be done, as stated above,[1] and as Aristotle teaches;[2] hence we find in the practical reason something that holds the same position in regard to operations, as, in the speculative intellect, the proposition holds in regard to conclusions. Suchlike universal propositions of the practical intellect that are directed to actions have the nature of law. And these propositions are sometimes under our actual consideration, while sometimes they are retained in the reason by means of a habit.

[1] Q. xiii. a. 3; Q. lxxvi. a. 1.   [2] *Eth. Nic.* vii. 3.

Reply Obj. 3. Reason has its power of moving from the will, as stated above; [1] for it is due to the fact that one wills the end, that the reason issues its commands as regards things ordained to the end. But in order that the volition of what is commanded may have the nature of law, it needs to be in accord with some rule of reason. And in this sense is to be understood the saying that the will of the sovereign has the force of law; otherwise the sovereign's will would savour of lawlessness rather than of law.

SECOND ARTICLE

WHETHER THE LAW IS ALWAYS DIRECTED TO THE COMMON GOOD?

We proceed thus to the Second Article.

Objection 1. It would seem that the law is not always directed to the common good as to its end. For it belongs to law to command and to forbid. But commands are directed to certain individual goods. Therefore the end of the law is not always the common good.

Obj. 2. Further, the law directs man in his actions. But human actions are concerned with particular matters. Therefore the law is directed to some particular good.

Obj. 3. Further, Isidore says: *If the law is based on reason, whatever is based on reason will be a law.*[2] But reason is the foundation not only of what is ordained to the common good, but also of that which is directed to private good. Therefore the law is not only directed to the good of all, but also to the private good of an individual.

[1] Q. xvii. a. 1.   [2] *Etym.* v. 3.

On the contrary, Isidore says that *laws are enacted for no private profit, but for the common benefit of the citizens.*[1]

I answer that as stated above [2] the law belongs to that which is a principle of human acts, because it is their rule and measure.   Now as reason is a principle of human acts, so in reason itself there is something which is the principle in respect of all the rest: wherefore to this principle chiefly and mainly law must needs be referred. Now the first principle in practical matters, which are the object of the practical reason, is the last end: and the last end of human life is bliss or happiness, as stated above.[3] Consequently the law must needs regard principally the relationship to happiness.   Moreover, since every part is ordained to the whole, as imperfect to perfect; and since one man is a part of the perfect community, the law must needs regard properly the relationship to universal happiness.   Wherefore Aristotle in the above definition of legal matters mentions both happiness and the body politic: for he says that we call legal matters *just, which are adapted to produce and preserve happiness and its parts for the body politic*: [4] since the state is a perfect community, as he says.[5]

Now in every genus, that which belongs to it chiefly is the principle of the others, and the others belong to that genus in subordination to that thing: thus fire, which is chief among hot things, is the cause of heat in mixed bodies, and these are said to be hot in so far as they have a share of fire.   Consequently, since the law is chiefly ordained to the common good, any other pre-

---

[1] *Etym.* v. 21.   [2] A. 1.   [3] Q. ii. a. 7; Q. iii. a. 1.
[4] *Eth. Nic.* v. 1.   [5] *Polit.* i. 1.

cept in regard to some individual work, must needs be devoid of the nature of a law, save in so far as it regards the common good. Therefore every law is ordained to the common good.

Reply Obj. 1. A command denotes an application of a law to matters regulated by the law. Now the order to the common good, at which the law aims, is applicable to particular ends. And in this way commands are given even concerning particular matters.

Reply Obj. 2. Actions are indeed concerned with particular matters: but those particular matters are referable to the common good, not as to a common genus or species, but as to a common final cause, according as the common good is said to be the common end.

Reply Obj. 3. Just as nothing stands firm with regard to the speculative reason except that which is traced back to the first indemonstrable principles, so nothing stands firm with regard to the practical reason, unless it be directed to the last end which is the common good: and whatever stands to reason in this sense, has run on the nature of a law.

9

QUESTION: OF THE VARIOUS KINDS OF LAW

WE must now consider the various kinds of law: under which head there are six points of inquiry: (1) Whether there is an eternal law? (2) Whether there is a natural law? (3) Whether there is a human law? (4) Whether there is a divine law? (5) Whether there is one divine law or several? (6) Whether there is a law of sin?

FIRST ARTICLE

WHETHER THERE IS AN ETERNAL LAW?

We proceed thus to the First Article.

Objection 1. It would seem that there is no eternal law. Because every law is imposed on someone. But there was not someone from eternity on whom a law could be imposed: since God alone was from eternity. Therefore no law is eternal.

Obj. 2. Further, promulgation is essential to law. But promulgation could not be from eternity: because there was no one to whom it could be promulgated from eternity. Therefore no law can be eternal.

Obj. 3. Further, a law implies order to an end. But nothing ordained to an end is eternal: for the last end alone is eternal. Therefore no law is eternal.

On the contrary, Augustine says, *that law which is the supreme reason cannot be understood to be otherwise than unchangeable and eternal.*[1]

I answer that, as stated above,[2] a law is nothing else but a dictate of practical reason emanating from the ruler who governs a perfect community. Now it is evident, granted that the world is ruled by divine providence, as was stated in the first part,[3] that the whole community of the universe is governed by divine reason. Wherefore the very idea of the government of things in God the Ruler of the universe, has the nature of a law. And since the divine reason's conception of things is not subject to time but is eternal according to Proverbs,[4] therefore it is that this kind of law must be called eternal.

---

[1] *De Lib. Arb.* i. 6.　　　　[2] Q. xc. a. 1, *r. obj.* 2; As. 3, 4.
[3] Q. xxii. as. 1, 2.　　　　[4] Prov. viii. 23.

Reply Obj. 1. Those things that are not in themselves, exist with God, inasmuch as they are foreknown and pre-ordained by Him, according to Romans, *Who calls those things that are not, as those that are.*[1] Accordingly, the eternal concept of the divine law bears the character of an eternal law, in so far as it is ordained by God to the government of things foreknown by Him.

Reply Obj. 2. Promulgation is made by word of mouth or in writing; and in both ways the eternal law is promulgated: because both the divine word and the writing of the Book of Life are eternal. But the promulgation cannot be from eternity on the part of the creature that hears or reads.

Reply Obj. 3. The law implies order to the end actively, in so far as it directs certain things to the end; but not passively—that is to say, the law itself is not ordained to the end—except accidentally, in a governor whose end is extrinsic to him, and to which end his law must needs be ordained. But the end of the divine government is God Himself, and His law is not distinct from Himself. Wherefore the eternal law is not ordained to another end.

SECOND ARTICLE

WHETHER THERE IS IN US A NATURAL LAW?

We proceed thus to the Second Article.

Objection 1. It would seem that there is no natural law in us. Because man is governed sufficiently by the eternal law, for Augustine says that *the eternal law is that by which it is right that all things should be most orderly.*[2] But nature does not abound in superfluities as neither

---

[1] Rom. iv. 17. [2] *De Lib. Arb.* i.

does she fail in necessaries. Therefore no law is natural to man.

Obj. 2. Further, by the law man is directed, in his acts, to the end, as stated above.[1] But the directing of human acts to their end is not a function of nature, as is the case in irrational creatures, which act for an end solely by their natural appetite; whereas man acts for an end by his reason and will. Therefore no law is natural to man.

Obj. 3. Further, the more a man is free, the less is he under the law. But man is freer than all the animals, on account of his free will, with which he is endowed above all other animals. Since therefore other animals are not subject to a natural law, neither is man subject to a natural law.

On the contrary, when the Gentiles, who have not the law, do by nature those things that are of the law, the gloss comments: *Although they have no written law, yet they have the natural law, whereby each one knows, and is conscious of, what is good and what is evil.*[2]

I answer that, as stated above,[3] law, being a rule and measure, can be in a person in two ways: in one way, as in him that rules and measures; in another way, as in that which is ruled and measured, since a thing is ruled and measured, in so far as it partakes of the rule or measure. Wherefore, since all things subject to divine providence are ruled and measured by the eternal law, as was stated above;[4] it is evident that all things partake somewhat of the eternal law, in so far as, namely, from its being imprinted on them, they derive their respective inclinations to their proper acts and ends.

---

[1] Q. xc. a. 2. [2] A gloss on Rom. ii. 14.
[3] Q. xc. a. 1, *r. obj.* 1. [4] A. 1.

Now among all others, the rational creature is subject to divine providence in the most excellent way, in so far as it partakes of a share of providence, by being provident both for itself and for others. Wherefore it has a share of the eternal reason, whereby it has a natural inclination to its proper act and end: and this participation of the eternal law in the rational creature is called the natural law. Hence the Psalmist, after saying, *Offer up the sacrifice of justice*,[1] as though someone asked what the works of justice are, adds: *Many say, Who showeth us good things?* In answer to which question he says: *The light of Thy countenance, O Lord, is signed upon us*; thus implying that the light of natural reason, whereby we discern what is good and what is evil, which is the function of the natural law, is nothing else than an imprint on us of the divine light. It is therefore evident that the natural law is nothing else than the rational creature's participation of the eternal law.

Reply Obj. 1. This argument would hold, if the natural law were something different from the eternal law: whereas it is nothing but a participation thereof, as stated above.

Reply Obj. 2. Every act of reason and will in us is based on that which is according to nature, as stated above;[2] for every act of reasoning is based on principles that are known naturally, and every act of appetite in respect of the means is derived from the natural appetite in respect of the last end. Accordingly the first direction of our acts to their end must needs be in virtue of the natural law.

Reply Obj. 3. Even irrational animals partake in their own way of the eternal reason, just as the rational

Ps. iv. 6.   [2] Q. x. a. 1.

creature does. But because the rational creature partakes thereof in an intellectual and rational manner, therefore the participation of the eternal law in the rational creature is properly called a law, since a law is something pertaining to reason, as stated above.[1] Irrational creatures, however, do not partake thereof in a rational manner, wherefore there is no participation of the eternal law in them, except by way of similitude.

10

QUESTION: OF THE MORAL PRECEPTS OF THE OLD LAW

We must now consider each kind of precept of the old law: and (1) the moral precepts, (2) the ceremonial precepts, (3) the judicial precepts. Under the first head there are twelve points of inquiry: (1) Whether all the moral precepts of the old law belong to the law of nature? (2) Whether the moral precepts of the old law are about the acts of all the virtues? (3) Whether all the moral precepts of the old law are reducible to the ten precepts of the decalogue? (4) How the precepts of the decalogue are distinguished from one another. (5) Their number. (6) Their order. (7) The manner in which they were given. (8) Whether they are dispensable? (9) Whether the mode of observing a virtue comes under the precept of the law? (10) Whether the mode of charity comes under the precept? (11) The distinction of other moral precepts. (12) Whether the moral precepts of the old law justified man?

[1] Q. xc. a. 1.

WHETHER ALL THE MORAL PRECEPTS OF THE OLD LAW BELONG TO THE LAW OF NATURE?

We proceed thus to the first article.

Objection 1. It would seem that not all the moral precepts belong to the law of nature. For it is written: *Moreover He gave them instructions, and the law of life for an inheritance.*[1] But instruction is in contradistinction to the law of nature; since the law of nature is not learnt, but instilled by natural instinct. Therefore not all the moral precepts belong to the natural law.

Obj. 2. Further, the divine law is more perfect than human law. But human law adds certain things concerning good morals to those that belong to the law of nature: as is evidenced by the fact that the natural law is the same in all men, while these moral institutions are various for various people. Much more reason therefore was there why the divine law should add to the law of nature ordinances pertaining to good morals.

Obj. 3. Further, just as natural reason leads to good morals in certain matters, so does faith: hence it is written that faith *worketh by charity.*[2] But faith is not included in the law of nature; since that which is of faith is above nature. Therefore not all the moral precepts of the divine law belong to the law of nature.

On the contrary, the apostle says that *the Gentiles, who have not the law, do by nature those things that are of the law*:[3] which must be understood of things pertaining to good morals. Therefore all the moral precepts of the law belong to the law of nature.

---

[1] Ecclus. xvii. 9.   [2] Gal. v. 6.   [3] Rom. ii. 14.

I answer that the moral precepts, distinct from the ceremonial and judicial precepts, are about things pertaining of their very nature to good morals. Now since human morals depend on their relation to reason, which is the proper principle of human acts, those morals are called good which accord with reason, and those are called bad which are discordant from reason. And as every judgment of speculative reason proceeds from the natural knowledge of first principles, so every judgment of practical reason proceeds from principles known naturally, as stated above;[1] from which principles one may proceed in various ways to judge of various matters. For some matters connected with human actions are so evident, that after very little consideration one is able at once to approve or disapprove of them by means of these general first principles: while some matters cannot be the subject of judgment without much consideration of the various circumstances, which all are not competent to do carefully, but only those who are wise: just as it is not possible for all to consider the particular conclusions of sciences, but only for those who are versed in philosophy: and lastly there are some matters of which man cannot judge unless he be helped by divine instruction; such as the articles of faith.

It is therefore evident that since the moral precepts are about matters which concern good morals; and since good morals are those which are in accord with reason; and since also every judgment of human reason must needs be derived in some way from natural reason; it follows, of necessity, that all the moral precepts belong to the law of nature; but not all in the same way. For there are certain things which the natural reason of

[1] Q. xciv. as. 2, 4.

every man, of its own accord and at once, judges to be done or not to be done: e.g. *Honour thy father and thy mother*, and *Thou shalt not kill, Thou shalt not steal*; and these belong to the law of nature absolutely. And there are certain things which, after a more careful consideration, wise men deem obligatory. Such belong to the law of nature, yet so that they need to be inculcated, the wiser teaching the less wise: e.g. *Rise up before the hoary head, and honour the person of the aged man*, and the like. And there are some things, to judge of which, human reason needs divine instruction, whereby we are taught about the things of God: e.g. *Thou shalt not make to thyself a graven thing, nor the likeness of anything ; thou shalt not take the name of the Lord thy God in vain.*

Thie suffices for the replies to the objections.

2 1. Qs. xc, xci, and c.

11

THAT ALL THINGS TEND TO BE LIKE UNTO GOD

FROM the fact that they acquire the divine goodness, creatures are made like unto God. Wherefore if all things tend to God as their last end, so as to acquire His goodness,[1] it follows that the last end of things is to become like unto God

Moreover. The agent is said to be the end of the effect forasmuch as the effect tends to be like the agent: wherefore *the form of the generator is the end of the act of generation*.[2] Now God is the end of things in such

[1] I. xviii. [2] 2 *Phys.* vii.

* D 953

wise as to be also their first active cause. Therefore all things tend to a likeness to God, as their last end.

Again, things give evidence that *they naturally desire to be*;[1] so that if any are corruptible, they naturally resist corruptives, and tend to where they can be safe-guarded, as the fire tends upwards and earth downwards. Now all things have being in so far as they are like God, Who is self-subsistent being: for they are beings only by participation. Therefore all things desire as their last end to be like God.

Further. All creatures are images of the first agent, namely God: since *the agent produces its like*.[2] Now the perfection of an image consists in representing the original by its likeness thereto; for this is why an image is made. Therefore all things are for the purpose of acquiring a divine similitude, as their last end.

Again, each thing by its movement or action tends to some good as its end, as proved above.[3] Now a thing partakes of the good, in so far as it is like to the sovereign goodness, which is God. Therefore all things, by their movements and actions, tend to a divine likeness as their last end.

12

HOW THINGS IMITATE THE DIVINE GOODNESS

FROM what has been said it is cl r that the last end of all things is to become like God. Now, that which has properly the aspect of an end, is the good.[4] Therefore,

---

[1] 9 *Eth. Nic.* vii.   [2] 1 *De Gen. et Corr.* vii. 6.
[3] xvi.   [4] xvi.

properly speaking, things tend to become like to God forasmuch as He is good.

Now, creatures do not acquire goodness in the way in which it is in God: although each thing imitates the divine goodness, according to its mode. For the divine goodness is simple, being, as it were, all in one. Because the divine being contains the whole fullness of perfection, as we proved.[1] Wherefore, since a thing is good so far as it is perfect, God's being is His perfect goodness; for in God, to be, to live, to be wise, to be happy, and whatever else is seen to pertain to perfection and goodness, are one and the same in God, as though the sum total of His goodness were God's very being. Again, God's being is the substance of the existing God.[2] But this cannot be so in other things. For it was proved in the Second Book,[3] that no created substance is its own being. Wherefore, if a thing is good so far as it is: and nothing is its own being: none is its own goodness, but each one is good by having a share of good, even as by having a share of being it is a being.

Also. All creatures are not placed on the same level of goodness. For in some the substance is both form and actuality; such, to wit, as are competent, by the mere fact that they exist, to be actually and to be good. Whereas in others, the substance is composed of matter and form: and such are competent to be actually and to be good, but by some part of their being, namely their form. Accordingly God's substance is His goodness: whereas a simple substance participates goodness, by the very fact that it exists; and a composite substance, by some part of itself.

In this third degree of substance, diversity is to be

<hr />

[1] xxviii. [2] xxi. [3] II. xv.

found again in respect of being. For in some composed of matter and form, the form fills the entire potentiality of matter; so that the matter retains no potentiality to another form, and consequently neither is there in any other matter a potentiality to this same form. Such are the heavenly bodies, which consist of their entire matter. In others the form does not fill the whole potentiality of matter; so that the matter retains a potentiality to another form; and in another part of matter there remains potentiality to this form; for instance in the elements and their compounds. Since, then, privation is the absence in substance of what can be in substance, it is clear that together with this form which does not fill the whole potentiality of matter, there is associated the privation of a form, which privation cannot be associated with a substance whose form fills the whole potentiality of matter, nor with that which is a form essentially, and much less with that one whose essence is its very being. And seeing that it is clear that there can be no movement where there is no potentiality to something else, for movement is *the act of that which is in potentiality*;[1] and since evil is the privation of good; it is clear that in this last order of substances, good is changeable, and has an admixture of the opposite evil; which cannot occur in the higher orders of substances. Therefore the substance answering to this last description stands lowest both in being and in goodness.

We find degrees of goodness also among the parts of this substance composed of matter and form. For since matter considered in itself is being in potentiality, and since form is its act; and again since a composite sub-

[1] 3 *Phys.* i.

stance derives actual existence from its form: it follows that the form is, in itself, good; the composite substance is good as having its form actually; and the matter is good, as being in potentiality to the form. And although a thing is good in so far as it is a being, it does not follow that matter, which is only being potentially, is only a potential good. For being is predicated absolutely, while good is founded on order, for a thing is said to be good, not merely because it is an end, or possesses the end; but even though it has not attained the end, so long as it is directed to the end, for this very reason it is said to be good. Accordingly matter cannot be called a being absolutely, because it is a potential being, whereby it is shown to have an order towards being: and yet this suffices for it to be called a good absolutely, on account of this very order. This shows that the good, in a sense, extends further than being; for which reason Dionysius says that *the good includes both existing and non-existing things.*[1] For even non-existent things, namely matter considered as subject to privation, seek a good, namely to exist. Hence it follows that matter also is good; for nothing but the good seeks the good.

In yet another way the creature's goodness falls short from God's. For as we have stated, God, in His very being, has supreme perfection of goodness. Whereas the creature has its perfection, not in one thing but in many: because what is united in the highest is manifold in the lowest. Wherefore, in respect of one and the same thing, virtue, wisdom, and operation are predicated of God; but of creatures, in respect of different things: and the further a creature is from the sovereign goodness,

[1] *De Div. Nom.* iv.

the more does the perfection of its goodness require to be manifold. And if it be unable to attain to perfect goodness, it will reach to imperfect goodness in a few respects. Hence it is that although the first and sovereign good is utterly simple, and the substances nearest to it in goodness, approach likewise thereto in simplicity; yet the lowest substances are found to be more simple than some that are higher; elements, for instance, than animals and men, because they are unable to reach the perfection of knowledge and understanding to which animals and men attain.

From what has been said, it is evident that, although God possesses His perfect and entire goodness in respect of His simple being, creatures nevertheless do not attain to the perfection of their goodness through their being alone, but through many things. Wherefore, although each one is good inasmuch as it exists, it cannot be called good absolutely if it lack other things that are required for its goodness: thus a man who being despoiled of virtue is addicted to vice, is said indeed to be good in a restricted sense, namely as a being, and as a man; but not absolutely; in fact rather should he be called evil. Accordingly it is not the same in every creature, to be and to be good: although each one is good, inasmuch as it exists: whereas in God to be and to be good are simply one and the same.

If, then, each thing tends to a likeness to God's goodness as its end; and a thing is like God's goodness in respect of whatever belongs to its goodness; and the goodness of a thing consists not merely in its being, but in whatever is required for its perfection, as we have proved: it is clear that things are directed to God as their end, not only in respect of their substantial being, but also in respect of such things as are accidental thereto and belong to its perfection, as well as in respect of their proper operation, which also belongs to a thing's perfection.[1]

13

THAT THINGS HAVE A NATURAL TENDENCY TO BE LIKE GOD FORASMUCH AS HE IS A CAUSE

IT is clear from the foregoing that things have a tendency to be like God also in the point of their being causes of others.

For the creature tends to be like God by its operation. Now, by its operation, one thing is the cause of another. Therefore things tend to a divine similitude in this also, that they are causes of other things.

Again. Things tend to be like God, forasmuch as He is good as stated above.[2] Now it is out of His goodness that God bestows being on others; for all things act forasmuch as they are actually perfect. Therefore all things seek to be like God, by being causes of others.

Moreover. Order towards good, is itself a good, as we have shown above.[3] Now everything forasmuch as it is the cause of another, is directed to a good: for good alone is caused *per se*, and evil is caused only by accident, as we have proved.[4] Therefore it is a good to be a cause of others. Now in respect of any good to which a thing tends, that thing's tendency is to a divine similitude; since every created good is by reason of a share in the divine goodness. Therefore things tend to a divine likeness by being causes of other things.

[1] Cf. xxvii.   [2] xx.   [3] Ibid.   [4] x.

Again. That the effect tends to be like the agent, amounts to the same as that the agent causes its likeness in its effect: for the effect tends to the end towards which it is directed by the agent. Now the agent tends to assimilate the patient to itself, not only in respect of its being, but also in respect of its causality: because the agent gives to its natural effect not only those natural principles whereby it subsists, but also those whereby it is a cause of other things; thus the animal, when begotten, receives from its getter both the power of self-nourishment, and the power of generation. Therefore the effect tends to be like the agent, not only in the point of species, but also in the point of its causality of other things. Now things tend to be like God, even as effects tend to be like the agent, as proved above.[1] Therefore things have a natural tendency towards a divine likeness in this, that they are causes of other things.

Moreover. A thing is most perfect when it is able to produce its like; for that light shines perfectly, which gives light to others. Now whatever tends to its own perfection, tends to a divine likeness. Wherefore a thing tends to a divine likeness from the very fact that it tends to be the cause of other things.

Since, however, a cause, as such, is higher than its effect, it is evident that to tend in this way to a divine likeness, so as to be a cause of other things, belongs to the highest grade among things.

Furthermore. A thing is perfect in itself before being able to cause another, as we have stated already. Hence to be the cause of other things is a perfection that accrues to a thing last. Since then the creature tends

[1] xix.

to a divine likeness in many points,[1] this remains last, that it seek a likeness to God by being a cause of others. Wherefore Dionysius says that it is of *all things most godlike to be God's co-operator*;[2] in which sense the apostle says: *We are God's coadjutors.*[3]

14

THAT IN ORDER TO ACQUIRE KNOWLEDGE OF GOD IT IS NECESSARY TO PROCEED BY THE WAY OF REMOTION

ACCORDINGLY having proved that there is a first being which we call God, it behoves us to inquire into His nature.

Now in treating of the divine essence the principal method to be followed is that of remotion. For the divine essence by its immensity surpasses every form to which our intellect reaches; and thus we cannot apprehend it by knowing what it is. But we have some knowledge thereof by knowing *what it is not*; and we shall approach all the nearer to the knowledge thereof according as we shall be enabled to remove by our intellect a greater number of things therefrom. For the more completely we see how a thing differs from others, the more perfectly we know it: since each thing has in itself its own being distinct from all other things. Wherefore when we know the definition of a thing, first we place it in a genus, whereby we know in general what it is, and afterwards we add differences, so as to mark its distinction from other things, and thus we arrive at the complete knowledge of a thing's essence.

[1] xx.   [2] *Cael. Hier.* iii.   [3] I Cor. iii. 9.

Since, however, we are unable in treating of the divine essence to take *what* as a genus, nor can we express its distinction from other things by affirmative differences, we must needs express it by negative differences. Now just as in affirmative differences one restricts another, and brings us the nearer to a complete description of the thing, according as it makes it to differ from more things, so one negative difference is restricted by another that marks a distinction from more things. Thus, if we say that God is not an accident, we thereby distinguish Him from all accidents; then if we add that He is not a body, we shall distinguish Him also from certain substances, and thus in gradation He will be differentiated by suchlike negations from all beside Himself: and then when He is known as distinct from all things, we shall arrive at a proper consideration of Him. It will not, however, be perfect, because we shall not know *what* He is in Himself.

Wherefore in order to proceed about the knowledge of God by the way of remotion, let us take as principle that which is already made manifest by what we have said above,[1] namely that God is altogether unchangeable. This is also confirmed by the authority of Holy Writ. For it is said: *I am God and I change not* ;[2] *With Whom there is no change;*[4] and *God is not as a man . . . that He should be changed.*[5]

---

[1] xiii.   [2] Mal. iii. 6.   [3] Vulg., 'the Lord.'
[4] James i. 17.   [5] Num. xxiii. 19.

15

THAT GOD IS ETERNAL

FROM the foregoing it is also clear that God is eternal.

For whatever begins or ceases to be, suffers this through movement or change. Now it has been shown that God is altogether unchangeable. Therefore He is eternal, having neither beginning nor end.

Again. Only things which are moved are measured by time: because *time is the measure of movement*, as stated.[1] Now God is absolutely without movement, as we have already proved.[2] Therefore we cannot mark *before* and *after* in Him. Therefore in Him there is not being after non-being, nor can He have non-being after being, nor is it possible to find any succession in His being, because these things cannot be understood apart from time. Therefore He is without beginning and end, and has all His being simultaneously; and in this consists the notion of eternity.[3]

Moreover. If anywhen He was not and afterwards was, He was brought by someone out of non-being into being. Not by Himself; because what is not cannot do anything. And if by another, this other is prior to Him. Now it has been shown[4] that God is the first cause. Therefore He did not begin to be. Therefore neither will He cease to be: because that which always was, has the power to be always. Therefore He is eternal.

Furthermore. We observe that in the world there are certain things which can be and not be, namely those that are subject to generation and corruption. Now whatsoever is possible to be has a cause, because, as in

[1] 4 *Phys.* xi. 5.   [2] xiii.   [3] 1 *Sum. Th.* Q. x.   [4] xiii.

itself it is equally related to two things, namely being and not being, it follows that if it acquires being this is the result of some cause. But, as proved above [1] by Aristotle's argument, we cannot go on to infinity in causes. Therefore we must suppose some thing, which it is necessary to be. Now every necessary thing either has a cause of its necessity from without, or has no such cause, but is necessary of itself. But we cannot go on to infinity in necessary things that have causes of their necessity from without. Therefore we must suppose some first necessary thing which is necessary of itself: and this is God, since He is the first cause, as proved above.[2] Therefore God is eternal, since whatever is necessary of itself is eternal.

Again. Aristotle [3] proves the everlastingness of movement from the everlastingness of time: and thence he goes on to prove the everlastingness of the substance that is the cause of movement.[4] Now the first moving substance is God. Therefore He is everlasting. And supposing the everlastingness of time and movement to be denied, there still remains the argument in proof of the everlastingness of substance. For if movement had a beginning, it must have had its beginning from some mover. And if this mover had a beginning, it had its beginning from some agent. And thus either we shall go on to infinity, or we shall come to something without a beginning.

Divine authority bears witness to this truth: wherefore the Psalm reads: *But Thou, O Lord, endurest for ever,*[5] and again: *But Thou art always the self-same, and Thy years shall not fail.*[6]

---

[1] xiii.   [2] Ibid.   [3] 8 *Phys.* i. 10 ff.
[4] vi. 3 ff.   [5] Ps. ci. 13.   [6] Ibid. 28.

16

THAT IN GOD THERE IS NO PASSIVE POTENTIALITY

Now if God is eternal, it follows of necessity that He is not in potentiality.

For everything in whose substance there is an admixture of potentiality, is possibly non-existent as regards whatever it has of potentiality, for that which may possibly be may possibly not be. Now God in Himself cannot not be, since He is eternal. Therefore in God there is no potentiality to be.

Again. Although that which is sometimes potential and sometimes actual, is in point of time potential before being actual, nevertheless actuality is simply before potentiality: because potentiality does not bring itself into actuality, but needs to be brought into actuality by something actual. Therefore whatever is in any way potential has something previous to it. Now God is the first being and the first cause, as stated above.[1] Therefore in Him there is no admixture of potentiality.

Again. That which of itself must necessarily be, can nowise be possibly, since what of itself must be necessarily, has no cause, whereas whatever can be possibly, has a cause, as proved above.[2] Now God, in Himself, must necessarily be. Therefore nowise can He be possibly. Therefore no potentiality is to be found in His essence.

Again. Everything acts according as it is actual. Wherefore that which is not wholly actual acts, not by its whole self, by but part of itself. Now that which does not act by its whole self is not the first agent,

[1] xiii.   [2] xv.

since it acts by participation of something and not by its essence. Therefore the first agent, which is God, has no admixture of potentiality, but is pure act.

Moreover. Just as it is natural that a thing should act in so far as it is actual, so is it natural for it to be passive in so far as it is in potentiality, for *movement is the act of that which is in potentiality*.[1] Now God is altogether impassible and immovable, as stated above.[2] Therefore in Him there is no potentiality, namely that which is passive.

Further. We notice in the world something that passes from potentiality to actuality. Now it does not reduce itself from potentiality to actuality, because that which is potential is not yet, wherefore neither can it act. Therefore it must be preceded by something else whereby it can be brought from potentiality to actuality. And if this again passes from potentiality to actuality, it must be preceded by something else, whereby it can be brought from potentiality to actuality. But we cannot go on thus to infinity. Therefore we must come to something that is wholly actual and nowise potential. And this we call God.

17

THAT IN GOD THERE IS NO MATTER

FROM this it follows that God is not matter.

For matter, such as it is, is in potentiality.

Again. Matter is not a principle of activity: wherefore, as Aristotle puts it,[3] efficient and material causes do not coincide. Now, as stated above,[4] it belongs to

---

[1] 3 *Phys.* i. 6.   [2] xiii.   [3] 2 *Phys.* vii. 3.   [4] xiii.

God to be the first efficient cause of things. Therefore
He is not matter.

Moreover. For those who referred all things to
matter as their first cause, it followed that natural things
exist by chance: and against these it is argued.[1] Therefore if God, who is the first cause, is the material cause of
things, it follows that all things exist by chance.

Further. Matter does not become the cause of an
actual thing, except by being altered and changed.
Therefore if God is immovable, as proved above,[2] He
can nowise be a cause of things as their matter.

The Catholic faith professes this truth, asserting that
God created all things not out of His substance, but out
of nothing.

The ravings of David of Dinant are hereby con-
founded, who dared to assert that God is the same as
primary matter, because if they were not the same, they
would needs differ by certain differences, and thus they
would not be simple: since in that which differs from
another thing by a difference, the very difference argues
composition. Now this proceeded from his ignorance
of the distinction between difference and diversity. For
as laid down,[3] a thing is said to be *different* in relation
to something, because whatever is different, differs by
something, whereas things are said to be *diverse* absolutely from the fact that they are not the same thing.[4]
Accordingly we must seek for a difference in things
which have something in common, for we have to point
to something in them whereby they differ: thus two
species have a common genus, wherefore they must needs
be distinguished by differences. But in those things

---

[1] 2 *Phys.* viii, ix.   [2] xiii.
[3] 10 *Metaph.* D. 9, iii. 6.   [4] 1. *Sum. Th.* Q. iii. a. 8, *r. obj.* 3.

which have nothing in common, we have not to seek in what they differ, for they are diverse by themselves. For thus are opposite differences distinguished from one another, because they do not participate in a genus as a part of their essence: and consequently we must not ask in what they differ, for they are diversified by their very selves. Thus, too, God and primary matter are distinguished, since, the one being pure act and the other pure potentiality, they have nothing in common.

18

THAT IN GOD THERE IS NO COMPOSITION

From the foregoing we are able to conclude that there is no composition in God. For in every composite thing there must needs be act and potentiality: since several things cannot become one simply, unless there be something actual there and something else potential. Because those things that are actually, are not united except as an assemblage or group, which are not one simply. In these moreover the very parts that are gathered together are as a potentiality in relation to the union: for they are actually united after being potentially unitable. But in God there is no potentiality.[1] Therefore in Him there is no composition.

Again. Every composite is subsequent to its components. Therefore the first being, namely God,[2] has no component parts.

Further. Every composite is potentially dissoluble, so far as its composite nature is concerned, although in

----
[1] xvi.   [2] xiii.

some there is something else incompatible with dissolution. Now that which is dissoluble is in potentiality to not-being. But this cannot be said of God, since of His very essence He is necessarily. Therefore there is no composition in Him.

Moreover. Every composition requires a compounder: for if there be composition, it results from several things: and things that are several in themselves would not combine together unless they were united by a compounder. If then God were composite, He would have a compounder: for He could not compound Himself, since no thing is its own cause, for it would precede itself, which is impossible. Now the compounder is the efficient cause of the composite. Therefore God would have an efficient cause: and thus He would not be the first cause, which was proved above.[1]

Again. In any genus the more simple a thing is the more excellent it is; such, in the genus *hot*, is fire which has no admixture of cold. Therefore that which obtains the summit of nobility among beings, must be in the summit of simplicity. Now that which obtains the summit of nobility in things is what we call God, since He is the first cause, because the cause is more excellent than its effect. Therefore there can be no composition in Him.

Moreover. In every composite thing the good does not belong to this or that part but to the whole, and I speak of good in reference to that goodness which is proper to, and is the perfection of, the whole: thus the parts are imperfect in relation to the whole: thus the parts of a man are not a man, nor have the parts of the number six the perfection of six, nor do the parts of

[1] xiii.

a line attain to the perfection of the measure found in
the whole line.   Therefore if God is composite, His
proper perfection and goodness are found in the whole
of God but not in any of His parts.   And thus the good
that is proper to Him will not be purely in Him; and
consequently He will not be the first and supreme good.

Further.   Before every multitude it is necessary to
find unity.   Now in every composite there is multitude.
Therefore that which is before all things, namely God,
must needs be devoid of all composition.

19

THAT IN GOD THERE IS NOTHING VIOLENT
OR BESIDE NATURE

HENCE Aristotle [1] concludes that in God there cannot
be anything violent or outside nature.   For whatever
has in itself anything violent or beside nature, has
something added to itself: since that which belongs to
a thing's essence cannot be violent or beside nature.
Now no simple thing has in itself anything that is
added, for this would argue its being composite.   Since
then God is simple, as shown above,[2] there can be nothing
in Him that is violent or beside nature.

Further.   The necessity resulting from compulsion is
a necessity imposed by another.   Now in God there is no
necessity imposed by another, for He is necessary of
Himself, and the cause of necessity in other things.[3]
Therefore nothing is compulsory in Him.

Moreover.   Wherever there is violence, there can be

---

[1] 5 *Metaph*. i. 6 (D. 4, v. 6).   [2] xviii.   [3] xv.

something besides what belongs to a thing by its very nature: since violence is contrary to that which is according to nature. But it is not possible for anything to be in God that does not belong to Him according to His nature, since by His very nature He is necessary being, as shown above.[1] Therefore there can be nothing violent in Him.

Again. Everything that is compelled or unnatural has a natural aptitude to be moved by another: because *that which is done by compulsion has an external principle, without any concurrence on the part of the patient.*[2] Now God is altogether immovable, as shown above.[3] Therefore nothing in Him can be violent or unnatural.

20

THAT GOD IS NOT A BODY

FROM the foregoing we are also able to prove that God is not a body.

For since every body is a continuous substance, it is composite and has parts. Now God is not composite, as we have shown.[4] Therefore He is not a body.

Further. Every quantitative substance is somehow in potentiality: for that which is continuous is potentially divisible to infinity; and the number can be infinitely augmented. Now every body is a quantitative substance. Therefore every body is in potentiality. But God is not in potentiality, but is pure act, as shown above.[5] Therefore God is not a body.

Again. If God were a body, He would needs be a

[1] xv.　　[2] 3 *Eth. Nic.* i. 3.　　[3] xiii.　　[4] xviii.　　[5] xvi.

physical body, for a mathematical body does not exist
by itself, as Aristotle proves,[1] since dimensions are
accidents.   Now He is not a physical body; for He is
immovable, as we have proved,[2] and every physical body
is movable.   Therefore God is not a body.

Moreover.   Every body is finite, which is proved in
regard both to spherical and to rectilinear bodies.[3]
Now we are able by our intellect and imagination to
soar above any finite body.   Wherefore, if God were a
body, our intellect and imagination would be able to
think of something greater than God: and thus God
would not exceed our intellect: which is inadmissible.
Therefore He is not a body.

Furthermore.   Intellective knowledge is more certain
than sensitive.   Now among natural things we find
some that are objects of sense: therefore there are also
some that are objects of intellect.   But the order of
powers is according to the order of objects, in the same
way as their distinction.   Therefore above all sensible
objects there is an intelligible object existing in natural
things.   But every body that exists among things is
sensible.   Therefore above all bodies it is possible to
find something more excellent.   Wherefore if God were
a body, He would not be the first and supreme
being.

Again.   A living thing is more excellent than any
body devoid of life.   Now the life of a living body is
more excellent than that body, since thereby it excels
all other bodies.   Therefore that which is excelled by
nothing, is not a body.   But such is God.   Therefore
He is not a body.

Moreover.   We find the philosophers proving the same

---

[1] 2 *Metaph.* v.   [2] xiii.   [3] *De Caelo,* v ff.

conclusion by arguments [1] based on the eternity of movement, as follows. In all everlasting movement the first mover must needs not be moved, neither *per se* nor accidentally, as we have proved above.[2] Now the body of the heavens is moved in a circle with an everlasting movement. Therefore its first mover is not moved, neither *per se* nor accidentally. Now no body causes local movement unless itself be moved, because moved and mover must be simultaneous; and thus the body that causes movement must be itself moved, in order to be simultaneous with the body that is moved. Moreover no power in a body causes movement except it be moved accidentally; since, when the body is moved, the power of that body is moved accidentally. Therefore the first mover of the heavens is neither a body nor a power residing in a body. Now that to which the movement of the heavens is ultimately reduced as to the first immovable mover, is God. Therefore God is not a body.

Again. No infinite power is a power residing in a magnitude. But the power of the first mover is an infinite power. Therefore it does not reside in a magnitude. And thus God, Who is the first mover, is neither a body nor a power residing in a body.

The first proposition is proved as follows. If a power residing in a magnitude be infinite, this magnitude is either finite or infinite. But there is no infinite magnitude, as proved.[3] And it is not possible for a finite magnitude to have an infinite power. Therefore in no magnitude can there be an infinite power.

That there cannot be an infinite power in a finite

---

[1] 7 and 8 *Phys.* See also above, xiii.　　　[2] xiii.
[3] 3 *Phys.* v, and *De Caelo*, v ff.

magnitude is proved thus. A great power produces in less time an equal effect, which a lesser power produces in more time: of whatever kind this effect may be, whether it be one of alteration, of local movement, or of any other kind of movement. Now an infinite power surpasses every finite power. It follows therefore that it produces its effect more rapidly, by causing a more rapid movement than any finite power. Nor can this greater rapidity be one of time. Therefore it follows that the effect is produced in an indivisible point of time. And thus moving, being moved, and movement will be instantaneous: the contrary of which has been proved.[1]

That an infinite power of a finite magnitude cannot cause movement in time, is proved thus. Let A be an infinite power; and AB a part thereof. This part therefore will cause movement in more time. And yet there must be proportion between this time and the time in which the whole power causes movement, since both times are finite. Suppose then these two times to be in proportion as 1 to 10, for it does not affect this argument whether we take this or any other ratio. Now if we increase the aforesaid finite power, we must decrease the time in proportion to the increase of the power, since a greater power causes movement in less time. If therefore we increase it tenfold, that power will cause movement in a time which will be one-tenth of the time occupied by the first part that we took of the infinite power, namely AB. And yet this power which is ten times the aforesaid power is a finite power, since it has a fixed proportion to a finite power. It follows therefore that a finite power and an infinite power cause movement in an equal time: which is impossible. There-

[1] 6 Phys. iii.

fore an infinite power of a finite magnitude cannot cause movement in any time.

That the power of the first mover is infinite is proved thus. No finite power can cause movement in an infinite time. Now the power of the first mover causes movement in an infinite time, since the first movement is eternal. Therefore the power of the first mover is infinite. The first proposition is proved thus. If any finite power of a body causes movement in infinite time, a part of that body having a part of that power, will cause movement during less time, since the greater power a thing has, for so much the longer time will it be able to continue a movement, and thus the aforesaid part will cause movement in finite time, and a greater part will be able to cause movement during more time. And thus always according as we increase the power of the mover, we increase the time in the same proportion. But if this increase be made a certain number of times we shall come to the quantity of the whole or even go beyond it. Therefore the increase also on the part of the time will reach the quantity of time wherein the whole causes movement. And yet the time wherein the whole causes movement was supposed to be infinite. Consequently a finite time will measure an infinite time: which is impossible.

However, there are several objections to this chain of reasoning. One of these is that it might be held that the body which moves the first thing moved is not divisible, as is the case of a heavenly body: whereas the argument given above supposes it to be divided.

To this we reply that a conditional clause may be true though its antecedent be impossible. And if there be anything to disprove such a conditional, the

antecedent is impossible.   Thus if any one disprove this
conditional, *If a man flies, he has wings*, the antecedent
would be impossible.   It is in this way that we are to
understand the process of the aforesaid reasoning.   For
this conditional is true, *If a heavenly body be divided, its
part will have less power than the whole*.   But this conditional is disproved if we suppose that the first mover
is a body, on account of the impossibilities that follow.
Wherefore it is clear that this is impossible.   We can
reply in the same way if objection be made to the increase
of finite powers.   Because it is impossible in natural
things to find powers according to any proportion that
there is between one time and any other time.   And yet
the conditional required in the aforesaid argument is
true.

The second objection is that, although a body be
divided, it is possible for a power of a body not to be
divided when the body is divided, thus the rational soul
is not divided when the body is divided.

To this we reply that by the above argument it is
not proved that God is not united to the body as the
rational soul is united to the human body, but that He
is not a power residing in a body, as a material power
which is divided when the body is divided.   Wherefore
it is also said of the human intellect that it is neither
a body nor a power in a body.[1]   That God is not united
to the body as its soul, is another question.[2]

The third objection is that if the power of every body is
finite, as is proved in the above process; and if a finite
power cannot make its effect to endure an infinite time;
it will follow that no body can endure an infinite time:
and consequently that a heavenly body will be neces-

[1] Cf. 2, lvi.   [2] Cf. xxvii.

sarily corrupted. Some reply to this that a heavenly
body in respect of its own power is defectible, but acquires
everlastingness from another that has infinite power.
Apparently Plato approves of this solution, for he
represents God as speaking of the heavenly bodies as
follows: *By your nature ye are corruptible, but by My
will incorruptible, because My will is greater than your
necessity.*[1]

But the Commentator refutes this solution.[2] For it
is impossible, according to him, that what in itself may
possibly not be, should acquire everlastingness of being
from another: since it would follow that the corruptible
is changed into incorruptibility; and this, in his opinion,
is impossible. Wherefore he replies after this fashion:
that in a heavenly body whatever power there is, is
finite, and yet it does not follow that it has all power;
for, according to Aristotle[3] the potentiality to (be)
somewhere is in a heavenly body, but not the potentiality
to be. And thus it does not follow that it has a potentiality to not-be. It must be observed, however, that
this reply of the Commentator is insufficient. Because,
although it be granted that in a heavenly body there is
no quasi-potentiality to be, which potentiality is that of
matter, there is nevertheless in it a quasi-active potentiality, which is the power of being: since Aristotle says
explicitly[4] that the heaven has the power to be always.
Hence it is better to reply that since power implies
relation to act, we should judge of power according to the
mode of the act. Now movement by its very nature has
quantity and extension, wherefore its infinite duration
requires that the moving power should be infinite. On

<hr>

[1] *Timaeus*, xli.   [2] 11 *Metaph.*
[3] 8 *Metaph.* D. 7, iv. 6.   [4] 1 *De Caelo*, iii. 4; xii. 3.

the other hand being has no quantitative extension, especially in a thing whose being is invariable, such as the heaven. Hence it does not follow that the power of being a finite body is infinite though its duration be infinite: because it matters not whether that power make a thing to last for an instant or for an infinite time, since that invariable being is not affected by time except accidentally.

The fourth objection is that the statement that what causes movement in infinite time must have an infinite power, does not necessarily apply to those movers which are not altered by moving. Because such a movement consumes nothing of their power; wherefore they can cause movement for no less time after they have moved for a certain time, than before. Thus the power of the sun is finite, and, because its power is not diminished on account of its action, it can act on this lower world for an infinite time, according to nature.

To this we reply that a body moves not unless it be moved, as we have shown. Therefore, supposing a body not to be moved, it follows that it does not move. Now in anything that is moved there is potentiality to opposites, since the terms of movement are opposite to one another. Consequently, considered in itself, every body that is moved is possibly not moved. And that which is possibly not moved, is not apt of itself to be moved for an everlasting time: and consequently neither is it apt to move for a perpetual time.

Accordingly the demonstration given above is based on the finite power of a finite body; which power cannot of itself move in an infinite time. But a body which of itself is possibly moved and not moved, and possibly moves and does not move, can acquire perpetual

movement from some cause; and this cause must needs
be incorporeal. Wherefore the first mover must needs
be incorporeal. Hence according to nature nothing
hinders a finite body, which acquires from another cause
perpetuity in being moved, from having also perpetuity
in moving: since also the first heavenly body, according
to nature, can cause a perpetual circular movement in
the lower bodies, according as one sphere moves another. Nor is it impossible, as the Commentator maintains,[1] for that which is, of itself, in potentiality to being
moved and not moved, to acquire perpetual movement
from something else, as he supposed it impossible as
regards perpetuity of being. For movement is a kind
of outflow from the mover to the thing movable, and
consequently a movable thing can acquire perpetual
movement from something else, without having it by
nature. On the other hand, *to be* is something fixed and
quiescent in a being, and consequently that which is,
of itself, in potentiality to not-be, cannot, as he says,
in the course of nature, acquire from something else
perpetuity of being.

The fifth objection is that according to the above
reasoning there does not appear to be more reason why
there should not be an infinite power in a magnitude
than outside a magnitude: for in either case it would
follow that it moves in not-time.

To this it may be replied that finite and infinite are
found in a magnitude, in time and in movement in a
univocal sense, as proved,[2] wherefore the infinite in
one of them removes a finite proportion in the others:
whereas in things devoid of magnitude there is neither

---

[1] See above: *But the Commentator* . . . , p. 113.
[2] 3 *Phys.* iv. 1; 6, ii. 8.

finite nor infinite unless equivocally. Hence the above course of reasoning has no place in suchlike powers.

But another and better answer is that the heaven has two movers.[1] One is its proximate mover, which is of finite power, and thence it is that its movement is of finite velocity. The other is its remote mover, which is of infinite power, whence it is that its movement can be of infinite duration. Thus it is clear that an infinite power which is not in a magnitude, can move a body not immediately in time: whereas a power which is in a magnitude must needs move immediately, since no body moves without itself being moved. Wherefore, if it moved, it would follow that it moves in not-time.

Better still it may be replied that a power which is not in a magnitude is an intellect, and moves by its will. Wherefore it moves according to the requirement of the movable and not according to the proportion of its strength. On the other hand, a power that is in a magnitude cannot move save by natural necessity, for it has been proved that the intellect is not a bodily force.[2] Wherefore it causes movement necessarily according to the proportion of its quantity. Hence it follows that if it moves anything it moves it instantaneously. In this sense then, the foregoing objections being refuted, proceeds the reasoning of Aristotle.

Moreover. No movement that proceeds from a bodily mover can be continuous and regular: because a bodily mover, in local movement, moves by attraction or repulsion, and that which is attracted or repelled is not disposed in the same way towards its mover from the beginning to the end of the movement, since at one

---

[1] Averroes, 12 *Metaph.* t. 41.
[2] See above: *To this we reply* . . . , p. 112.

time it is nearer to it and at another time further from it: and thus no body can cause a continuous and regular movement. On the other hand the first movement is continuous and regular, as is proved.[1] Therefore the mover of the first movement is not a body.

Again, no movement that tends towards an end which passes from potentiality to actuality, can be perpetual: since, when it arrives at actuality, the movement ceases. If therefore the first movement is perpetual, it must be towards an end which is always and in every way actual. Now such is neither a body nor a power residing in a body; because these are all movable either *per se* or accidentally. Therefore the end of the first movement is not a body nor a power residing in a body. Now the end of the first movement is the first mover, which moves as the object of desire:[2] and that is God. Therefore God is neither a body nor a power residing in a body.

Now though, according to our faith, it is false that the movement of the heavens is everlasting, as we shall show further on;[3] it is nevertheless true that that movement will not cease, either on account of lack of power in the mover, or on account of the substance of the movable being corrupted, since we do not find that the movement of the heavens slackens in the course of time. Wherefore the aforesaid proofs lose nothing of their efficacy.

The truth thus demonstrated is in accordance with divine authority. For it is said: *God is a spirit, and they that adore Him, must adore Him in spirit and in truth*;[4] and again: *To the King of ages, immortal,*

---

[1] 8 *Phys.* vii ff.   [2] Cf. xiii.
[3] 4, xcvii.   [4] John iv. 24.

invisible, the only God;[1] and: *The invisible things of God
. . . are clearly seen, being understood by the things that
are made*,[2] for things that are clearly seen not by the
eye but by the mind, are incorporeal.

Hereby is refuted the error of the early natural philosophers,[3] who admitted none but material causes, such as
fire, water, and the like, and consequently asserted that
the first principles of things were bodies, and called
them gods. Among these also there were some who
held that the causes of movement were *sympathy* and
antipathy: and these again are refuted by the above
arguments. For since according to them sympathy
and antipathy are in bodies, it would follow that the
first principles of movement are forces residing in a
body. They also asserted that God was composed of the
four elements and sympathy: from which we gather that
they held God to be a heavenly body. Among the
ancients Anaxagoras alone came near to the truth, since
he affirmed that all things are moved by an intellect.

By this truth, moreover, those heathens are refuted
who maintained that the very elements of the world,
and the forces residing in them, are gods; for instance
the sun, moon, earth, water, and so forth, being led
astray by the errors of the philosophers mentioned above.

Again, the above arguments confound the extrava-
gances of the unlettered Jews, of Tertullian, of the
Vadiani or Anthropomorphite heretics, who depicted
God with human features; and again of the Manichees,
who affirmed God to be an infinite substance composed
of light and spread abroad throughout boundless space.
The occasion of all these errors was that in their thoughts

---

[1] 1 Tim. i. 17.   [2] Rom. i. 20.
[3] Cf. 1 *Phys*. ii.

about divine things they had recourse to their imagination, which can reflect none but corporeal likenesses. Wherefore it behoves us to put the imagination aside when we meditate on things incorporeal.

21

THAT GOD IS HIS OWN ESSENCE

FROM what has been laid down we are able to conclude that God is His own essence, quiddity, or nature.

In everything that is not its own essence or quiddity there must needs be some kind of composition: for since each thing contains its own essence, if a thing contained nothing besides its own essence, all that a thing is would be its essence. Therefore if a thing were not its own essence, there must be something in it besides its essence: and consequently there must be composition therein. For which reason the essence in composite things has the signification of a part, as humanity in a man. Now it has been shown [1] that in God there is no composition. Therefore God is His own essence.

Again, seemingly that alone which does not enter into the definition of a thing is beside the essence of that thing: for a definition signifies what a thing is.[2] Now only the accidents of a thing do not enter into its definition: and consequently only accidents are in a thing besides its essence. But in God there are no accidents, as we shall show further on.[3] Accordingly, there is nothing in Him besides His essence. Therefore He is His own essence.

[1] xviii.　　　　[2] 4 *Metaph*. viii. 4.　　　　[3] xxiii.

Moreover. Forms that are not predicated of subsistent things, whether the latter be taken universally or singly, are not single *per se* subsistent forms individualized in themselves. For we do not say that Socrates, or man, or an animal is whiteness, because whiteness is not singly *per se* subsistent, but is individualized by its subsistent subject. Likewise, natural forms do not *per se* subsist singly, but are individualized in their respective matters: wherefore we do not say that this individual fire, or that fire in general, is its own form. Moreover, the essences or quiddities of genera or species are individualized by the signate matter of this or that individual, although indeed the quiddity of a genus or species includes form and matter in general: wherefore we do not say that Socrates, or man, is humanity. Now the divine essence exists *per se* singly and is individualized in itself, since it is not in any matter, as shown above.[1]   Hence the divine essence is predicated of God, so that we say: *God is His own essence.*

Further. The essence of a thing is either the thing itself, or is related to it in some way as cause: since a thing derives its species from its essence. But nothing can in any way be a cause of God: for He is the first being, as shown above.[2]   Therefore, God is His own essence.

Again, that which is not its own essence, is related in respect of some part of itself to that essence, as potentiality to act: wherefore the essence is signified by way of form, for instance *humanity*. But there is no potentiality in God, as shown above,[3] therefore it follows that He is His own essence.

[1] xvii.   [2] xiii.   [3] xvi.

22

THAT IN GOD EXISTENCE AND ESSENCE ARE THE SAME

FROM what has been shown above, we may go on to prove that in God essence or quiddity is not distinct from His existence.

For it has been shown above [1] that there is a thing which exists of itself necessarily, and this is God. Now necessary existence, if it belong to a quiddity which is not that existence itself, is either inconsistent with or repugnant to that quiddity, as *per se* existence is to the quiddity of whiteness, or else is consistent or akin thereto, for instance that whiteness exist in some other thing. In the former supposition it will not belong to that quiddity to exist *per se* necessarily, for instance it becomes not whiteness to exist *per se*. In the second hypothesis, either this existence must be dependent on the essence, or both of them on some other cause, or the essence on the existence. The first two are in contradiction with the very notion of necessary *per se* existence: for if it depend on something else, it no longer exists necessarily. From the third supposition it follows that this quiddity is added accidentally to the thing which exists *per se* necessarily: because whatever follows on the essence of a thing is accidental thereto. Therefore, God has not an essence distinct from His existence.

Against this, however, it might be urged that this existence does not depend absolutely on this essence,

[1] xiii.

and in such a way that it would not be at all unless the essence were: but that it depends as regards the conjunction whereby they are united together. And thus this existence is *per se* necessary, while the conjunction is not *per se* necessary.

But this answer does not avoid the above impossibility. For if this existence can be understood without this essence, it will follow that this essence is related accidentally to this existence. Now this existence is that which exists *per se* necessarily. Therefore this essence is related accidentally to that which exists *per se* necessarily. Therefore it is not its quiddity. But God is that which exists *per se* necessarily. Therefore this existence is not God's essence, but something subsequent thereto. On the other hand if this existence cannot be understood apart from this essence, then this existence depends absolutely on that on which depends its conjunction with this essence: and thus the same conclusion follows.

Further, each thing exists by its own existence. Wherefore that which is not its own existence does not exist *per se* necessarily. But God exists *per se* necessarily. Therefore God is His own existence.

Moreover, if God's existence is not His essence; and it cannot be a part of Him, since the divine essence is simple, as shown above; [1] it follows that this existence is something besides His essence. Now whatever is becoming to a thing besides its essence, is becoming to it through some cause: for those things which are not one *per se*, if they be united together, must needs be united through some cause. Therefore existence is becoming to that quiddity through some cause. Either, then, this

[1] xviii.

cause is something essential to that thing, or the essence itself, or else it is some other thing. If the former; and the essence exists according to that existence; it follows that a thing is a cause of its own existence. But this is impossible, because according to the understanding the cause exists before the effect; and consequently if a thing is the cause of its own existence, it would be understood to exist before having existence, which is impossible:—unless it be understood that a thing is the cause of its own accidental existence, which is a relative existence. For this is not impossible: for we find an accidental being caused by the principles of its subject, before the substantial being of the subject is understood to exist. Now, however, we are speaking, not of accidental, but of substantial existence. If, on the other hand, existence be becoming to the essence, by reason of some other cause; then whatever acquires existence from another cause, is caused and is not the first cause: whereas God is the first cause, having no cause, as shown above.[1] Wherefore this quiddity that acquires existence elsewhere is not the quiddity of God. Therefore it is necessary that God's existence be His own quiddity.

Moreover. Existence denotes a kind of actuality: since a thing is said to exist, not through being in potentiality, but through being in act. Now everything to which an act is becoming, and which is distinct from that act, is related thereto as potentiality to act: since act and potentiality are reciprocal terms. Accordingly, if the divine essence is distinct from its existence, it follows that His essence and existence are mutually related as potentiality and act. Now it has been proved

[1] xiii.

that in God there is nothing of potentiality, and that
He is pure act.[1]   Therefore God's essence is not distinct
from His existence.

Again.   Whatsoever cannot exist unless several things
concur, is composite.   Now no thing in which essence
and existence are distinct from one another can exist
except several things concur, to wit its essence and
existence.   Therefore every thing, in which essence
and existence are distinct, is composite.   But God is
not composite, as proved above.[2]   Therefore God's
existence is His essence.

Further.   Everything exists through having existence.
Therefore nothing the essence of which is not its existence, exists by its essence, but by participation of
something, namely existence.   Now that which exists
by participation of something cannot be the first being,
because that in which a thing participates in order to
exist, is previous to that thing.   But God is the first
being, to which nothing is previous.[3]   Therefore God's
essence is His existence.

This sublime truth Moses was taught by the Lord:
for when he asked the Lord: *If* the children of Israel
*should say to me: What is His name? what shall I say to
them?* the Lord answered: I AM WHO AM. . . . *Thus shalt
thou say to the children of Israel :* HE WHO IS *hath sent me
to you*;[4] thus declaring His own name to be: HE WHO IS.
Now every name is appointed to signify the nature or
essence of a thing.   Wherefore it follows that God's
very existence itself is His essence or nature.

Moreover.   The Catholic doctors have professed this
truth.   For Hilary says: *Existence is not an accident in*

[1] xvi.   [2] xviii.
[3] xiii.   [4] Exod. iii. 13, 14.

God, but the subsisting truth, the abiding cause, and the natural property of His essence.[1] And Boethius says that *the divine substance is existence itself, and all other existence proceeds therefrom.*[2]

23

THAT THERE IS NO ACCIDENT IN GOD

FROM this truth it follows of necessity that nothing can accrue to God besides His essence, nor anything be accidentally in Him.

For existence itself cannot participate in something that is not of its essence; although that which exists can participate in something else. Because nothing is more formal or more simple than existence. Hence existence itself can participate in nothing. Now the divine substance is existence itself.[3] Therefore He has nothing that is not of His substance. Therefore no accident can be in Him.

Moreover. Whatever is in a thing accidentally, has a cause of being there: since it is added to the essence of that in which it is. Therefore if anything is in God accidentally, this must be through some cause. Consequently the cause of the accident is either the divine substance itself, or something else. If it is something else, this other thing must act on the divine substance; since nothing introduces a form, whether substantial or accidental, into some recipient, unless in some way it act upon that recipient: because to act is nothing but to make something to be actual, and it is this by a form. Wherefore God will be passive and movable to some

---

[1] *De Trin.* vii. 11.   [2] Ibid. ii.   [3] xxii.

agent: which is against what has been decided above.[1]
If, on the other hand, the divine substance itself is the
cause of the accident that is in it, then it is impossible
for it to be its cause as receiving it, since then the same
thing in the same respect would make itself to be in act.
Therefore, if there is an accident in God, it follows that
He receives that accident in one respect, and causes it
in another, even as bodies receive their proper accidents
through the nature of their matter, and cause them
through their form: so that God, therefore, will be composite, the contrary of which has been proved above.[2]

Again. Every subject of an accident is compared
thereto as potentiality to act: because an accident is a
kind of form making a thing to exist actually according
to accidental existence. But there is no potentiality in
God, as shown above.[3] Therefore there can be no accident in Him.

Moreover. Everything in which something is accidentally is in some way changeable as to its nature:
since an accident, by its very nature, may be in a thing
or not in it. Therefore if God has something that becomes Him accidentally, it follows that He is changeable:
the contrary of which has been proved above.[4]

Further. Everything that has an accident in itself,
is not whatever it has in itself, because an accident is
not of the essence of its subject. But God is whatever
He has in Himself. Therefore no accident is in God.
The middle proposition is proved as follows. A thing
is always to be found more excellently in the cause
than in the effect. But God is the cause of all things.
Therefore whatever is in Him, is found in Him in the
most perfect way. Now that which is most perfectly

becoming to a thing, is that thing itself: because it is more perfectly one than when one thing is united to another substantially as form is united to matter: which union again is more perfect than when one thing is in another accidentally. It follows therefore that God is whatever He has.

Again. Substance is not dependent upon accident, although accident depends on substance. Now that which is not dependent upon another, can sometimes be found without it.[1] Therefore some substance can be found without an accident: and this seemingly is most becoming to a supremely simple substance, such as the divine substance.[2] Therefore the divine substance is altogether without accidents.

The Catholic tractarians also are in agreement with this statement. Wherefore Augustine says that *there is no accident in God*.[3]

Having established this truth we are able to refute certain erroneous statements in the law of the Saracens to the effect that the divine essence has certain forms added thereto.

24

THAT THE DIVINE BEING CANNOT BE SPECIFIED BY THE ADDITION OF ANY SUBSTANTIAL DIFFERENCE

AGAIN. From what we have said above, it can be shown that we cannot add anything to the divine being so as to specify it by an essential specification, as a genus is specified by differences. For it is impossible that a

[1] Cf. xiii.   [2] xviii.   [3] *De Trin.* v. 4.

thing be in act unless there be also all those things whereby its substantial being is specified: for an animal cannot be in act unless it be either a rational or an irrational animal. Wherefore also the Platonists who postulated ideas, did not postulate *per se* existing ideas of genera, which derive specification from essential differences, but they postulated *per se* existing ideas of the species alone, which need not to be specified by essential differences. If, then, the divine being can receive an essential specification from something added to it, that being will not be in act without something added to it. But God's very being is His substance as shown above.[1] Therefore the divine substance cannot be in act without some addition: the contrary of which has been shown above.[2]

Again. Whatever needs something added to it, in order to exist, is in potentiality to that thing. But the divine substance is not in potentiality in any way, as proved above:[3] and God's substance is His being. Therefore His being cannot receive essential specification from something added to it.

Moreover. Whatever makes a thing to be in act, and is intrinsic to that thing, is either the whole essence thereof or part of its essence. Now that which specifies a thing by an essential specification, makes a thing to be in act, and is intrinsic to the thing specified: otherwise the latter could not be specified essentially thereby. Therefore it must be either the very essence or part of the essence of that thing. But if something be added to the divine being, it cannot be the whole essence of God, for it has already been proved[4] that God's existence is not distinct from His essence. Therefore it

[1] xxii.   [2] xiii.   [3] xvi.   [4] xxii.

follows that it is a part of the divine essence: and thus God would be composed of essential parts, the contrary of which was proved above.[1]

Again. That which is added to a thing by way of essential specification, does not constitute the notion of that thing, but only makes it to be in act: for *rational* added to *animal* makes animal to be in act, but does not constitute the notion of an animal as such: because the difference does not enter into the definition of the genus. Now if something be added to God to specify Him with an essential specification, it must give that to which it is added the notion of its proper quiddity or nature: since what is added thus, gives the thing actual being. Now this, namely actual being, is the divine essence itself, as shown above.[2] It follows, therefore, that nothing can be added to the divine being to give it an essential specification, as a difference specifies a genus.

25

THAT GOD IS NOT IN ANY GENUS

HENCE it follows of necessity that God is not in any genus.

For whatever is in a genus, has in itself something whereby its generic nature is specified: for nothing is in a genus without being in some one of its species. But in God this is impossible, as shown above.[3] Therefore it is impossible that God be in any genus.

Moreover. If God be in a genus, He is either in the genus of accident, or in that of substance. He is not in

---

[1] xviii.　　　[2] xxii.　　　[3] xxiv.

the genus of accident: for an accident cannot be the first being and first cause. Nor can He be in the genus of substance: for substance that is a genus is not being itself, otherwise every substance would be its own being, and thus would not be caused by something else, which is impossible, as is clear from what we have said above.[1] Now God is being itself.[2] Therefore He is not in any genus.

Again. Whatever is in a genus differs as to being from the other things contained in the same genus: otherwise a genus would not be predicated of several things. Now all things that are contained in one same genus, must agree in the *whatness* of the genus, because the genus is predicated of all in respect of *what a thing is*. Therefore the being of anything contained in a genus is beside the *whatness* of the genus. But this is impossible in God.[3] Therefore God is not in a genus.

Further. A thing is placed in a genus by the nature of its *whatness*, for genus is predicated of what a thing is. But the *whatness* of God is His very being.[4] Now a thing is not placed in a genus according to its being, because then *being* would be a genus signifying being itself. It remains therefore that God is not in a genus.

That being cannot be a genus is proved by Aristotle as follows.[5] If being were a genus, it would be necessary to find a difference in order to contract it to a species. Now no difference participates in the genus, so that, to wit, the genus be contained in the notion of the difference, for thus the genus would be placed twice in the definition of the species: but the difference must be something besides that which is contained in the notion of the genus. Now there can be nothing besides that

[1] xiii.   [2] xxii.   [3] xxiv.   [4] xxii.   [5] 2 *Metaph.* iii. 8.

which is understood by being, if being belong to the
notion of those things of which it is predicated. And
thus by no difference can being be contracted. It remains, therefore, that being is not a genus: wherefore it
follows of necessity that God is not in a genus.

Wherefore it is likewise evident that God cannot be
defined: since every definition is composed of genus and
difference.

It is also clear that no demonstration is possible in
regard to Him: because the principle of a demonstration
is the definition of that about which the demonstration
is made.

Someone, however, might think that, although the
name of substance cannot properly be applied to God,
because God does not subsist under (*substat*) accidents:
yet the thing signified by that term is applicable to Him,
and consequently He is in the genus *substance*. For
substance is a *per se being*, and it is clear that this can
be applied to God, from the fact that it has been proved [1]
that He is not an accident. But to this we reply,
according to what has been said, that *per se* being is not
in the definition of substance. For from the fact that
it is described as *a being* it cannot be a genus, since it
has been already proved that *being* has not the conditions of a genus: and again from the fact that it is
described as being *per se*, for this would seem to denote
nothing else than a negation, since it is said to be a
per se being, through not being in another, which is a
pure negation. And this cannot satisfy the conditions
of a genus, for then a genus would not express what a
thing is, but what it is not. Therefore we must understand the definition of substance in this way, that a

[1] xxiii.

substance is *a thing to which it is fitting not to be in a subject*: the word *thing* being taken from its quiddity, just as *being* is from existence: so that the meaning of substance is that it has a quiddity to which it is fitting to exist not in another. Now this does not apply to God, for He has no quiddity besides His existence.[1] Hence it follows that He is nowise in the genus of substance: and consequently that He is in no genus, since it has been proved [2] that He is not in the genus of accident.

26

THAT GOD IS NOT THE FORMAL BEING OF ALL THINGS

FROM the foregoing we are able to refute the error of some who have asserted that God is nothing else than the formal being of everything.[3]

For this being is divided into substantial and accidental being. Now the divine being is neither the being of a substance nor the being of an accident, as shown above.[4] Therefore it is impossible for God to be the being whereby everything is formally.

Again. Things are not distinct from one another in that they have being, since in this they all agree. If, then, things differ from one another, it follows that either being itself is specified by certain differences added thereto, so that different things have a specifically different being, or that things differ in that being itself is attached to specifically different natures. But the former of these is impossible, because an addition cannot

[1] xxii.   [2] xxiii.
[3] I *Sum. Th.* Q. iii. a. 8.   [4] xxv.

be attached to being in the same way as a difference is added to a genus, as already stated.[1] It remains, therefore, that things differ because they have different natures, to which being is attached in different ways. Now the divine being is not attached to another nature, but is the nature itself, as shown above.[2] If, therefore, the divine being were the formal being of all things, it would follow that all things are simply one.

Moreover. The principle is naturally prior to that which flows from it. Now in certain things being has something by way of principle: since the form is said to be the principle of being; and in like manner the agent which gives certain things actual being. Therefore if the divine being is the being of each thing, it will follow that God, Who is His own being, has a cause, and thus is not *per se* necessary being. The contrary of which has been shown above.[3]

Further. That which is common to many is not something besides those many except only logically: thus *animal* is not something besides Socrates and Plato and other animals except as considered by the mind, which apprehends the form of animal as divested of all that specifies, and individualizes it: for man is that which is truly an animal, else it would follow that in Socrates and Plato there are several animals, namely animal in general, man in general, and Plato himself. Much less, therefore, being itself in general is something apart from all things that have being; except only as apprehended by the mind. If, therefore, God is being in general, He will not be an individual thing except only as apprehended in the mind. Now it has been shown above [4] that God is something not merely in the

[1] xxv.   [2] xxii.   [3] xv.   [4] xiii.

intellect, but in reality. Therefore God is not the common being of all.

Again. Generation is essentially the way to being, and corruption the way to not-being. For the term of generation is the form, and that of corruption privation, for no other reason than because the form makes a thing to be, and corruption makes a thing not to be, for supposing a certain form not to give being, that which received that form would not be said to be generated. If, then, God were the formal being of all things it would follow that He is the term of generation. Which is false, since He is eternal, as we have shown above.[1]

Moreover. It would follow that the being of every thing has been from eternity: wherefore there would be neither generation nor corruption. For if there were, it would follow that a thing acquires anew a being already pre-existing. Either then it is acquired by something already existing, or else by something nowise pre-existing. In the first case, since according to the above supposition all existing things have the same being, it would follow that the thing which is said to be generated, receives not a new being but a new mode of being, and therefore is not generated but altered. If on the other hand the thing nowise existed before, it would follow that it is made out of nothing, and this is contrary to the essence of generation. Consequently this supposition would wholly do away with generation and corruption: and therefore it is clear that it is impossible.

Moreover. The Sacred Doctrine refutes this error, by confessing that God is *high and elevated*,[2] and that He is *over all* things.[3] For if He were the being of all, He would be something in all, and not above all.

[1] xv.   [2] Isa. vi. 1.   [3] Rom. ix. 5.

Those who erred thus are condemned by the same sentence as idolaters who *gave the incommunicable name,*[1] i.e. of God, *to wood and stones.*[2] For if God is the being of all it would be no truer to say *a stone is a being* than to say *a stone is God.*

Now there are four things which apparently fostered this error. The first was a wrong understanding of certain authorities. For they found Dionysius saying: *The being of all is the super-essential Godhead*;[3] and from this they wished to conclude that God is the formal being of all things, not perceiving that this meaning is irreconcilable with the words. For if the Godhead were the formal being of all, it would not be above all, but in the midst of all, in fact something of all. Wherefore when he said that the Godhead is *above* all, he declares It to be by Its nature distinct from all and placed above all. And by saying that the Godhead is the *being of all*, he declares that all things derive from God a likeness to the divine being. Moreover he elsewhere expressly proscribes their wrong interpretation where he declares that *there can be no contact with God nor mingling of Him with other things, as of point with line, or of the shape of the seal on wax.*[4]

The second cause of this error was defective reason. For·since that which is common is specified or individualized by addition, they deemed the divine being, to which nothing is added, not to be some proper being, but the common being of all, not perceiving that the common or universal cannot be without some addition, though it be considered apart from any addition: for *animal* cannot be apart from the difference of *rational* or

[1] Vulg., *names.* [2] Wisd. of Sol. xiv. 21.
[3] *Cael. Hier.* iv. [4] *Div. Nom.* ii.

irrational, although we think of it apart from these differences.   Moreover although we think of the universal without an addition, we do not think of it apart from its receptivity of addition: for if no difference could be added to *animal*, it would not be a genus; and the same applies to all other names of things.   Now the divine being is without addition, not only in thought but also in reality; and not only is it without addition, but also without receptivity of addition.   Wherefore from the very fact that it neither receives nor can receive addition, we should conclude rather that God is not common but proper being; since His being is distinct from all others for the very reason that nothing can be added to it.   Hence the Commentator says [1] that the first cause, by reason of the very purity of its goodness, is distinct from others and, so to speak, individualized.

The third cause of this error is the consideration of the divine simplicity.   For since God is the extreme of simplicity, they thought that if we make an analysis of all that is in us, the last thing, being the most simple, must be God; for we cannot proceed indefinitely in the composition of the things that are in us.   In this again their reason was lacking, that they failed to observe that what is most simple in us, is not so much a complete thing as some part of a thing: whereas simplicity is ascribed to God as to a perfect subsistent being.

The fourth thing that might lead them into this error, is the expression whereby we say that God is in all things: for they failed to perceive that He is in things, not as part thereof, but as the cause of things, which is nowise wanting to its effect.   For we do not say that the form is in the body in the same sense as we say that the sailor is in the boat.

[1] *De Causis*, prop. ix.

27

THAT GOD IS NOT THE FORM OF A BODY

ACCORDINGLY, having shown that God is not the being of all, it can be proved in like manner that God is not the form of any thing.

For the divine being cannot be the being of a quiddity that is not its own being, as shown above.[1] Now that which is the divine being itself is no other than God. Therefore it is impossible for God to be the form of any other thing.

Further. The form of a body is not its very being but the principle of its being. But God is being itself. Therefore God is not the form of a body.

Again. The union of form and matter results in a composite, and this is a whole in respect of form and matter. Now the parts are in potentiality with respect to the whole: but in God there is no potentiality.[2] Therefore it is impossible for God to be the form united to any thing.

Again. That which has being *per se*, is more excellent than what has being in another. Now every form of a body has being in another. Since then God is the most excellent being, as the first cause of being,[3] He cannot be the form of any thing.

Moreover, this can also be proved from the eternity of movement, as follows.[4] If God were the form of a movable thing, since He is the first mover, the composite will be its own mover. But that which moves itself can be moved and not moved. Therefore it is in it to be either. Now a thing of this kind has not of itself indefectibility of movement. Therefore above

[1] xxii.   [2] xvi.   [3] xiii.   [4] Cf. xiii, xx.

that which moves itself we must place something else as first mover, which confers on it perpetuity of movement. And thus God Who is the first mover is not the form of a body that moves itself.

This argument avails for those who hold the eternity of movement. Yet if this be not granted the same conclusion may be drawn from the regularity of the heavenly movement. For just as that which moves itself can both be at rest and be moved, so can it be moved with greater or less velocity. Wherefore the necessity of uniformity in the heavenly movement depends on some higher principle that is altogether immovable, and that is not the part, through being the form, of a body which moves itself.

The authority of Scripture is in agreement with this truth. For it is written in the psalm: *Thy magnificence is elevated above the heavens;*[1] and, *He is higher than heaven, and what wilt thou do? . . . the measure of Him is longer than the earth, and deeper [2] than the sea.*[3]

Hence we are able to refute the error of the pagans who asserted that God was the soul of the heaven or even the soul of the whole world:[4] which led them to defend the idolatrous doctrine whereby they said that the whole world was God, not in reference to the body but to the soul, even as man is said to be wise in reference not to his body but to his soul: which being supposed they deemed it to follow that divine worship is not unduly shown to the world and its parts. The commentator also says that *this occasioned the error of the Zabian people,*[5] i.e. of idolaters, because, to wit, they asserted that God was the soul of heaven.

---

[1] Ps. viii. 2.　　　[2] Vulg., *broader.*　　　[3] Job xi. 8, 9.
[4] 1 *Sum. Th.* Q. iii. a. 8.　　　[5] *Metaph.* xi.

28

OF THE DIVINE PERFECTION

Now although things that exist and live are more perfect than those which only exist, yet God Who is not distinct from His own existence, is universally perfect being.[1] And by universally perfect I mean that He lacks not the excellence of any genus.

For every excellence of any being whatsoever is ascribed to a thing in respect of its being, since no excellence would accrue to man from his wisdom, unless thereby he *were* wise, and so on. Wherefore, according as a thing has being, so is its mode of excellence: since a thing, according as its being is contracted to some special mode of excellence more or less great, is said to be more or less excellent. Hence if there be a thing to which the whole possibility of being belongs, no excellence that belongs to any thing can be lacking thereto. Now to a thing which is its own being, being belongs according to the whole possibility of being: thus if there were a separate whiteness, nothing of the whole possibility of whiteness could be wanting to it: because something of the possibility of whiteness is lacking to a particular white thing through a defect in the recipient of whiteness, which receives it according to its mode and, maybe, not according to the whole possibility of whiteness. Therefore God, Who is His own being, as shown above,[2] has being according to the whole possibility of being itself: and consequently He cannot lack any excellence that belongs to any thing.

[1] 1 *Sum. Th.* Q. iv. a. 2.   [2] xxii.

And just as every excellence and perfection is in a thing according as that thing is, so every defect is in a thing according as that thing in some sense is not. Now just as God has being wholly, so is not-being wholly absent from Him, since according as a thing has being it fails in not-being. Therefore all defect is removed from God, and consequently He is universally perfect.

But those things which only exist are imperfect, not on account of an imperfection in absolute being itself, for they have not being according to its whole possibility, but because they participate being in a particular and most imperfect way.

Again.   Every imperfect thing must needs be preceded by some perfect thing: for seed is from some animal or plant. Wherefore the first being must be supremely perfect. Now it has been shown [1] that God is the first being. Therefore He is supremely perfect.

Moreover.   A thing is perfect in so far as it is in act, and imperfect in so far as it is in potentiality and void of act. Wherefore that which is nowise in potentiality but is pure act, must needs be most perfect. Now such is God.[2]   Therefore He is most perfect.

Further.   Nothing acts except according as it is in act: wherefore action follows upon the mode of actuality in the agent; and consequently it is impossible for the effect that results from an action to have a more excellent actuality than that of the agent, although it is possible for the actuality of the effect to be more imperfect than that of the active cause, since action may be weakened on the part of that in which it terminates. Now in the genus of efficient cause we come at length to the one cause which is called God, as explained above,[3]

[1] xiii.   [2] xvi.   [3] xiii.

from Whom all things proceed, as we shall show in the sequel.[1] Wherefore it follows that whatever is actual in any other thing, is found in God much more eminently than in that thing, and not conversely. Therefore God is most perfect.

Again. In every genus there is some thing most perfect relatively to that genus, by which every thing in that genus is measured: since every thing is shown to be more or less perfect according as it approaches more or less to the measure of that genus: thus white is said to be the measure in all colours, and the virtuous among all men.[2] Now the measure of all beings can be none other than God Who is His own being. Therefore no perfection that belongs to any thing is lacking to Him, otherwise He would not be the universal measure of all.

Hence it is that when Moses sought to see the face of God, the Lord answered him: *I will show thee all good*,[3] giving thus to understand that the fullness of all good is in Him. And Dionysius says: *God exists not in any single mode, but embraces and prepossesses all being within Himself, absolutely and without limit*.[4]

It must however be observed that perfection cannot fittingly be ascribed to God if we consider the meaning of the word in respect of its derivation: since what is not *made*, cannot seemingly be described as *perfect*. Yet since whatever is made has been brought from potentiality to act, and from not-being to being, when it was made; it is rightly described as perfect, i.e. *completely made*, when its potentiality is completely reduced to act, so that it retains nothing of not-being, and has complete being. Accordingly by a kind of extension

---

[1] II. xv.   [2] *Eth. Nic.* iv. 5; v. 10.
[3] Exod. xxxiii. 18, 19.   [4] *Div. Nom.* v.

of the term, *perfect* is applied not only to that which has arrived at complete act through being made, but also to that which is in complete act without being made at all. It is thus that we say that God is perfect, according to: *Be ye perfect as also your heavenly Father is perfect.*[1]

29

OF THE LIKENESS OF CREATURES

IN sequence to the above we may consider in what way it is possible to find in things a likeness to God, and in what way it is impossible.[2]

For effects that fall short of their causes do not agree with them in name and ratio, and yet there must needs be some likeness between them, because it is of the nature of action that a like agent should produce a like action, since every thing acts according as it is in act. Wherefore the form of the effect is found in its transcendent cause somewhat, but in another way and another ratio, for which reason that cause is called *equivocal*. For the sun causes heat in lower bodies by acting according as it is in act; wherefore the heat generated by the sun must needs bear some likeness to the sun's active power by which heat is caused in those lower bodies and by reason of which the sun is said to be hot, albeit in a different ratio. And thus it is said to be somewhat like all those things on which it efficaciously produces its effects, and yet again it is unlike them all in so far as these effects do not possess heat and so forth in the same

[1] Matt. v. 48.   [2] *I Sum. Th.* Q. iv. a. 3.

way as they are found in the sun. Thus also God bestows all perfections on things, and in consequence He is both like and unlike all.

Hence it is that Holy Writ sometimes recalls the likeness between Him and His creatures, as when it is said: *Let Us make man to Our image and likeness*; [1] while sometimes this likeness is denied, according to the words: *To whom then have you likened God ; or what image will you make for Him ?* [2] and of the psalm: *O God, who shall be like to Thee ?* [3]

Dionysius is in agreement with this argument, for he says: *The same things are like and unlike to God ; like, according as they imitate Him, as far as they can, who is not perfectly imitable; unlike, according as effects fall short of their causes.* [4]

However,[5] according to this likeness, it is more fitting to say that the creature is like God than vice versa. For one thing is like another when it possesses a quality or form thereof. Since then what is in God perfectly is found in other things by way of an imperfect participation, that in which likeness is observed is God's simply but not the creature's. And thus the creature has what is God's, and therefore is rightly said to be like God. But it cannot be said in this way that God has what belongs to His creature: wherefore neither is it fitting to say that God is like His creature; as neither do we say that a man is like his portrait, although we declare that his portrait is like him.

And much less properly can it be said that God is assimilated to the creature. For assimilation denotes movement towards similarity, and consequently applies

---

[1] Gen. i. 26. [2] Isa. xl. 18. [3] Ps. lxxxii. 1.
[4] *Div. Nom.* ix. [5] *Sum. Th. l.c., r. obj.* 4.

to one that receives its similarity from another. But the creature receives from God its similarity to Him, and not vice versa. Therefore God is not assimilated to His creature, but rather vice versa.

30

WHAT TERMS CAN BE PREDICATED OF GOD

AGAIN in sequel to the above we may consider what can and what cannot be said of God; also what is said of Him alone, and what is said of Him together with other beings.

For since every perfection of creatures is to be found in God, albeit in another and more eminent way, whatever terms denote perfection absolutely and without any defect whatever, are predicated of God and of other things; for instance, goodness, wisdom, and so forth. But any term that denotes suchlike perfections together with a mode proper to creatures, cannot be said of God except by similitude and metaphor, whereby that which belongs to one thing is applied to another, as when a man is said to be a stone on account of the denseness of his intelligence. Such are all those terms employed to denote the species of a created thing, as *man* and *stone*: for its proper mode of perfection and being is due to each species: likewise whatever terms signify those properties of things that are caused by the proper principles of the species, therefore they cannot be said of God otherwise than metaphorically. But those which express these perfections together with the mode of supereminence in which they belong to God, are said of God alone, for instance, *the sovereign good*, the *first being*, and the like.

Now, I say that some of the aforesaid terms denote perfection without defect, as regards that which the term is employed to signify: for as regards the mode of signification every term is defective. For we express things by a term as we conceive them by the intellect: and our intellect, since its knowledge originates from the senses, does not surpass the mode which we find in sensible objects, wherein the form is distinct from the subject of the form, on account of the composition of form and matter. Now in those things the form is found to be simple indeed, but imperfect, as being non-subsistent: whereas the subject of the form is found to be subsistent, but not simple, nay more, with concretion. Wherefore whatever our intellect signifies as subsistent, it signifies it with concretion, and whatever it signifies as simple, it signifies it not as subsisting but as qualifying. Accordingly in every term employed by us, there is imperfection as regards the mode of signification, and imperfection is unbecoming to God, although the thing signified is becoming to God in some eminent way: as instanced in the term *goodness* or *the good*: for goodness signifies by way of non-subsistence, and the good signifies by way of concretion. In this respect no term is becomingly applied to God, but only in respect of that which the term is employed to signify. Wherefore, as Dionysius teaches,[1] such terms can be either affirmed or denied of God: affirmed, on account of the signification of the term; denied, on account of the mode of signification. Now the mode of supereminence in which the aforesaid perfections are found in God, cannot be

---

[1] *Cael. Hier.* ii. 3.

expressed in terms employed by us, except either by negation, as when we say God is *eternal* or *infinite*, or by referring Him to other things, as when we say that He is the *first cause* or the *sovereign good*. For we are able to grasp, not what God is, but what He is not, and the relations of other things to Him, as explained above.[1]

31

THAT THE DIVINE PERFECTION AND THE PLURALITY OF DIVINE NAMES ARE NOT INCONSISTENT WITH THE DIVINE SIMPLICITY

FROM what has been said we are also able to see that the divine perfection and the various names applied to God are not inconsistent with His simplicity.

For we asserted that all the perfections to be found in other things are to be ascribed to God in the same way as effects are found in their equivocal causes:[2] which causes are in their effects virtually, as heat is in the sun. Now this virtue unless it were in some way of the genus of heat, the sun acting thereby would not generate its like. Wherefore by reason of this virtue the sun is said to be hot, not only because it causes heat, but because the virtue whereby it does this, is something in conformity with heat. Now by this same virtue by which the sun causes heat, it causes also many other effects in lower bodies, such as dryness. And so heat and dryness, which are distinct qualities in fire, are ascribed to the sun in respect of the one virtue. And so too, the perfections of all things, which are becoming

[1] xiv.   xxix.

to other things in respect of various forms, must needs
be ascribed to God in respect of His one virtue.   And
this virtue is not distinct from His essence, since nothing
can be accidental to Him, as we have proved.[1]   Accordingly God is said to be *wise* not only because He causes
wisdom, but because in so far as we are wise, we imitate
somewhat the virtue whereby He makes us wise.   He
is not, however, called a *stone*, although He made the
stones, because by the term stone we understand a
definite mode of being, in respect of which a stone differs
from God.[2]   But a stone imitates God as its cause, in
respect of being, goodness, and so forth, even as other
creatures do.

The like of this may be found in human cognitive
powers and operative virtues.   For the intellect by its
one virtue knows all that the sensitive faculty apprehends by various powers, and many other things besides.   Again, the intellect, the higher it is, the more
things is it able to know by means of one, while an
inferior intellect can arrive at the knowledge of those
things only by means of many.   Again, the royal power
extends to all those things to which the various subordinate powers are directed.   And so, too, God by His
one simple being possesses all manner of perfections,
which in a much lower degree other things attain by
certain various means.   Whence it is clear how it is
necessary to give several names to God.   For since we
cannot know Him naturally except by reaching Him
from His effects,[3] it follows that the terms by which we
denote His perfection must be diverse, as also are the
perfections which we find in things.   If, however, we
were able to understand His very essence as it is, and

[1] xxiii.   [2] xxx.   [3] Cf. xi.

to give Him a proper name, we should express Him by one name only: and this is promised in the last chapter of Zacharias, to those who will see Him in His essence: *In that day there shall be one Lord, and His name shall be one.*[1]

32

THAT NOTHING IS PREDICATED UNIVOCALLY OF GOD AND OTHER THINGS

FROM the above it is clear that nothing can be predicated univocally of God and other things. For an effect which does not receive the same form specifically as that whereby the agent acts, cannot receive in a univocal sense the name derived from that form: for the sun and the heat generated from the sun are not called hot univocally. Now the forms of things whereof God is cause do not attain to the species of the divine virtue, since they receive severally and particularly that which is in God simply and universally.[2] It is evident therefore that nothing can be said univocally of God and other things.

Further. If an effect attain to the species of its cause, the name of the latter will not be predicated of it univocally unless it receive the same specific form according to the same mode of being: for *house* in art is not univocally the same as *house* in matter, since the form of house has an unlike being in the one case and in the other. Now other things, even though they should receive entirely the same form, do not receive it

---

[1] xiv. 9.   [2] xxviii, xxix.

according to the same mode of being: because there is nothing in God that is not the divine being itself, as shown above,[1] which does not apply to other things. Therefore it is impossible for anything to be predicated univocally of God and other things.

Moreover. Whatever is predicated of several things univocally is either genus, or species, or difference, or proper accident. Now nothing is predicated of God as genus or as difference, as we have proved above,[2] and consequently neither as definition nor as species, which consists of genus and difference. Nor can anything be accidental to Him, as was shown above,[3] and consequently nothing is predicated of God, either as accidental or as proper, for the proper is a kind of accident. It follows therefore that nothing is predicated of God and other things univocally.

Again. That which is predicated univocally of several things is more simple than either of them, at least in our way of understanding. Now nothing can be more simple than God, either in reality or in our way of understanding. Therefore nothing is predicated univocally of God and other things.

Further. Whatever is predicated univocally of several things belongs by participation to each of the things of which it is predicated: for the species is said to participate the genus, and the individual the species. But nothing is said of God by participation, since whatever is participated is confined to the mode of a participated thing, and thus is possessed partially and not according to every mode of perfection. It follows therefore that nothing is predicated univocally of God and other things.

Again. That which is predicated of several things

[1] xxiii.   [2] xxiv, xxv.   [3] xxiii.

according to priority and posteriority is certainly not predicated of them univocally, since that which comes first is included in the definition of what follows, for instance substance in the definition of accident considered as a being. If therefore we were to say *being* univocally of substance and accident, it would follow that substance also should enter into the definition of being as predicated of substance: which is clearly impossible. Now nothing is predicated in the same order of God and other things, but according to priority and posteriority: since all predicates of God are essential, for He is called being because He is very essence, and good because He is goodness itself: whereas predicates are applied to others by participation; thus Socrates is said to be a man, not as though he were humanity itself, but as a subject of humanity. Therefore it is impossible for any thing to be predicated univocally of God and other things.

33

THAT NOT ALL TERMS APPLIED TO GOD AND CREATURES ARE PURELY EQUIVOCAL

It is also clear from what has been said that things predicated of God and other things are not all pure equivocations, as are the effects of an equivocal cause. For in the effects of an equivocal cause we find no mutual order or relationship, and it is altogether accidental that the same name is applied to various things; since the name applied to one does not signify that thing to have any relationship to another. Whereas it is not so with the terms applied to God and creatures:

for in employing these common terms we consider the order of cause and effect, as is clear from what we have said.[1] Therefore certain things predicated of God and other things are not pure equivocations.

Moreover. Where there is pure equivocation, we observe no likeness of things, but merely sameness of name. Now there is some kind of likeness of things to God, as shown above.[2] Therefore it follows that they are not said of God by pure equivocation.

Again. When one thing is predicated of several by pure equivocation, we cannot be led from one to the knowledge of the other, for the knowledge of things depends not on words but on the meaning of names. Now we come to the knowledge of things divine from our observation of other things, as shown above.[3] Therefore the like are not pure equivocations when said of God and other things.

Further. The use of equivocal terms breaks the continuity of an argument. Therefore if nothing were said of God and creatures except by pure equivocation, no argument could be made by proceeding to God from creatures, whereas the contrary is evidenced by all who speak of divine things.

Moreover. It is useless to predicate a name of a thing unless by that name we understand something about that thing. Now if names are predicated altogether equivocally of God and creatures, we understand nothing of God by those names: since the meanings of those names are known to us only as applied to creatures. It would therefore be to no purpose to prove about God that God is being, good, or any thing else of the kind.

If, however, it be asserted that by suchlike terms we

[1] xxxii.   [2] xxix.   [3] In various places.

only know of God what He is not, so that, to wit, He be called *living* because He is not in the genus of inanimate beings, and so forth, it follows at least that *living* when said of God and creatures agrees in the negation of inanimate being: and thus it will not be a pure equivocation.

34

THAT TERMS APPLIED TO GOD AND CREATURES ARE EMPLOYED ANALOGICALLY

IT follows, then, from what has been said [1] that those things which are said of God and other things are predicated neither univocally nor equivocally, but analogically, that is according to an order or relation to some one thing.

This happens in two ways. First, according as many things have a relation to some one thing: thus in relation to the one health, an animal is said to be *healthy* as its subject, medicine as effective thereof, food as preserving it, and urine as its sign. Secondly, according as order or relation of two things may be observed, not to some other thing, but to one of them: thus being is said of substance and accident, in so far as accident bears a relation to substance, and not as though substance and accident were referred to a third thing.

Accordingly such names are not said of God and other things analogically in the first way, for it would be necessary to suppose something previous to God; but in the second way.

Now in this analogical predication the relationship is

[1] xxxii, xxxiii.

sometimes found to be the same both as to the name and as to the thing, and sometimes it is not the same. For the relationship of the name is consequent upon the relationship of knowledge, since the name is the sign of intellectual conception. Accordingly when that which comes first in reality is found to be first also in knowledge, the same thing is found to be first both as to the meaning of the name and as to the nature of the thing: thus substance is prior to accident both in nature, in as much as substance is the cause of accident, and in knowledge, in as much as substance is placed in the definition of accident. Wherefore *being* is said of substance previously to being said of accident, both in reality and according to the meaning of the word. On the other hand, when that which comes first according to nature, comes afterwards according to knowledge, then, in analogical terms, there is not the same order according to the reality and according to the meaning of the name: thus the healing power in health-giving (medicines) is naturally prior to health in the animal, as cause is prior to effect; yet as we know this power through its effect, we name it from that effect. Hence it is that *health-giving* is first in the order of reality, and yet *healthy* is predicated of animal first according to the meaning of the term.

Accordingly, since we arrive at the knowledge of God from other things, the reality of the names predicated of God and other things is first in God according to His mode, but the meaning of the name is in Him afterwards. Wherefore He is said to be named from His effects.

I. xiv–xxxiv.

35

ARISTOTLE'S 'METAPHYSICS'

'CAUSE' means: (1) That from which (as immanent material) a thing comes into being, e.g. the bronze of the statue and the silver of the dish, and the classes which include these. (2) The form or pattern, i.e. the formula of the essence, and the classes which include this (e.g. the ratio 2 : 1 and number in general are causes of the octave) and the parts of the formula. (3) The initial origin of change or rest; e.g. the adviser is the cause of the action, and the father a cause of the child, and in general the agent a cause of the deed and the originator of change a cause of the change. (4) The end, i.e. that for the sake of which a thing is, e.g. health is the cause of walking. For why does one walk? We say 'that one may be healthy,' and in speaking thus we think we have given the cause. The same is true of all the means that intervene before the end when something else has put the process in motion (as e.g. the reduction of humours or purging or drugs or instruments intervene before health is reached, for all these are for the sake of the end, though they differ from one another in that some are instruments and others are actions.

These, then, are, broadly speaking, all the senses in which causes are spoken of; and as they are spoken of in several senses it follows that there are several causes of the same thing, and in no accidental sense; e.g. both the art of sculpture and the bronze are causes of the statue not in virtue of anything else but *qua* statue; not, however, in the same way, but the one as matter and the other as source of the movement. And things can be causes of one another, e.g. exercise of good condition, and the latter of exercise; not, however, in the same way, but the one as end and the other as source of movement. Again, the same thing is sometimes cause of contraries; for that which when present causes a particular thing, we sometimes charge, when absent, with the contrary; e.g. we impute the shipwreck to the absence of the steersman, whose presence was the cause of safety; and both—the presence and the privation—are causes as sources of movement.

Metaph. 13 a, 24—b, 16.

Thomas divides 13 a, 24—14 a, 25 *as follows :*

(*a*) 'Cause' means first . . . in which causes are spoken of;

(*b*) and as they are spoken of . . . sources of movement.

(*c*) All the causes now mentioned . . . of the kinds,

(*d*) but the varieties . . . same time as the builder.

Book V, Lesson II begins by announcing this division :

Aristotle here distinguishes the meanings of the word 'cause.' He first assigns their species (*a, b, c*) and then their varieties (*d*). His enumeration (*a*) and explanation (*b*) of the species is followed by their reduction to four main types (*c*).

Leaving (c d) to Lesson III, Lesson II treats (a b) only :

He says then that 'cause' first of all means 'that, starting from which a thing comes into being, and which continues to inhere in that thing.' This is added in order to exclude privations and contraries. For things are said to come into being even from that which does not continue to inhere in them; to become white, for example, after being black, the privation of white, or after being non-white, the contrary of white. A statue, on the other hand, springs from bronze and continues to be of bronze; a dish springs from silver and continues to be of silver. For when a statue is brought into being, the bronze nature is not lost, nor the silver nature when a dish is made. The bronze of a statue, therefore, and the silver of a dish, are causes in the sense of being 'materials.' *And the classes which include these* is added because, whenever any species is matter relative to a thing, the corresponding genus is also matter relative to that same thing. For instance, if a statue has bronze for its matter, it will also have 'metal' for its matter, 'compound' for its matter, and 'physical body' for its matter, and so in other cases.

The word 'cause' has also a second meaning, that of 'form,' 'pattern,' or 'exemplar.' This is the formal cause, which is related to the effect in two ways: first as its intrinsic form or 'species,' and secondly as something extrinsic in whose likeness the thing is said to be made, and in this sense the exemplar is also called the 'form' of a thing. It was in this sense that Plato held that ideas are forms. Now since everything acquires its generic or specific nature through its form, and since that generic or specific nature is the content of the definition declaring what a thing is, it follows that the form of a thing is its determinative predicate, its 'ratio' or logical definition, by which we know what a thing is. For although a definition may contain certain material elements, nevertheless its chief component must derive from the form of the thing defined. This, therefore, is the reason why forms are causes: that they give the completeness of the logical nature (ratio) of a thing's essence (quidditas). And just as the genus of the matter of a thing was itself the matter of that thing, so is the genus of the form of a thing itself the form of that thing. For example, the form of the octave interval is the ratio 2 : 1. For when two notes have [their frequencies in] the ratio 2 : 1, their interval is one octave; and duality being the form of the ratio 2 : 1, it is also the form of an octave interval. Again, since duality falls under the genus number, it follows that, more generally still, number is the form of an octave interval, so that we may cite the octave interval as an instance of the ratio of one number to another. Moreover, not only the whole definition is related to the definitum as its form, but also its parts, or such at least as occur directly in it. For inasmuch as 'biped animal capable of stepping' is the form of man, so also is 'biped' and 'animal' and 'capable of stepping.' On the other hand, matter sometimes occurs in a definition indirectly, as when we say that the soul is the 'act of an organic physical body capable of life.'

A third meaning of the word 'cause' is: 'that from which change or lack of change takes its origin.' This is the 'moving' or 'efficient' cause. The words *or rest* are added because change and lack of change, whether both natural or both forced, are traceable to the same cause. For rest at a place and motion towards a place both arise from the same cause. *As advisers are causes*, for the changes, which take place in him who safeguards something by acting upon advice, themselves take their origin from the counsellor. In the same way too, the *father is a cause of the child*. These two examples of Aristotle cover the two sources of all changes and of all happenings: intention, illustrated by the adviser, and nature, illustrated by the father. It is always in this sense that the agent is the cause of what is done, and he who changes, the cause of alteration.

On the theory of Ibn-Sīnā, it should be noted, there are four varieties of efficient cause: the perfective, the dispositive, the auxiliary, and the consiliary cause. An efficient cause is *perfective*, when it gives the final completeness to a thing, for example, in natural bodies that which induces the substantial form, and in artificial ones that which induces the artificial form, as does the builder in a house. It is *dispositive* if it does not induce the ultimate and completing form, but merely prepares the matter to receive form, for example, as the hewer of wood or stone is also said to build a house, yet not in the full and strict sense, for what he makes is not actually but only potentially a house. Such an agent is less improperly called an efficient cause if he induces an ultimate disposition upon which the form follows of necessity, as in the case of a man generating a man without causing his intellect, which comes otherwhence. An *auxiliary* efficient cause is one that contributes to the effect, differing from the principal agent in not acting for its own but another's ends. Thus, whoever helps a king in war, acts for that which the king intends. This same relation holds between a secondary and a primary cause; for among agents whose nature is to be in a certain order among themselves, the secondary cause acts for the ends proper to the primary cause. The action of a soldier, for instance, is directed to the aims intended by the statesman. An *adviser* differs from a principal agent by laying down the scope and manner of the action. This same relation obtains between the primary agent, acting through his intellect, and the secondary agent — whether this be a physical body or another intelligent being. For in all cases the secondary agent accepts the purpose and manner of his action from a primary agent endowed with intellect, the shipwright from the naval architect, and the universe of nature from the supreme mind. This third kind of cause also includes whatever brings about, not substantial being only, but also accidental being; so that not only is the maker called the cause of what he makes, but he who changes something is also called the cause of its alteration.

The fourth meaning of 'cause' is 'end or purpose.' It is that for the sake of which a thing is made or done, as walking for the sake of health. Now a purpose achieves existence last of all, and for this reason its causal character was at first less evident, so that (as was pointed out in Book I) the earlier philosophers overlooked it. Aristotle, therefore, gives a formal proof that purposes are causes. In fact, to ask why and wherefore is to ask for a cause. When it is asked why and wherefore someone walks, it is a suitable answer to say: 'To recover his health.' We believe that in giving this answer, we have assigned a cause. It is clear from this that purposes really are causes.[1] Not only, however, do we call the ultimate purpose of an agent an end relative to each intermediate cause, but we also call each separate intermediate cause an end relative to its predecessors no less than an origin of change relative to all

---

[1] Does trust in the chances of linguistic usage amount to positive proof?

its successors. For example, between a doctor [1] as
first agent and health as an ultimate purpose we may
have the following intermediates: first, and nearest in
this chain to health, the *reduction* [2] of humours in those
who superabound in them; in the second place, *purgation* as a means of reducing humours; in the third place,
laxatives as a means of purgation; and in the fourth and
last intermediate place, *instruments* by which the medicine is prepared and administered. All this kind of
thing is there for the sake of the ultimate purpose, and
nevertheless one thing among them is the end of another.
Reduction, for example, is an end relative to purgation,
and purgation relative to the medicine. And this, not-
withstanding the differences here present, in that some
of these things are instruments—such as the apparatus
used to prepare and administer the medicine, and indeed, the medicine too, whose nature is itself used as an
instrument—while others are actions, operations, and
effects—such as purgation and reduction of humours.
Aristotle concludes that the word 'cause' is used in
so-and-so many, namely in four senses. He adds,
practically, either because of the varieties yet to be
mentioned, or perhaps because the above four causes
are not found in the same manner in all cases.

[1] Reading *medicus* for *medicina*, not on manuscript authority, which
is available neither directly nor indirectly, but merely to avoid an
otherwise unavoidable kink in the chain of intermediates.

[2] ἰσχνασία surely derives from ἰσχναίνω with the primary meaning
'to dry up'? This would then be a process carried out in the first
recourse, and by means of purgatives, upon the corporeal humours.
Leanness would then be merely a collateral effect. Since Aristotle
came of a medical family, and was for this very reason more interested
in the biological than in the exact sciences, his use of medical terms is
as likely as not to be the technical one. At any rate, their interpretation can hardly be final until the medical terminology has been con-
sulted. Quite separate from this are, of course, the two further questions: Why did Moerbeke translate ἰσχνασία by *attenuatio*, and : What
did Thomas think that *attenuatio* meant?

In the passage beginning: *As they are spoken of in several senses*, he goes on to draw certain conclusions about causes. These are three in number. The first is, that the same thing can have many causes, and this essentially, not accidentally only. The latter point is, indeed, hard to miss, for a thing which is the essential cause of some effect can itself be possessed of many accidents, all of which can be called accidental causes of that effect. The former point, that a plurality of essential causes is possible, manifests itself by the fact that the word 'cause' is used with many meanings. The sculptor and the bronze are both essential and not merely accidental causes of a statue, though not in the same way. What really is impossible, is that the same thing should have many causes of the same kind and of the same degree of propinquity. It is possible, however, for there to be two causes of which one is proximate and the other remote, or two of which neither is sufficient by itself but which suffice when taken together, as in the case of many men pulling a ship along. In the example, however, two beings are causes of the statue: the bronze as material cause, and the sculptor as efficient cause.

The second conclusion is that mutual causality can take place. This is not possible, indeed, within the same genus of causality, but given different genera, it becomes plainly possible. For example, pain from the incision of a wound is the efficient cause of health, while health is the final cause of the pain. It is impossible, however, for the same thing to be effect and cause relative to the same kind of causation. Another and better reading has it thus: 'exertion is the cause of fitness,' viz. of a good habit of body (εὐεξία) which is brought about by moderate labour promoting digestion and carrying off superfluous humours.

It should be noticed that the above four causes fall into two corresponding pairs. The efficient and final causes correspond, for the one is the starting point of change and the other its terminus. Likewise the material and formal causes, for form confers being and matter receives it. The efficient cause is a cause of the final cause, and the final cause is a cause of the efficient cause. Yet with a difference: the agent is a cause of the end even in respect of existence, since by producing change it leads to the end coming to be. The end, however, is not a cause of the agent in respect to existence, but only in respect to its causal functioning. For the agent is a cause inasmuch as it acts, yet it does not act save for the sake of the end. The agent, therefore, owes to the end the fact of its being a cause.

In respect to existence, form and matter are mutual causes—form of matter by conferring actual existence upon it, matter of form by giving it something to inhere in. These two can be mutual causes of existence either in an unqualified sense (*simpliciter*) or in a qualified sense (*secundum quid*). For *substantial* form confers existence upon matter in an unqualified sense, but *accidental* form only in a qualified sense, being itself a form only in a qualified sense. Moreover, matter sometimes sustains form, not in an unqualified sense, but only to the extent that it is the form of this particular object and grounds its existence upon this object: such is the relation between the human body and its rational soul.

The third conclusion is, that the same thing can be the cause of contraries. This would seem to be difficult or impossible if it bore exactly the same relation to both contraries. In point of fact, it is their cause in *different* ways. When the presence of A is the cause of B, we impute the absence of B to A, and so call A the cause of the contrary of B. Thus, the presence of a helmsman causes the safety of a ship, and we call his absence the cause of its wrecking. To counter the misapprehension that this third point, like the first two, be due to existence of different kinds of cause, Aristotle adds that both the presence and the absence belong to the same kind of cause, namely to the class of efficient causes. For non-A is in the same way the cause of non-B, as A is of B.

Metaph. 5 1. ii.

36

ON BEING AND ESSENCE

IT now remains to be seen in what way essence exists in the separate substances, namely in the soul, in intelligences, and in the first cause. Now, although all admit that the first cause is simple, some nevertheless endeavour to introduce in intelligences and in souls a composition of matter and form. The originator of this theory seems to have been Avicebron, the author of the *Fons Vitae*.[1] This, however, runs counter to what philosophers commonly say, since they call those substances separate from matter and prove that they are altogether without matter. And the most convincing reason they have for saying this is drawn from the power of understanding which is in those substances. For we see that forms are not actual intelligibles except inasmuch as they are separated from matter and its conditions, nor are they made actual intelligibles except through the power of an intelligent substance inasmuch as they are received in it and are acted upon by it. And so it is necessary that in any intelligent substance there be complete immunity from matter, so that those substances neither have matter as a part of themselves nor are as a form impressed in matter as is the case with material forms.

Nor can any one say that intelligibility is not hindered by matter in general, but only by corporeal matter.

[1] Tr. IV. i–vi. Cf. Bäumke, *Avencebrolis* (*Ibn-Gebirol*) *Fons Vitae*, Münster, 1895.

For if this came about by reason of corporeal matter only, since matter is not called corporeal except inasmuch as it exists under a corporeal form, then it would necessarily follow that matter would have this quality of hindering intelligibility in virtue of its corporeal form. And this cannot be, since even the corporeal form itself is actually intelligible, as are also the other forms, whenever it is abstracted from matter. Therefore, in the human soul, or in an intellectual nature, there is no composition of matter and form that would lead one to suppose that matter is in them exactly as it is in corporeal substances. But there is in them a composition of form and existence, and so it is said in the commentary on the ninth proposition of the *Liber de Causis* [1] that an intellectual nature is a being having form and existence, and form is taken there for the essence itself, or the simple nature.

How this comes about can be clearly seen. For wherever things bear such relation to one another that one is the cause of the other's existence, that one which is the cause of the other can have existence without the other, but the converse does not hold true. The relation of matter and form, however, is found to be of such kind because the form gives existence to the matter, and therefore it is impossible for the matter to be without some form, but it is not impossible that there be a form without matter, for the form as form has no dependence on matter. But if some forms should be discovered which cannot exist save in matter, this happens to them by reason of their distance from the first cause which is the first act and pure act. And therefore those forms

[1] St Thomas.   Edit. Parm. 21, 735a.   Cf. Bardenhewer, *Die pseudo-aristotelische Schrift, Ueber das reine Gute bekannt unter den Namen 'Liber de Causis,'* Freiburg i. B. 1882, 68, p. 173.

which are closest to the first cause subsisting in themselves without matter. For form as such, understood generically, does not need matter, as has been said, and intellectual natures are forms of this kind; and therefore it is not necessary that the essences or quiddities of these substances be anything other than the form itself.

In this lies the difference between the essence of a composite substance and that of a simple substance, that the essence of a composite substance is not form alone but embraces form and matter, whereas the essence of a simple substance is form alone. And from this two other differences arise. The first is that the essence of a composite substance can be used in predication as a whole or as a part, which happens because of the quantification of matter, as has been said. And therefore the essence of a composite thing is not to be predicated in any random fashion of the composite thing itself, as it cannot, for instance, be said that man is his essence. But the essence of a simple thing, which is its form, cannot be used in predication except as a whole since there is nothing there beyond the form to be, as it were, receptive of the form, and therefore in whatever way the essence of a simple substance be taken, the predication is concerned with that form. And therefore Avicenna says [1] that the essence of a simple substance is the simple substance itself, because there is not anything else to be receptive of this essence. The second difference is that the essences of composite things, from the fact that they are received in quantified matter, are multiplied according to its division, and that is how it happens that some things are the same in species, but different numerically. But since the essence of a simple

1 *Metaph.* v. 5, fol. 90 r.

substance is not received in matter, there cannot be in it any such multiplication. And therefore, in these substances there cannot be found many individuals of the same species, but there are as many species among them as there are individuals, as Avicenna expressly says.[1]

Therefore, although substances of this kind are only forms without matter, nevertheless there is not absolute simplicity in them so as to make them pure act, but they have an admixture of potency, and this is clear from the following: for whatever does not belong to the notion of essence or quiddity is something added to it from without, and entering into composition with the essence, because no essence can be understood without those things which are parts of the essence. But every essence or quiddity can be understood without anything being known of its existence; for I can understand what a man or a phoenix is, and yet not know whether it has existence in the external world.

Therefore it is clear that existence is a different thing from essence or quiddity, unless perchance there be something whose essence is its very existence. And this thing must needs be unique and the primary reality, because there cannot be a multiplication of anything without either the addition of some difference, as the nature of genus is multiplied into species, or the reception of the forms in different matters, as the nature of species is multiplied in different individuals, or the existence of a thing primarily by itself and secondarily as received in something else, just as, if there were something that was 'heat by itself,' it would be a different thing from heat in some object in virtue of its very isolation. But if we posit something which is

[1] *Metaph.* ix. 4, fol. 105 r.

existence only, such that its very existence be subsistent, this existence will not admit of the addition of differences, because then it would not be existence only, but existence, and in addition to this a certain form; and much less would it admit of the addition of matter, because then it would be an existence not subsisting, but material. And so it remains that such a thing which is its own existence can be but one. And from this it is necessary that in anything whatsoever outside of this existence must be one thing, and the quiddity or nature or form another. Therefore it follows that in intellectual nature there is existence over and above form, and on this account it has been said that an intellectual nature is form and existence.

But everything which belongs to any being is either caused from principles of the being's nature, as risibility in man, or it comes to it through some extrinsic principle, as light in the air from the influence of the sun. But it cannot be that existence itself should be caused by the very form or quiddity of the thing; caused, that is, as by an efficient cause, since if it were so something would bring itself into existence; but this is impossible. Therefore, everything which is such that its existence is different from its nature must needs have its existence from another. And because everything which exists through another must be referred back to that which exists through itself, as to its first cause, there must be something which is the cause of existence in all things, because it is existence only, otherwise there would be an infinite series of causes, since everything which is not existence only would have a cause of its existence, as has been said. Therefore it is clear that an intellectual nature is form and existence, and that it has its existence from the first being which is existence only, and this is the first cause which is God.

But everything which receives something from another is in potency in respect to that other, and what is received in it is its act. Therefore it is necessary that the essence itself, or the form which is the intellectual nature, be in potency in respect to the existence which it receives from God, and that existence is received after the manner of act. And so potency and act are found in intellectual natures, but not, however, matter and forms, unless equivocally. On this account also, to suffer, to receive, to be a subject, and all things of this sort which are seen to belong to things because of their matter, belong equivocally to intellectual substances and to corporeal substances, as Averroes says.[1] And because, as has been said, the quiddity of an intelligence is the intellectual nature itself, therefore its quiddity or essence is the same thing as itself, and its existence received from God is that by which it subsists as a thing among things. And on this account such a substance is said by some to be composed of that by which it is, and that which it is (*quo est et quod est*), or of what it is, and existence (*quod est et esse*), as Boethius says.[2]

And since we posit potency and act in intellectual natures, it will not be hard to find a multitude of intellectual natures, which would be impossible if there were no potency in them. And on this account Averroes says [3] that if the nature of the possible intellect were unknown we could not find multiplicity in separate substances. Therefore, the distinction of these in regard

---

[1] 3 *De Anima*, comm. 14, fol. 108 r.   [2] P.L. 64, 1311.
[3] 3 *De Anima*, comm. 5, fol. 103 r.

to one another is according to their degree of potency and act, so that a superior intelligence which is closer to the first being has more of act and less of potency, and so of the others. And this is realized also in the case of the human soul which holds the lowest rank among intellectual substances. Hence its possible intellect has the same relation to intelligible forms as prime matter, which holds the lowest rank in sensible existence, has to sensible forms, as Averroes says.[1] On this account also Aristotle compares it to a tablet on which nothing is written.[2] And on this account, because compared to other intelligible substances it has more potency, it is thereby made to be so very close to material things that a material thing is brought to share its existence, so that from soul and body results a single existence in a single composite, although that existence regarded as the existence of the soul is not dependent on the body. And therefore, lower than that form which the soul is, are found other forms which have more potency and are closer to matter, inasmuch as their existence is impossible without matter. In these also there is found an order and gradation down to the first forms of elements which are closest to matter. And so they have no operation except according to the demands of their active and passive qualities, and of those other qualities by which matter is disposed to form.

4 *De Ente et Essentia.*

[1] 3 *De Anima*, comm. 5, fol. 103 r.   [2] 3 *De Anima*, 403 a 1.

37

THE ACT OF FAITH

THIRD ARTICLE

WHETHER IT IS NECESSARY FOR SALVATION TO BELIEVE ANYTHING ABOVE THE NATURAL REASON?

We proceed thus to the Third Article.

Objection 1. Faith does not seem to be necessary for salvation. For the salvation and perfection of a thing seem to be sufficiently ensured by its natural endowments. Now matters of faith surpass man's natural reason, since they are things unseen as stated above.[1] Therefore to believe seems unnecessary for salvation.

Obj. 2. Further, it is dangerous for man to assent to matters, wherein he cannot judge whether that which is proposed to him be true or false: *Doth not the ear discern words?*[2] Now a man cannot form a judgment of this kind in matters of faith, since he cannot trace them back to first principles, by which all our judgments are guided. Therefore it is dangerous to believe in such matters. Therefore to believe is not necessary for salvation.

Obj. 3. Further, man's salvation rests on God: *But the salvation of the just is from the Lord. Now the invisible things* of God *are clearly seen, being understood by the things that are made;*[3] *His eternal power also and Divinity,*[4] and that which is clearly seen by the understanding is not an object of belief. Therefore it is not

[1] Q. i. a. 4.
[2] Job xii. 11.
[3] Ps. xxxvi. 39.
[4] Rom. i. 20.

necessary for man's salvation, that he should believe certain things.

On the contrary, it is written: *Without faith it is impossible to please God.*[1]

I answer that wherever one nature is subordinate to another, we find that two things concur towards the perfection of the lower nature, one of these being in virtue of the proper motion of that nature, the other coming from the influence of the higher nature. Thus, water by its proper movement moves towards the centre (of the earth), while according to the movement of the moon, water is subject to the tidal motion about that centre. In like manner the planets have their proper movements from west to east, while in accordance with the movement of the first heaven, they have a movement from east to west. Now the created rational nature alone is immediately subordinate to God, since other creatures do not attain to universal ideas, but only to something particular, while they partake of the divine goodness either in *being* only, as inanimate things, or also in *living,* and in *knowing individual things* as plants and animals; whereas the rational nature, inasmuch as it apprehends the universal notion of good and being, is immediately related to the universal of principle being.

Consequently the perfection of the rational creature consists not only in what belongs to it in respect of its nature, but also in that which it acquires supernaturally by becoming a beneficiary of the divine goodness. Hence it was said above [2] that man's ultimate happiness consists in a supernatural vision of God: to which vision man cannot attain unless he be taught by God: *Every one that hath heard of the Father and hath learned cometh*

---

[1] Heb. xi. 6.　　　　　[2] I. Q. iii. a. 8.

to Me.[1] Now man gets the benefit of this learning, not indeed all at once, but by little and little, according to the mode of his nature: and every one who learns thus must needs believe, in order that he may acquire science in a perfect degree; thus also Aristotle says that *it behoves a learner to believe.*[2]

Hence, in order that a man arrive at the perfect vision of heavenly happiness, he must first of all believe God, as a disciple believes the master who is teaching him.

Reply Obj. 1. Since man's nature is dependent on a higher nature, natural knowledge does not suffice for its perfection, and some supernatural knowledge is necessary, as stated above.

Reply Obj. 2. Just as man assents to first principles, by the natural light of his intellect, so does a virtuous man, by the habit of virtue, judge aright of things concerning that virtue; and in this way, by the light of faith which God bestows on him, a man assents to truths of faith and not to their contraries. Consequently *there is no* danger or *condemnation to them that are in Christ Jesus,* and whom He has enlightened by faith.

Reply Obj. 3. In many respects faith perceives the invisible things of God in a higher way than natural reason does in proceeding to God from His creatures. Hence it is written: *Many things are shown to thee above the understanding of man.*[3]

2 II. Q. ii. a. 3.

---

[1] John vi. 45.   [2] *De Soph. Elench.* 165 b, 3.   [3] Ecclus. iii. 25.

38

THAT THE CONSIDERATION OF CREATURES IS USEFUL FOR BUILDING UP OUR FAITH

THIS meditation on the divine works is indeed necessary in order to build up man's faith in God.

First, because through meditating on His works we are able somewhat to admire and consider the divine wisdom. For things made by art are illustrative of the art itself, since they bear the imprint of that art. Now God brought things into being by His wisdom: for which reason it is said in the psalm: *Thou hast made all things in wisdom.*[1] Hence we are able to gather the wisdom of God from the consideration of His works, since by a kind of communication of His likeness it is spread abroad in the things He has made. For it is said: *He poured her out,* namely wisdom, *upon all His works*:[2] wherefore the psalmist, after saying, *Thy knowledge is become wonderful to me; it is high, and I cannot reach to it,* and after referring to the aid of the divine enlightening, when he says: *Night shall be my light,* etc., confesses himself to have been helped to know the divine wisdom by the consideration of the divine works, saying: *Wonderful are Thy works, and my soul knoweth right well.*[3]

Secondly, this consideration leads us to admire the sublime power of God, and consequently begets in men's hearts a reverence for God. For we must needs conclude that the power of the maker transcends the things made.

[1] Ps. ciii. 24.   [2] Ecclus. i. 10.   [3] Ps. cxxxviii. 6, etc.

Wherefore it is said: *If they*, the philosophers, to wit, *admired their power and their effects*, namely of the heavens, stars, and elements of the world, *let them understand . . . that He that made them is mightier than they*.[1] Also it is written: *The invisible things of God* [2] *. . . are clearly seen, being understood by the things that are made; His eternal power also and divinity*.[3] And this admiration makes us fear and reverence God. Hence it is said: *Great is Thy name in might. Who shall not fear Thee, O King of nations?* [4]

Thirdly, this consideration inflames the souls of men to the love of the divine goodness. For whatever goodness and perfection is scattered severally among various creatures, is all united together in Him universally, as in the source of all goodness, as we proved.[5] Wherefore if the goodness, beauty, and sweetness of creatures are so alluring to the minds of men, the fountain-head of the goodness of God Himself, in comparison with the rivulets of goodness which we find in creatures, will set on fire the minds of men and draw them wholly to itself. Hence it is said in the psalm: *Thou hast given me, O Lord, a delight in Thy doings; and in the works of Thy hands I shall rejoice* ; [6] and elsewhere it is said of the children of men: *They shall be inebriated with the plenty of Thy house*, that is of all creatures, *and Thou shalt make them drink of the torrent of Thy pleasure. For with Thee is the fountain of life*.[7] Again it is said against certain men: *By these good things that are seen*, namely creatures that are good by participation, *they could not understand Him*,[8] Who is good indeed, nay more, that is goodness itself, as we have shown in the First Book.

[1] Wisd. of Sol. xiii. 4.   [2] Vulg., *of Him.*   [3] Rom. i. 20.
[4] Jer. x. 6, 7.   [5] I. xxviii, xl.   [6] Ps. xci. 5.
[7] Ps. xxxv. 9, 10.   [8] Wisd. of Sol. xiii. 1.

Fourthly, this consideration bestows on man a certain likeness to the divine perfection. For it was shown[1] that God, by knowing Himself, beholds all other things in Himself. Since then the Christian faith teaches man chiefly about God, and makes him to know creatures by the light of divine revelation, there results in man a certain likeness to the divine wisdom. Hence it is said: *But we all beholding the glory of the Lord with open face, are transformed into the same image.*[2]

Accordingly it is evident that the consideration of creatures helps to build up the Christian faith. Wherefore it is said: *I will . . . remember the works of the Lord, and I will declare the things I have seen; by the words of the Lord are His works.*[3]

2, ii.

[1] i, xlix ff.   [2] 2 Cor. iii. 18.   [3] Ecclus. xlii. 15.

39

TREATISE ON TRUTH

WHETHER THE MIND, CONSIDERED AS CONTAINING THE
IMAGE OF THE TRINITY, IS THE ESSENCE OF THE SOUL
OR A MERE FACULTY THEREOF

1. The question deals with the mind, which contains
the image of the Trinity, and firstly it is asked whether
the mind, holding within itself the image of the Trinity,
is the essence of the soul or a mere faculty thereof. It
seems that the mind *is* the very essence of the soul;
for Augustine says [1] that the terms 'mind' and 'spirit'
are not relative but denote the essence and nothing but
the essence of the soul. Hence the mind is the very
essence of the soul.

2. Further, diversities of faculty are not found in
the soul except in its essence. Now the appetitive and
intellectual powers are diverse faculties of the soul.
(It is laid down in Aristotle,[2] that there are five kinds
of faculty of the soul, i.e. vegetative, sensitive, appetitive,
locomotive, and intellectual.) Since then the mind
includes in itself appetitive and intellectual powers (for
Augustine [3] places in the mind intelligence and will)
it would seem that the mind is not a mere faculty but
the very essence of the soul.

3. Further, Augustine says [4] that we are in the image
of God by the fact that we exist, that we know that we

[1] *De Trin.* ix. 4. [2] *De Anima*, 414, and 31.
[3] *De Trin.* ix. 3–4. [4] *De Civ. Dei*, xi. 36.

exist, and that we love both this knowledge and this
existence; while in another place [1] he ascribes the likeness of God in us to our mind, knowledge, and love.
Now since loving is the perfection of love, and knowing
the perfection of knowledge, it seems that existence is
the perfection of mind. But existence is the perfection
of essence. Therefore mind is the essence of the soul.

4. Further, the image of God is of the same nature in
the angel and in ourselves. But the mind of the angel
is the very essence of his soul (and thus Dionysius
frequently calls the angels 'divine or intellectual
minds').[2] Therefore our mind, too, is the very essence
of our soul.

5. Further, Augustine says [3] that memory, understanding, and will are one mind, one essence, and one
life. Therefore, just as life belongs to the essence, so
does mind.

6. Further, an accident cannot be the basis of a substantial difference. But man differs substantially from
the brute by his possession of mind. Thus mind is not
an accident. But a faculty of the soul is a property
of the soul, according to Avicenna, and so is classified
with the accidents. Hence mind is not a faculty but
is the essence of the soul.

7. Further, specifically different activities do not issue
from one faculty. But from mind there issue remember-
ing, knowing, willing; which are specifically different
activities.[4] Therefore, mind is not a mere faculty of
the soul but its essence.

8. Further, one faculty is not the foundation of another. But the mind is the foundation of the image of

---

[1] *De Trin.* ix. 4.
[2] *De Div. Nom.* vii.
[3] *De Trin.* x. 2.
[4] Cf. pseudo-Aug. *De Spiritu et Anima.*

God, which is constituted by the three faculties. Therefore mind is not a faculty but the essence of the soul.

9. Further, no faculty includes other faculties within itself. But mind includes intellect and will. Hence it it not a faculty but the essence.

But against this: the soul has no parts other than its faculties. Yet the mind 'is a certain higher part of the soul,' as Augustine says.[1] Therefore mind is a faculty.

Further, the essence of the soul is common to all the faculties, for all are grounded in it. But mind is not common to all the faculties, being differentiated from sense. Therefore mind is not the essence of the soul.

Further, in the essence of the soul there is no room to distinguish between a higher and a lower. But in the soul there is a higher and a lower, for Augustine [2] distinguishes between a higher and a lower reason in mind. Therefore mind is a faculty of the soul, not the essence.

Further, the essence of the soul is the principle of life. But mind is not the principle of life, but the principle of knowledge. Therefore mind is not the essence of the soul, but a faculty.

Further, a subject is not predicated of an accident. But mind is predicated of memory, understanding, and will which are in the essence of the soul as in a subject. Therefore mind is not the essence of the soul.

Further, according to Augustine,[3] the soul (in its entirety) is not in the image of God, but the soul in some part of itself is in that image; and the image of God in the soul is the mind. Therefore the mind does not denote the entire soul but some part thereof.

---

[1] *De Trin.* xii. 2–4.   [2] *De Trin.* xii. 3–4.
[3] *De Trin.* xii. 4–7.

Further, the words for 'mind' and 'reminiscence' (*mens, memini*) are connected. Now memory is a faculty of the soul. Therefore mind is so too, and is not the essence.

I answer by saying that the name for mind (*mens*) is taken from the verb 'to measure' (*mensurare*). Now things of a kind are measured by that which is least and most primitive in their kind,[1] and so the word 'mind' is used for the soul in the same way as the word 'intellect.' For the intellect acquires knowledge of things only by measuring them, as it were, against its own primitive elements. Intellect, however, being a term used in contrast with act or perfection, denotes a potency or faculty; and faculty lies between essence and activity.[2] Since, however, the essences of things are unknown to us and their faculties or powers become known to us by their activities, we frequently make use of the terms for their faculties to denote the essences. Then, as nothing can become known except by what is proper to it, the essence which is designated by one of its powers must be designated by a power or faculty proper to it. Again, it is commonly true of powers that the greater includes the less, but not conversely; just as a man who can carry a hundred pounds can carry twenty, as Aristotle says.[3] Hence, if a thing has to be designated by one of its powers, it should be designated by the most comprehensive or the highest. Now the soul that is in a plant has a very meagre faculty and is denoted by the same, being called nutritive or vegetable. The soul of the brute reaches a higher degree in that it has sensation, and the soul is therefore called sensitive or sometimes

---

[1] Cf. *Phys.* 265 b. 10.   [2] Cf. Dionysius, *Cael. Hier.* xi.
[3] *De Caelo*, 281, a. 13.

even a sense-soul. But the human soul reaches to the highest degree among the powers of the soul and derives its name from that, being called intellectual or sometimes intellect or mind, seeing that this intellectual faculty is contained within it and is ready to put forth its activity, and this faculty is proper to man alone of the animals. It is clear, then, that the mind is the highest faculty in our soul, and hence, since we resemble God by what is highest in ourselves, this image of God will not belong to the essence of the soul save in so far as that essence has mind for its highest faculty. Thus, mind, considered as containing the image of God, denotes a faculty and not the essence of the soul, or if it denotes the soul itself, this happens only in so far as that faculty issues from the soul.

In reply therefore to the first difficulty, it must be said that 'mind' does not denote essence as that is distinguished from power or faculty, but as absolute essence is distinguished from relative; thus mind is distinct from self-knowledge, for in self-knowledge mind is related to itself, whereas 'mind' by itself is an absolute term. Alternatively it might be said that Augustine is using 'mind' to signify the essence along with the faculty.

To the second it must be said that there are two ways of classifying the faculties of the soul, according to their objects, and according to the nature of the activity, i.e. according to the subject. If, then, they are differentiated according to the objects of their activity, there are found to be the five classes enumerated above. But if they are differentiated according to the subjective mode of acting, there are three classes, vegetative, sensitive, and intellectual; since the activity of the soul can be related to its material in three ways. The first of these is that which operates as a natural activity, having its source in the nutritive faculty and making use in its activity of active and passive qualities, just as any other physical or chemical activity. The second manner is that in which the activity of the soul is not concerned with the material object but with its conditions, as in the activity of the sensitive faculty. There the sense-organ receives a form or 'species' without matter but with material conditions. The third manner is that in which the activity of the soul oversteps both matter and material conditions, and this is the intellectual activity of the soul. It thus comes about that according to these two different classifications two activities of the soul may be in the same or in different groups. Thus sensitive appetite and intellectual appetite or will, considered in regard of their objects, belong to the same group, for the object of each is the good. But if they are considered in regard of their manner of operating, they belong to different classes, for the lower appetite is of the sensitive class and the higher is of the intellectual. Just as sense does not apprehend its object without material conditions, i.e. those of time and place, so the sensitive appetite is directed towards its object in the same manner, i.e. to a good that is particularized. On the other hand, the higher appetite is directed to its object in the same manner in which the intellect apprehends that object, and so, as far as the manner of operating is concerned, the will belongs to the intellectual group. The manner of operating depends on the disposition of the agent, for the more perfect the agent, the more perfect the activity. Thus, if these faculties are considered as they issue from the essence of the soul, which is their ground, then the will is found to be in the same group as the intellect, but the lower appetite, which is divided into concupiscence and the irascible passion, is not. Therefore, mind can include intellect and will without having to be the essence of the soul; i.e. 'mind' denotes a certain group of faculties and in this group are understood to be those faculties which in their operation dispense entirely with matter and material conditions.

To the third it must be said that Augustine and other saints find the image of the Trinity in man in many ways, and there is no need for one of these to agree with another. Thus it is clear that Augustine discerns the image in mind, knowledge, and love, and at another time in memory, understanding, and will; and although love will correspond, and likewise understanding and knowledge, it is not necessary that memory should answer to mind. Similarly, Augustine's account of the image which this objection discusses is different from the two preceding. Therefore it is not necessary that, as loving corresponds to love and knowing to knowledge, existence should correspond to mind as the proper perfection of that which is mind.

To the fourth it must be said that angels are called 'minds' not because the angelic mind or intellect is the essence of the angel, when that mind is considered as a faculty, but because the angels have no other faculties of the soul save those that can be grouped under the heading of 'mind,' and so they are purely 'mind.' To the human soul, on the other hand, there are added other faculties that cannot be grouped under the heading of mind, since the human soul is the 'form' of a body. These are the sensitive and nutritive faculties.

Therefore the human soul cannot be called a 'mind' in the same way as that of an angel.

To the fifth it must be said that living is a higher perfection than being, and understanding is higher than living. Now for the image of God to be found in anything, it is necessary that the thing should be in the highest degree of perfection that is possible to a creature. Thus if the thing have being alone, as the rocks, or being and life, as the flowers and the beasts, the image of God is not realized therein; but to realize the image perfectly, it is necessary that the creature have being, life, and intellect, for only thus is it most fittingly related to the essential attributes of God. Now although in explaining the image mind is put in place of the divine essence, and memory, understanding, and will in place of the Three Persons, and although Augustine thus bases his account of the image in the creature upon mind, saying: 'Memory, understanding, and will are one life, one mind, one essence,' it is not necessary to conclude that the creature is called mind in the same way as it is called life or essence. In us being, life, and intellect are not, as they are in God, one and the same thing; these three are, however, called one essence because they proceed from the one essence of mind, and one life because they all appertain to one kind of life, and one mind because they all can be grouped under the one mind as parts of a whole, just as sight and hearing are grouped together as parts of the sensitive soul.

To the sixth it must be said that since according to Aristotle[1] the substantial differences of things are unknown to us, the makers of definitions sometimes use in

[1] *Metaph.* 1040, a. 5–29.

their stead accidentals which declare or make known the essence as a true effect makes known a cause. Therefore the property of being sensitive, which is the constitutive difference of the brute, is not drawn from sensation considered as a faculty but from the essence of the soul from which such a faculty issues. The same is true of reason or of that creature which possesses it.

To the seventh it must be said that just as the sensitive soul is not understood to be an extra faculty over and above those various faculties of sensation which it comprehends, but is a unit-faculty embracing them all as its parts, in the same way the mind is not an extra faculty over and above memory, understanding, and will but is a unit-faculty embracing the three. So, too, for example, the faculty of house-building includes those of hewing the stones and building the walls, and so on.

To the eighth it must be said that the mind does not stand to intellect and will as their ground, but rather as a whole to its parts, at least when the mind is taken to be the faculty itself. But when mind is taken to be the essence of the soul with that faculty issuing from it, then it does denote the ground of the faculties.

To the ninth it must be said that a single faculty does not comprise within itself other faculties, but there is nothing to prevent a unit-faculty including others as its parts, just as one part of the body can include other organic parts, as the hand includes the fingers.

De Veritate, Q. x. a. 1.

40

THE BOOK OF BLESSED DIONYSIUS CONCERNING THE DIVINE NAMES

THEREFORE we must inquire how we know God, Who cannot be grasped by the mind or the senses. Would it be true to say that we do not know Him according to His nature? For this is unknown and is beyond the reach of reason and intuition. Yet by means of the ordering of all things, which has been as it were projected out of Him and which bears certain images and likenesses of its divine patterning, we ascend in ordered degrees so far as we are able, to that which is above all things, by the ways of negation and transcendence and the conception of a universal cause.

Thus God is known in all things and yet apart from all things; and He is known through knowledge and through ignorance. On the one hand, He is apprehended by intuition, reason, understanding, touch, sense, opinion, imagination, name, and so on; while on the other hand He cannot be grasped by intuition nor can He be uttered or named, and He is not anything in the world nor is He known in any existent thing. He is all things in all, and nothing in any, and is known in all, and is not known from any to any man. For this do we say rightly concerning God, and from all existing things does He receive praise according to the quality of all those things of which He is the cause. Yet there is, on the other hand, that most divine knowledge of God, which

is attained by unknowing in a union that transcends
the mind, when the mind recedes from all things and
then leaves even itself, and is united to the super-
resplendent rays, being illumined in them and from them
by the unsearchable depth of wisdom.   Yet this wisdom
is to be known, as I have said, from all things.   For it
is, as Scripture says, the efficient cause of all things,
ordering them all in harmony.   Wisdom is the cause
of the indissoluble concord of all things and the cause of
order, ever fitting the end of one part to the beginning
of the second, and producing one beautiful harmony
and agreement of all things.

                                   De Div. Nom. vii, lect. 4.

Therefore we must inquire how we know God.

After Dionysius has shown how God knows other
things, here he shows how God is known, making three
comments on this. First he proposes a doubt, and
secondly he solves it,[1] and thirdly he draws a conclusion
from the preceding.[2]

He says in the first place that, after the statement
that God knows everything through His essence which
is above mind and sense and all that is, it remains that
we should inquire how we can know God, seeing that
He is not intelligible but above things intelligible, and
not sensible but above things sensible, and is not to be
numbered among existent things but is above them all,
whereas our knowledge is through intellect or sense,
and we know not what does not exist.

*Would it be true to say that we do know Him but not
according to His nature ?*

---

[1] In the phrase: *Would it be true to say* . . .
[2] In the paragraph: *Thus God is known* . . .

Here Dionysius solves the doubt proposed; and because the solution is tentative, he puts it in the form of a question. The solution is this, that we know God but not by His nature, seeing as it were His very essence: for that essence is unknown to creatures and surpasses not only sense-knowledge, but every human intellect and the mind of every angel operating with natural power and vigour, and cannot be known to any one otherwise than by the gift of some grace. We do not, therefore, know God by seeing His essence, but from the pattern of the whole universe. The entirety of creatures is set before us by God that thereby we may know Him; for the ordered universe has some likeness and faint resemblance to the divine nature which is its pattern and archetype. Thus from consideration of the ordered universe, *we ascend in ordered degrees, so far as we are able* by our intellect, to God Who is above all, and this in three ways: first *by the way of negation*, in so far as we esteem nothing of what we see to be God or worthy of God; secondly, by transcendence (for such perfections among creatures as life, wisdom and so on are not to be denied of God owing to any defect in Him, but since He stands above all creaturely perfection we must therefore not allow Him wisdom Who exceeds all wisdom); and thirdly by way of causality, considering that all that there is in creatures comes from God as from a cause. Thus our knowledge of God is the counterpart of His knowledge, for He knows creatures by His own nature and we know His nature by creatures.

Thus God is known in all things and apart from all. Here Dionysius draws the conclusion from what has been said, in three stages, first the conclusion itself, then the manner in which it follows from the premisses (in the

sentence: *For this do we say rightly* . . .), and finally he
explains an assumption he had made (in the sentence:
Yet this wisdom is to be known . . .). First, then, he
declares that because we ascend from creatures to God
*by the ways of negation and transcendence and the con-
ception of a universal cause* God is known in all things
as in the effects of His action, and apart from all things
since He stands aloof from them and overtops them all,
and thus is God known *through our knowledge* (for whatever falls within our ken we receive as coming to us
from Him) and *through our ignorance* for the recognition
that we are ignorant of God's essence is itself a knowledge of God.   What he has said of knowledge in general
he then explains in detail, saying that God *is apprehended by intuition and by speech* (or *by reason* as
the other version has it), by understanding (i.e.
by the united powers of intuition and reason), and
by *touch*. This last he adds as it is the sensitive
faculty common to all animals, and he gives the more
general term *sense* immediately afterwards. Then he
lists the imperfect forms of knowledge, *opinion and
imagination*, which are the degenerate forms of rational
knowledge and sure sense-awareness. *Name* is added
as it is the outward sign of knowledge, and the *etcetera*
covers the other subsidiaries of knowing and of expression.   Contrariwise, God *cannot be grasped by intuition*
nor by sense, *nor can He be uttered or named*. How
these two positions are reconciled he explains by saying
that God *is not anything in the world*, but, above all
things that are, and thus knowledge, by intuition or by
other ways, of things that are in the world does not
amount to knowledge of God.   Again, *God is all things
in all* by His causality, though He is not of the number

of existent things by His essence, and thus knowledge of an existent thing by intuition or by any other of the aforesaid means is knowledge of God as a cause, though not of Him as He is.

For this do we say rightly concerning God, and from all existing things does He receive praise according to the quality of all those things of which He is the cause. Here Dionysius shows how the conclusion follows from the premisses, saying that in this we are right, that God is known and is not known. He is known from all that exists, and receives praise therefrom, since all things stand related to Him as to their cause. Again, there is another very lofty manner of knowing God, by negation, i.e. we know God by unknowing, by a manner of uniting with God that exceeds the compass of our minds, *when the mind recedes from all things and then leaves even itself and is united with the super-resplendent rays* of the Divinity. Here the mind knows not only that God is above all that is non-mental, but also that He is above its own nature and all that it can comprehend. In this state of knowledge of God, the mind is enlightened from out the depths of the divine wisdom which defy our scrutiny; for to understand that God is not only above all that exists but even above all that we can comprehend comes to us from the divine wisdom.

Yet this wisdom is to be known, as I have said, from all things. Here Dionysius explains an assumption made previously, i.e. that God is known from all things. He says that this is so because the divine wisdom is the efficient cause wherefrom all things receive their being, and not their being only, but also their order in the cosmos, in so far as things conspire together and collaborate to one last end. Further, wisdom is the cause that gives stability to this harmony and concord which are perpetual in spite of all changes among created things. He explains the manner of this harmony, saying that wisdom is *ever fitting the end of one part to the beginning of the second*, i.e. the inferior qualities of a higher being to the higher qualities of an inferior, so that the highest type of body, the human, comes into union with the lowest intellect, or rational soul; and in like manner for other things. Thus wisdom fashions the beauty of the universe, *producing one beautiful harmony and agreement of all things*, in due order and proportion.

De Div. Nom., C. 7, l. 4

41

QUESTION : OF THE CONTEMPLATIVE LIFE

(*In Eight Articles*)

WE must now consider the contemplative life, under which head there are eight points of inquiry: (1) Whether the contemplative life belongs to the intellect only, or also to the affections? (2) Whether the moral virtues pertain to the contemplative life? (3) Whether the contemplative life consists in one act or in several? (4) Whether the consideration of any and every truth pertains to the contemplative life? (5) Whether the contemplative life of man on this earth can arise to the vision of God? (6) Of the movements of contemplation assigned by Dionysius.[1] (7) Of the pleasure of contemplation. (8) Of the duration of contemplation.

FIRST ARTICLE

WHETHER THE CONTEMPLATIVE LIFE HAS NOTHING TO DO WITH THE AFFECTIONS, AND PERTAINS WHOLLY TO THE INTELLECT?

We proceed thus to the First Article.

Objection 1. It would seem that the contemplative life has nothing to do with the affections and pertains wholly to the intellect. For Aristotle says that *the end of contemplation is truth*.[2] Now truth pertains wholly to

---

[1] *De Div. Nom.* 4.   [2] *Metaph.* 993, b. 21.

the intellect. Therefore it would seem that the contemplative life wholly regards the intellect.

Obj. 2. Further, Gregory says that *Rachel, which is interpreted 'vision of the principle,'* [1] signifies the contemplative life.[2] Now the vision of a principle belongs properly to the intellect. Therefore the contemplative life belongs properly to the intellect.

Obj. 3. Further, Gregory says that it belongs to the contemplative life, *to rest from external action.*[3] Now the affective or appetitive power inclines to external actions. Therefore it would seem that the contemplative life has nothing whatever to do with the appetitive faculty.

On the contrary, Gregory says that *the contemplative life is to cling with our whole mind to the love of God and our neighbour, and to desire nothing beside our Creator.*[4] Now desire and love pertain to the affective or appetitive power, as stated above.[5] Therefore the contemplative life has also something to do with the affective or appetitive power.

I answer that, as stated above,[6] the life of those is called contemplative who are chiefly intent on the contemplation of truth. Now intention is an act of the will, as stated above,[7] because intention is the seeking of an end which is the object of the will. Consequently the contemplative life, as regards the essence of the action, pertains to the intellect, but as regards the motive cause of the exercise of that action it belongs to

---

[1] Or rather, *One seeing the principle* if derived from ראה and הוּן. Cf. Jerome, *De Nom. Hebr.*

[2] *Moral.* vi. 37.   Cf. *Hom.* xiv *in Ezech.*

[3] *Hom.* xiv *in Ezech.*

[4] Ibid.

[5] 2 I. Q. xv. a. 2; Q. xxvi. a. 2.

[6] Q. clxxix. a. 1.

[7] 2 I. Q. xii. a. 1.

the will, which moves all the other powers, even the intellect, to their actions, as stated above.[1]

Now the appetitive power moves one to observe things either with the senses or with the intellect, sometimes for love of the thing seen because, as it is written, *where thy treasure is, there is thy heart also*,[2] sometimes for love of the very knowledge that one acquires by observation. Wherefore Gregory makes the contemplative life to consist in the *love of God*, inasmuch as through loving God we are aflame to gaze on His beauty. And since every one rejoices when he obtains what he loves, it follows that the contemplative life terminates in delight, which is seated in the affective power, the result being that love also becomes more intense.

Reply Obj. 1. From the very fact that truth is the end of contemplation, truth can be regarded as an appetible good, both lovable and delightful, and in this respect it pertains to the appetitive power.

Reply Obj. 2. We are urged to the vision of the first principle, namely God, by the love thereof; wherefore Gregory says that *the contemplative life tramples on all cares and longs to see the face of its Creator*.[3]

Reply Obj. 3. The appetitive power moves not only the bodily members to perform external actions, but also the intellect to practise the act of contemplation, as stated above.

[1] I. Q. lxxxii. a. 4; 2 I. Q. ix. a. 1.   [2] Matt. vi. 21.
[3] *Hom*. xiv *in Ezech*.

SECOND ARTICLE

WHETHER THE MORAL VIRTUES PERTAIN TO THE CONTEMPLATIVE LIFE

We proceed thus to the Second Article.

Objection 1. It would seem that the moral virtues pertain to the contemplative life. For Gregory says that *the contemplative life is to cling to the love of God and our neighbour with the whole mind.*[1] Now all the moral virtues whose exercise is prescribed by the Commandments, are reducible to the love of God and of our neighbour, for *love . . . is the fulfilling of the Law.*[2] Therefore it would seem that the moral virtues belong to the contemplative life.

Obj. 2. Further, the contemplative life is chiefly directed to the contemplation of God; for Gregory says *that the mind tramples on all cares and longs to gaze on the face of its Creator.*[3] Now no one can accomplish this without cleanness of heart, which is a result of moral virtue.[4] For it is written: *Blessed are the clean of heart, for they shall see God,*[5] and, *Follow peace with all men, and holiness, without which no man shall see God.*[6] Therefore it would seem that the moral virtues pertain to the contemplative life.

Obj. 3. Further, Gregory says that *the contemplative life gives beauty to the soul,*[7] wherefore it is signified by Rachel, of whom it is said that she was *of a beautiful countenance.*[8] Now the beauty of the soul consists in the moral virtues, especially temperance, as Ambrose

---

[1] Ibid.
[2] Rom. xiii. 10.
[3] *Hom.* xiv *in Ezech.*
[4] Cf. Q. viii. a. 7.
[5] Matt. v. 8.
[6] Heb. xii. 14.
[7] *Hom.* xiv *in Ezech.*
[8] Gen. xxix. 17.

says.[1] Therefore it seems that the moral virtues pertain to the contemplative life.

On the contrary, the moral virtues are directed to external actions. Now Gregory says that it belongs to the contemplative life *to rest from external action*.[2] Therefore the moral virtues do not pertain to the contemplative life.

I answer that a thing may belong to the contemplative life in two ways, essentially or as a predisposition. The moral virtues do not belong to the contemplative life essentially, because the end of the contemplative life is the consideration of truth: and as Aristotle says, *knowledge*, which pertains to the consideration of truth, *has little influence on the moral virtues*:[3] wherefore he declares[4] that the moral virtues pertain to active but not to contemplative happiness.

On the other hand, the moral virtues belong to the contemplative life as a predisposition. For the act of contemplation, wherein the contemplative life essentially consists, is hindered both by the impetuosity of the passions which withdraw the soul's intention from intelligible to sensible things, and by outward disturbances. Now the moral virtues curb the impetuosity of the passions, and quell the disturbance of outward occupations. Hence moral virtues belong to the contemplative life as a predisposition.

Reply Obj. 1. As stated above,[5] the contemplative life has its motive cause on the part of the affections, and in this respect the love of God and our neighbour is requisite to the contemplative life. Now motive causes

---

[1] *De Offic.* i. 43, 45, 46.
[2] *Moral.* vi. Cf. *Hom.* xiv *in Ezech.* Cf. A. 1, r. obj. 3.
[3] *Eth. Nic.* 1103, b. 27, 1179, b. 2.
[4] *Eth. Nic.* 1178, a. 8.   [5] A. 1.

do not enter into the essence of a thing, but dispose and perfect it. Wherefore it does not follow that the moral virtues belong essentially to the contemplative life.

Reply Obj. 2. Holiness or cleanness of heart is caused by the virtues that are concerned with the passions which hinder the purity of the reason; and peace is caused by justice which deals with human acts: *The work of justice shall be peace,*[1] since he who refrains from wronging others lessens the occasions of quarrels and disturbances. Hence the moral virtues dispose one to the contemplative life by causing peace and cleanness of heart.

Reply Obj. 3. Beauty, as stated above,[2] consists in a certain clarity and due proportion. Now each of these is found fundamentally in the reason; because both the light that makes beauty seen, and the establishing of due proportion among things, belong to reason. Hence, since the contemplative life consists in an act of the reason, there is beauty in it by its very nature and essence; wherefore it is written of the contemplation of wisdom: *I became a lover of her beauty.*[3]

On the other hand, beauty is in the moral virtues by participation, in so far as they belong to the rational order; and especially is it in temperance, which restrains the concupiscences which especially darken the light of reason. Hence it is that the virtue of chastity most of all makes man apt for contemplation, since venereal pleasures most of all weigh the mind down to sensible objects, as Augustine says.[4]

---

[1] Isa. xxxii. 17.   [2] Q. cxlv. a. 2.
[3] Wisd. of Sol. viii. 2.   [4] *Soliloq.* i. 10.

THIRD ARTICLE

WHETHER THERE ARE VARIOUS ACTIONS PERTAINING TO THE CONTEMPLATIVE LIFE?

We proceed thus to the Third Article.

Objection 1. It would seem that there are various actions pertaining to the contemplative life. For Richard of S. Victor distinguishes between *contemplation*, *meditation*, and *cogitation*.[1] Yet all these apparently pertain to contemplation. Therefore it would seem that there are various actions pertaining to the contemplative life.

Obj. 2. Further, the apostle says:[2] *But we . . . beholding* (speculantes) *the glory of the Lord with open face, are transformed into the same clarity.*[3] Now this belongs to the contemplative life. Therefore in addition to the three aforesaid, vision (*speculatio*) belongs to the contemplative life.

Obj. 3. Further, Bernard says that *the first and greatest contemplation is admiration of the Majesty.*[4] Now according to Damascene [5] admiration is a kind of fear. Therefore it would seem that several acts are requisite for the contemplative life.

Obj. 4. Further, *prayer, reading,* and *meditation* [6] are said to belong to the contemplative life. Again, *hearing* belongs to the contemplative life: since it is stated that Mary (by whom the contemplative life is signified) *sitting . . . at the Lord's feet, heard His word.*[7] There-

---

[1] *De Grat. Contempl.* i. 3, 4.   [2] 2 Cor. iii. 18.
[3] Vulg., *into the same image from glory to glory.*
[4] *De Consid.* v. 14.   [5] *De Fide Orth.* ii. 15.
[6] Hugh of S. Victor, *Alleg. in N. T.* iii. 4.
[7] Luke x. 39.

fore it would seem that several acts are requisite for the contemplative life.

On the contrary, 'life' signifies here the operation on which a man is chiefly intent. Wherefore if there are several operations of the contemplative life, there will be, not one, but several contemplative lives.

I answer that we are now speaking of the contemplative life as applicable to man. Now according to Dionysius,[1] between man and angel there is this difference, that an angel perceives the truth by simple apprehension, whereas man becomes acquainted with a simple truth by a process from manifold data. Accordingly, then, the contemplative life has one act wherein it is finally completed, namely the contemplation of truth, and from this act it derives its unity. Yet it has many acts whereby it arrives at this final act. Some of these pertain to the reception of principles, from which it proceeds to the contemplation of truth; others are concerned with the elaboration from these principles of the truth which is sought; and the last and crowning act is the contemplation itself of the truth.

Reply Obj. 1. According to Richard of S. Victor *cogitation* would seem to regard the consideration of the many things from which a person intends to gather one simple truth. Hence cogitation may comprise not only the perceptions of the senses in taking cognizance of certain effects, but also the data of the imagination and the discourse of reason concerning the various indications, or whatever they may be, that lead to the truth in view: although, according to Augustine,[2] cogitation may signify any actual operation of the intellect.—*Meditation* would seem to be the process of reason from certain principles

<hr>

[1] *De Div. Nom.* vii.　　　　[2] *De Trin.* xiv. 7.

that lead to the contemplation of some truth: and *consideration* has the same meaning, according to Bernard,[1] although, according to Aristotle,[2] every operation of the intellect may be called *consideration*.—But *contemplation* regards the simple act of gazing on the truth; wherefore Richard says again that *contemplation is the soul's clear and free dwelling upon the object of its gaze; meditation is the survey of the mind while occupied in searching for the truth; and cogitation is the mind's glance which is prone to wander.*[3]

Reply Obj. 2. According to a gloss[4] of Augustine on this passage, *beholding* (*speculatio*) denotes *seeing in a mirror* (*speculo*), not *from a watch-tower* (*specula*). Now to see a thing in a mirror is to see a cause in its effect wherein its likeness is reflected. Hence *beholding* would seem to be reducible to meditation.

Reply Obj. 3. *Admiration* is a kind of fear resulting from the apprehension of a thing that surpasses our *faculties*: hence it results from the contemplation of the sublime truth. For it was stated above[5] that contemplation terminates in the affections.

Reply Obj. 4. Man reaches the knowledge of truth in two ways. First, by means of things received from another. In this way, as regards the things he receives from God, he needs *prayer*: *I called upon* God, *and the spirit of wisdom came upon me*:[6] while as regards the things he receives from man, he needs *hearing*, in so far as he receives from the spoken word, and *reading*, in so far as he draws upon documents committed to writing. Secondly, he needs to apply himself by his personal study, and thus he requires *meditation*.

[1] *De Consid.* ii. 2.   [2] *De Anima*, 427, a. 17.
[3] *De Grat. Contempl.* i. 4.   [4] Cf. *De Trin.* xv. 8.
[5] A. I.   [6] Wisd. of Sol. vii. 7.

WHETHER THE CONTEMPLATIVE LIFE CONSISTS IN THE
    MERE CONTEMPLATION OF GOD, OR ALSO IN THE
    CONSIDERATION OF ANY AND EVERY TRUTH

We proceed thus to the Fourth Article.

Objection 1. It would seem that the contemplative life
consists not only in the contemplation of God, but also
in the consideration of any truth. For it is written:
Wonderful are Thy works, and my soul knoweth right well.[1]
Now the knowledge of God's works is effected by any
contemplation of the truth. Therefore it would seem
that it pertains to the contemplative life to contemplate
not only the divine truth, but also any other.

Obj. 2. Further, Bernard says that *contemplation
consists in admiration first of God's majesty, secondly of
His judgments, thirdly of His benefits, fourthly of His
promises.*[2] Now of these four the first alone regards the
divine truth, and the other three pertain to His effects.
Therefore the contemplative life consists not only in the
contemplation of the divine truth, but also in the consideration of truth regarding the effects of God's activity.

Obj. 3. Further, Richard of S. Victor[3] distinguishes
six species of contemplation. The first belongs to *the
imagination alone*, and consists in thinking of corporeal
things. The second is in *the imagination guided by reason*,
and consists in considering the order and disposition of
sensible objects. The third is in *the reason based on the
imagination*; when, to wit, from the consideration of the
visible we rise to the invisible. The fourth is in *the*

---

[1] Ps. cxxxviii. 14.   [2] *De Consid.* v. 14.
[3] *De Grat. Contempl.* i. 6.

reason and conducted by the reason, when the mind is intent on things invisible of which the imagination has no cognizance. The fifth is *above the reason*, but not contrary to reason, when by divine revelation we become cognizant of things that cannot be comprehended by the human reason. The sixth is *above reason and contrary to reason*; when, to wit, by the divine enlightening we know things that seem contrary to human reason, such as the doctrine of the mystery of the Trinity. Now only the last of these would seem to pertain to the divine truth. Therefore the contemplation of truth regards not only the divine truth, but also that which is considered in creatures.

Obj. 4. Further, in the contemplative life the contemplation of truth is sought as being the perfection of man. Now any truth is a perfection of the human intellect. Therefore the contemplative life consists in the contemplation of any truth.

On the contrary, Gregory says that *in contemplation we seek God, who is the first principle.*[1]

I answer that, as stated above,[2] a thing may belong to the contemplative life in two ways: principally, and secondarily or as a predisposition. That which belongs principally to the contemplative life is the contemplation of the divine truth, because this contemplation is the end of the whole human life. Hence Augustine says that *the contemplation of God is promised us as being the goal of all our actions and the everlasting perfection of our joys.*[3] This contemplation will be perfect in the life to come, when we shall see God face to face, wherefore it will make us perfectly happy: whereas now the contemplation of the divine truth is competent to us im-

---

[1] *Moral.* vi. 37.   [2] A. 2.   [3] *De Trin.* i. 8.

perfectly, namely *through a glass* and *in a dark manner*.[1]
Hence it bestows on us a certain inchoate beatitude,
which begins now and will be continued in the life to
come; wherefore Aristotle [2] places man's ultimate
happiness in the contemplation of what is best, i.e. of
the intelligible.

Since, however, God's effects show us the way to the
contemplation of God Himself: *The invisible things of
God . . . are clearly seen, being understood by the things
that are made*,[3] it follows that the contemplation of the
effects of God's activity also belongs to the contemplative
life, inasmuch as man is guided thereby to the knowledge
of God. Hence Augustine says that *in the study of
creatures we must not exercise an empty and futile curiosity,
but should make them the stepping-stones to things imperishable and everlasting*.[4]

Accordingly it is clear from what has been said [5]
that four things pertain, in a certain order, to the contemplative life: first, the moral virtues; secondly, other
acts exclusive of contemplation; thirdly, contemplation
of the effects of God's activity; fourthly, the comple-
ment of all which is the contemplation of the divine
truth itself.

Reply Obj. 1. David sought the knowledge of God's
works, so that he might be led by them to God; wherefore he says elsewhere: *I meditated on all Thy works :
I meditated upon the works of Thy hands : I stretched forth
my hands to Thee*.[6]

Reply Obj. 2. By considering the divine judgments
man is guided to the consideration of the divine justice;
and by considering the divine benefits and promises,

---

[1] I Cor. xiii. 12.
[2] *Eth. Nic.* 1177 a. 12–18.
[3] Rom. i. 20.
[4] *De Vera Relig.* xxix.
[5] As. 1, 2, 3.
[6] Ps. cxlii. 5, 6.

man is led to the knowledge of God's mercy or goodness, as by effects already manifested or yet to be vouchsafed.

Reply Obj. 3. These six denote the steps whereby we ascend by means of creatures to the contemplation of God. For the first step consists in the mere consideration of sensible objects; the second step consists in going forward from sensible to intelligible objects; the third step is to judge of sensible objects according to intelligible things; the fourth is the absolute consideration of the intelligible objects to which one has attained by means of sense-data; the fifth is the contemplation of those intelligible objects that are unattainable by way of sense-data, but which the reason is able to grasp; the sixth step is the consideration of such intelligible things as the reason can neither discover nor grasp, which pertain to the sublime contemplation of divine truth, wherein contemplation is ultimately perfected.

Reply Obj. 4. The ultimate perfection of the human intellect is the divine truth: and other truths perfect the intellect in relation to the divine truth.

Fifth Article

Whether in the Present State of Life the Contemplative Life can reach to the Vision of the Divine Essence?

We proceed thus to the Fifth Article.

Objection 1. It would seem that in the present state of life the contemplative life can reach to the vision of the divine essence. For, as stated, Jacob said: *I have seen God face to face, and my soul has been saved.*[1] Now

---

[1] Gen. xxxii. 30.

the vision of God's face is the vision of the divine essence. Therefore it would seem that in the present life one may come, by means of contemplation, to see God in His essence.

Obj. 2. Further, Gregory says that *contemplative men withdraw within themselves in order to explore spiritual things, nor do they ever carry with them the shadows of things corporeal, or if these follow them they prudently drive them away : but being desirous of seeing the incomprehensible light, they suppress all the images of their limited comprehension, and through longing to reach what is above them, they overcome that which they are.*[1] Now man is not hindered from seeing the divine essence, which is the incomprehensible light, save by the necessity of turning to imagery drawn from bodily things. Therefore it would seem that the contemplation of the present life can extend to the vision of the incomprehensible light in its essence.

Obj. 3. Further, Gregory says: *All creatures are small to the soul that sees its Creator: wherefore when the man of God*, the blessed Benedict, to wit, *saw a fiery globe upon the tower and angels returning to heaven, without doubt he could only see such things by the light of God.*[2] Now the blessed Benedict was still in this life. Therefore the contemplation of the present life can extend to the vision of the essence of God.

On the contrary, Gregory says: *As long as we live in this mortal flesh, no one reaches such a height of contemplation as to fix the eyes of his mind on the ray itself of incomprehensible light.*[3]

I answer that, as Augustine says, *no one seeing God lives this mortal life wherein the bodily senses have their*

[1] *Moral.* vi. 37.   [2] *Dial.* ii. 35.   [3] *Hom.* xiv *in Ezech.*

*play : and unless in some way he depart this life, whether
by going altogether out of his body, or by withdrawing from
his carnal senses, he is not caught up into that vision.*[1]
This has been carefully discussed above [2] where we spoke
of rapture, and in the First Part [3] where we treated of
the vision of God.

Accordingly we must state that one may be in this
life in two ways. First, in actual fact, that is to say,
by actually making use of the bodily senses, and thus
contemplation in the present life can nowise attain to
the vision of God's essence. Secondly, one may be in
this life potentially and not in actual fact, that is to say,
when the soul is united to the mortal body as to its form,
yet so as to make use neither of the bodily senses, nor
even of the imagination, as happens in rapture; and in
this way the contemplation of the present life can attain
to the vision of the divine essence. Consequently the
highest degree of contemplation in the present life is
that which Paul had in rapture, whereby he was in a
middle state between the present life and the life to
come.

Reply Obj. 1. As Dionysius says, *if any one seeing God,
understood what he saw, he saw not God himself, but something belonging to God.*[4] And Gregory says: *By no means
is God seen now in His glory; but the soul sees something
of lower degree, and therefore it goes forward by the straight
road and afterwards it attains to the glory of vision.*[5]
Accordingly the words of Jacob, *I saw God face to face*,
do not imply that he saw God's essence, but that he saw
some shape,[6] imaginary, of course, wherein God spoke
to him.—Or, *since we know a man by his face, by the face*

---

[1] *Gen. ad Lit.* xii. 27. [2] Q. clxxv. as. 4, 5.
[3] Q. xii. a. 2. [4] *Ad Caium Monach.* i.
[5] *Hom.* xiv *in Ezech.* [6] Cf. 1. Q. xii, a. 11, *r. obj.* 1.

of God he signified his knowledge of Him, according to a gloss of Gregory on the same passage.

Reply Obj. 2. In the present state of life human contemplation is impossible without sense-imagery, because it is connatural to man to see the intelligible species in the phantasms, as Aristotle says.[1] Yet the intellect when gaining knowledge does not rest content with this sense-imagery, but contemplates therein the purity of the intelligible truth: and this not only in natural knowledge, but also in that which we obtain by revelation. For Dionysius says that *the divine glory shows us the angelic hierarchies under certain symbolic figures, and by its power we are brought back to the single ray of light*,[2] i.e. to the simple knowledge of the intelligible truth. It is in this sense that we must understand the statement of Gregory that *contemplatives do not carry along with them the shadows of things corporeal*, since their contemplation is not fixed on them, but on the consideration of the intelligible truth.

Reply Obj. 3. By these words Gregory does not imply that the blessed Benedict, in that vision, saw God in His essence, but he wishes to show that because *all creatures are small to him that sees God*, it follows that all things can easily be seen through the enlightenment of the divine light. Wherefore he adds: *For however little he may see of the Creator's light, all created things become petty to him.*

[1] *De Anima*, 431. b. 2.   [2] *Cael Hier.* i.

SIXTH ARTICLE

WHETHER THE OPERATION OF CONTEMPLATION IS
FITTINGLY DIVIDED INTO A THREEFOLD MOVEMENT,
CIRCULAR, STRAIGHT, AND OBLIQUE?

We proceed thus to the Sixth Article.

Objection 1. It would seem that the operation of contemplation is unfittingly divided into a threefold movement, *circular, straight,* and *oblique.*[1] For contemplation pertains exclusively to rest: *When I go into my house, I shall repose myself with her.*[2] Now movement is opposed to rest. Therefore the operations of the contemplative life should not be described as movements.

Obj. 2. Further, the action of the contemplative life pertains to the intellect, whereby man is like the angels. Now Dionysius describes these movements as being different in the angels from what they are in the soul. For he says that the *circular* movement in the angel is *according to his enlightenment by the beautiful and the good.*[3] On the other hand, he assigns the circular movement of the soul to several things: the first of which is the *withdrawal of the soul into itself from externals*; the second is *a certain concentration of its powers, whereby it is rendered free of error and of outward occupation*; and the third is *union with those things that are above it.*—Again, he describes differently their respective straight movements. For he says that the straight movement of the angel is that by which he proceeds to the care of those things that are beneath him. On the other hand, he describes the straight movement of the soul as being twofold:

[1] *De Div. Nom.* iv.　　[2] Wisd. of Sol. viii. 16.
[3] *De Div. Nom.* iv.

first, *its progress towards things that are near it*; secondly, *its uplifting from external things to simple contemplation.*—Further, he assigns a different oblique movement to each. For he assigns the oblique movement of the angels to the fact that *while providing for those who have less they remain unchanged in relation to God*: whereas he assigns the oblique movement of the soul to the fact that *the soul is enlightened in divine knowledge by reasoning and discoursing.*—Therefore it would seem that the operations of contemplation are unfittingly assigned according to the ways mentioned above.

Obj. 3. Further, Richard of S. Victor mentions many other different movements in likeness to the birds of the air. *For some of these rise at one time to a great height, at another swoop down to earth, and they do so repeatedly; others fly now to the right, now to the left again and again; others go forwards or lag behind many times; others fly in a circle now more now less extended; and others hover almost immovably in one place.*[1] Therefore it would seem that there are only three movements of contemplation.

On the contrary, stands the authority of Dionysius.[2]

I answer that, as stated above,[3] the operation of the intellect, wherein contemplation essentially consists, is called a movement, in so far as movement is the act of a perfect thing, according to Aristotle.[4] Since, however, it is through sensible objects that we come to the knowledge of intelligible things, and since sensible operations do not take place without movement, the result is that even intelligible operations are described as movements, and are differentiated in likeness to

---

[1] *De Contempl.* i. 5.
[2] *De Div. Nom.* iv.
[3] Q. clxxix. a. 1, *r. obj.* 3.
[4] *De Anima*, 431. a. 7.

various movements. Now of bodily movements, local movements are the most perfect and come first, as proved;[1] wherefore the foremost among intelligible operations are described by being likened to them. These movements are of three kinds; for there is the *circular* movement, by which a thing moves uniformly round one point as centre, another is the *straight* movement by which a thing goes from one point to another; the third is *oblique*, being composed as it were of both the others. Consequently, in intelligible operations, that which is simply uniform is compared to circular movement; the intelligible operation by which one proceeds from one point to another is compared to the straight movement; while the intelligible operation which unites something of uniformity with progress to various points is compared to the oblique movement.

Reply Obj. 1. External bodily movements are opposed to the quiet of contemplation, which consists in rest from outward occupations: but the movements of intellectual operations belong to the quiet of contemplation.

Reply Obj. 2. Man is like the angels in intellect generically, but the intellective power is much higher in the angel than in man. Consequently these movements must be ascribed to souls and angels in different ways, according as the two intellects differ in point of uniformity of knowledge. For the angelic intellect has uniform knowledge in two respects. First, because it does not acquire intelligible truth from the variety of composite objects; secondly, because it understands the truth of intelligible objects not discursively, but by simple intuition. On the other hand, the intellect of the soul acquires intelligible truth from sensible

[1] *Phys.* viii. 7.

objects, and understands it by a certain discourse of the reason.

Wherefore Dionysius assigns the *circular* movement of the angels to the fact that their intuition of God is uniform and unceasing, having neither beginning nor end: even as a circular movement having neither beginning nor end is uniformly around the one same centre. But on the part of the soul, ere it arrive at this uniformity, its twofold lack of uniformity needs to be removed. First, that which arises from the variety of external things: this is removed by the soul withdrawing from externals, and so the first thing he mentions regarding the circular movement of the soul is *the soul's withdrawal into itself from external objects.* Secondly, another lack of uniformity requires to be removed from the soul, and this is owing to the discoursing of reason. This is done by directing all the soul's operations to the simple contemplation of the intelligible truth, and this is indicated by his saying in the second place that *the soul's intellectual powers must be uniformly concentrated,* in other words that discourse must be laid aside and the soul's gaze fixed in the contemplation of the one simple truth. In this operation of the soul there is no error, even as there is clearly no error in the understanding of first principles which we know by simple intuition. Afterwards, these two things being premised, he mentions thirdly the uniformity which is like that of the angels, for then all things being laid aside, the soul continues in the contemplation of God alone. This he expresses by saying: *Then being thus made uniform unitedly,* i.e. in harmony, *and with united powers, it is conducted to the good and the beautiful.* The *straight* movement of the angel cannot apply to his proceeding from one thing to another by considering them, but only to the order of his providence, namely to the fact that the higher angel enlightens the lower angels through the angels that are intermediate.   He indicates this when he says: *The angel's movement takes a straight line when he proceeds to the care of things subject to him, taking in his course whatever things are direct,* i.e. in keeping with the dispositions of the direct order.   Whereas he ascribes the *straight* movement in the soul to the soul's proceeding from exterior sensibles to the knowledge of intelligible objects.   The *oblique* movement in the angels he describes as being composed of the straight and circular movements, inasmuch as their care for those beneath them is in accordance with their contemplation of God: while the *oblique* movement in the soul he also declares to be partly straight and partly circular, in so far as in reasoning it makes use of the light received from God.

Reply Obj. 3. These varieties of movement that are taken from the distinction between above and below, right and left, forwards and backwards, and between wider and sharper curves, are all comprised under either straight and oblique movement, because they all denote discursions of reason.   For if the reason pass from the genus to the species, or from the part to the whole, it will be, as he explains, from above to below: if from one opposite to another, it will be from right to left; if from the cause to the effect, it will be backwards and forwards; if it be about accidents that surround a thing near at hand or far remote, there will be motion in a curve. The discoursing of reason from sensible to intelligible objects, if it be according to the order of natural reason, belongs to the straight movement; but if it be according to the divine enlightenment, it will belong to the oblique movement as explained above.[1] That alone which he describes as immobility belongs to the circular movement.

Wherefore it is evident that Dionysius describes the movement of contemplation with much greater fullness and depth.

WHETHER THERE IS DELIGHT IN CONTEMPLATION?

We proceed thus to the Seventh Article.

Objection 1. It would seem that there is no delight in contemplation. For delight belongs to the appetitive power; whereas contemplation resides chiefly in the intellect. Therefore it would seem that there is no delight in contemplation.

Obj. 2. Further, all strife and struggle is a hindrance to delight. Now there is strife and struggle in contemplation. For Gregory says that *when the soul strives to contemplate God, it is in a state of struggle; at one time it almost overcomes, because by understanding and feeling it tastes something of the incomprehensible light, and at another time it almost succumbs, because even while tasting it fails.*[2] Therefore there is no delight in contemplation.

Obj. 3. Further, delight is the result of a perfect operation, as stated.[3] Now the contemplation of men on earth is imperfect: *We see now through a glass in a dark manner.*[4] Therefore seemingly there is no delight in the contemplative life.

Obj. 4. Further, a lesion of the body is an obstacle to delight. Now contemplation causes a lesion of the body; wherefore it is stated that after Jacob had said '*I have*

---

[1] *R. obj.* 2. [2] *Hom.* xiv *in Ezech.*
[3] *Eth. Nic.* 1174, b. 32. [4] 1 Cor. xiii. 12.

seen God face to face' . . . *he halted on his foot* . . .
because he touched the sinew of his thigh and it shrank.[1]
Therefore seemingly there is no delight in contemplation.

On the contrary, it is written of the contemplation of
wisdom: *Her conversation hath no bitterness, nor her
company any tediousness, but joy and gladness*:[2] and
Gregory says that *the contemplative life is sweetness
exceedingly lovable*.[3]

I answer that there may be delight in any particular
contemplation in two ways. First by reason of the
operation itself,[4] because each individual delights in
the operation which befits him according to his own
nature or habit. Now contemplation of the truth befits
a man according to his nature as a rational animal: the
result being that *all men naturally desire to know*, so that
consequently they delight in the knowledge of truth.
And more delightful still does this become to one who
has the habit of wisdom and knowledge, the result
of which is that he contemplates without difficulty.
Secondly, contemplation may be delightful by reason of
its object, in so far as one contemplates that which one
loves; even as bodily vision gives pleasure, not only
because to see is pleasurable in itself, but because one
sees a person whom one loves. Since, then, the contemplative life consists chiefly in the contemplation of
God, of which charity is the motive, as stated above,[5]
it follows that there is delight in the contemplative life,
not only by reason of the contemplation itself, but also
by reason of the divine love.

In both respects the delight thereof surpasses all
human delight, both because spiritual delight is greater

---

[1] Gen. xxxii.   [2] Wisd. of Sol. viii. 16.   [3] *Hom.* xiv *in Ezech.*
[4] Cf. 2 I. Q. iii. a. 5.   [5] As. 1, 2, *r. obj.* 1.

than carnal pleasure, as stated above,[1] when we were treating of the passions, and because the love whereby God is loved out of charity surpasses all love. Hence it is written: *O taste and see that the Lord is sweet.*[2]

Reply Obj. 1. Although the contemplative life consists chiefly in an act of the intellect, it has its beginning in the appetite, since it is through charity that one is urged to the contemplation of God. And since the end corresponds to the beginning, it follows that the term also and the end of the contemplative life is found in the appetite, since one delights in seeing the object loved, and the very delight in the object seen arouses a yet greater love. Wherefore Gregory says that *when we see one whom we love, we are so aflame as to love him more.*[3] And this is the ultimate perfection of the contemplative life, namely that the divine truth be not only seen but also loved.

Reply Obj. 2. Strife or struggle arising from the disagreeable nature of an external thing, hinders delight in that thing. For a man delights not in a thing against which he strives. But in that for which he strives; when he has obtained it, other things being equal, he delights yet more: wherefore Augustine says that *the more peril there was in the battle, the greater the joy in the triumph.*[4] But there is no strife or struggle in contemplation from the side of the truth which we contemplate, though there is on the part of our defective understanding and our corruptible body which drags us down to lower things: *The corruptible body is a load upon the soul, and the earthly habitation presseth down the mind that museth upon many things.*[5] Hence it is that when man attains to the contemplation of truth, he loves it

---

[1] I II. Q. xxxi. a. 5.   [2] Ps. xxxiii. 9.   [3] *Hom.* xiv *in Ezech.*
[4] *Conf.* viii. 3.   [5] Wisd. of Sol. ix. 15.

yet more, while he hates the more his own deficiency and the weight of his corruptible body, so as to say with the apostle: *Unhappy man that I am, who shall deliver me from the body of this death ?* [1] Wherefore Gregory says: *When God is once known by desire and understanding, He withers all carnal pleasure in us.* [2]

Reply Obj. 3. The contemplation of God in this life is imperfect in comparison with the contemplation in heaven; and in like manner the delight of contemplation to men upon earth is imperfect as compared with the delight of contemplation in heaven, of which it is written: *Thou shalt make them drink of the torrent of Thy pleasure.* [3] Yet, though the contemplation of divine things which is to be had by men upon earth is imperfect, it is more delightful than all other contemplation however perfect, on account of the excellence of that which is contemplated. Hence Aristotle says: *It is our lot to have less clear intuitions of those noble and god-like substances, . . . and though we establish contact with them even feebly, that knowledge owing to the sublime nature of its object gives us more pleasure than all that is round about us;* [4] and Gregory says in the same sense: *The contemplative life is sweetness exceedingly lovable; for it carries the soul away above itself, it opens heaven and discovers the spiritual world to the eyes of the mind.* [5]

Reply Obj. 4. After contemplation Jacob was lame of one foot, *because we need to grow weak in the love of the world ere we wax strong in the love of God,* as Gregory says: *Thus when we have known the sweetness of God, we have one foot sound while the other halts; since every one who halts on one foot leans only on that foot which is sound.* [6]

---

[1] Rom. vii. 24.
[2] *Hom.* xiv *in Ezech.*
[3] Ps. xxxv. 9.
[4] *De Part. Anim.* 644 b 24, 31.
[5] *Hom.* xiv *in Ezech.*
[6] Ibid.

WHETHER THE CONTEMPLATIVE LIFE IS CONTINUOUS?

We proceed thus to the Eighth Article.

Objection 1. It would seem that the contemplative life is not continuous. For the contemplative life consists essentially in things pertaining to the intellect. Now all the intellectual perfections of this life will be made void: *Whether prophecies shall be made void, or tongues shall cease, or knowledge shall be destroyed.*[1] Therefore the contemplative life is made void.

Obj. 2. Further, a man tastes the sweetness of contemplation by snatches and for a short time only: wherefore Augustine says: *Thou admittest me to a most unwonted affection in my inmost soul, to a strange sweetness, . . . yet through my grievous weight I sink down again.*[2] Again, Gregory commenting on the words of Job: *When a spirit passed before me,*[3] says: *The mind does not remain long at rest in the sweetness of inward contemplation, for it is recalled to itself and beaten back by the very immensity of the light.*[4] Therefore the contemplative life is not continuous.

Obj. 3. Further, that which is not connatural to man cannot be continuous. Now the contemplative life, according to Aristotle, *is a life above human measure.*[5] Therefore seemingly the contemplative life is not continuous.

On the contrary, our Lord said: *Mary hath chosen the best part, which shall not be taken away from her,*[6] since,

---

[1] 1 Cor. xiii. 8.
[3] Job iv. 15.
[5] *Eth. Nic.* 1177, b. 26.

[2] *Conf.* x. 40.
[4] *Moral.* v. 33.
[6] Luke x. 32.

as Gregory says, *the contemplative life begins here so as it may be perfected in our heavenly home.*[1]

I answer that a thing may be described as continuous in two ways: first, in its nature; secondly, in our practice of it.   It is evident that in regard to itself contemplative life is continuous for two reasons: first, because it is about incorruptible and unchangeable things; secondly, because it has no contrary, for there is nothing contrary to the pleasure of contemplation, as stated.[2]   But even in our practice contemplative life is continuous,—both because it belongs to us in virtue of the activity of the incorruptible part of the soul, namely the intellect, wherefore it can endure after this life,—and because in the works of the contemplative life we work not with our bodies, so that we are the more able to persevere in the works thereof, as Aristotle remarks.[3]

Reply Obj. 1. The manner of contemplation is not the same here as in heaven: yet the contemplative life is said to remain by reason of charity, wherein it has both its beginning and its end.   Gregory speaks in this sense: *The contemplative life begins here, so as to be perfected in our heavenly home, because the fire of love which begins to burn here is aflame with a yet greater love when we see Him Whom we love.*[4]

Reply Obj. 2.   No action can last long at its highest pitch.   Now the highest point of contemplation is to reach the uniformity of divine contemplation, according to Dionysius, and as we have stated above.[5]   Hence although contemplation cannot last long in this respect, it can be of long duration in the other contemplative acts.

Reply Obj. 3. Aristotle declares the contemplative life

---

[1] *Hom.* xiv *in Ezech.*   [2] *Top.* i. 13.   [3] *Eth. Nic.* 1177, a. 21.
[4] *Hom.* xiv *in Ezech.*   [5] A. 6, r. obj. 2; cf. *Cael. Hier.* iii.

to be above man, because it befits us *so far as there is in us something divine*,[1] namely the intellect, which is incorruptible and impassible in itself, wherefore its act can endure longer.

2 II. Q. clxxx.

42

WHETHER THE CONTEMPLATIVE LIFE CONSISTS ONLY IN AN ACT OF THE UNDERSTANDING

We proceed thus to the Second Article.

1. First of all, it seems that the contemplative life consists only in an act of the understanding, since the aim of this life is the attainment of truth.   Now truth pertains to the understanding alone, and so it follows that the contemplative life must consist only in an act of the understanding.

Further, the contemplative life has been called a state of leisure by holy men.   Aristotle also has described it as a holiday.[2]   Now leisure and immunity from service are opposed to action, which issues from the will. In a similar way, therefore, the contemplative life would seem to be opposed to will-action, and to consist only in understanding.

Again, there are qualities such as wisdom and understanding, which bring to maturity the contemplative life; and these pertain to the province of knowledge. From this it seems to follow that contemplation itself consists only in knowledge, for a proportion always exists between operations and their habits.

---

[1] *Eth. Nic.*, ibid.   [2] *Eth. Nic.* 1177, b. 22.

Yet against these reasons Isidore writes that *the contemplative life is that which is untrammelled by all human commerce, and delights only in the love of God.*[1] If this be so, the contemplative life does not consist only in knowledge, because love has to do with the affections.

And further, just as sight is to understanding, so taste pertains to appetite. But Gregory writes that *the contemplative life gives one already an intimate taste of future happiness.*[2] Hence the contemplative life does not consist only in understanding.

2. It seems, however, that the contemplative life consists in an operation of reason, because the contemplative life is a human life, and thus is led in a human fashion. Now it is the way of men to act according to reason, as reasoning animals, and therefore the contemplative life would seem to consist principally in reasoning.

Again, the contemplative life principally consists in knowledge of divine things. But the invisible things of God *are clearly seen, being understood by the things that are made.*[3] But it is the work of reason, thus to deduce conclusions from given data.

Moreover, Richard of S. Victor writes: *The flight of our spirit in contemplation varies in many ways: now it ascends from lower things to the highest, now it descends from higher to lower; now it deduces from part to whole, now from whole to part; now it argues from greater truth, at another time from less.*[4] Hence the contemplative life would seem to consist primarily in act of the reason, for this movement of the mind demands the use of reason.

But against this we have S. Bernard maintaining that

[1] *Lib. Diff. sive de Prop. Ser.*   [2] *Hom.* iii *in Ezech.*
[3] Rom. i.   [4] *De Contemplatione.*

pondering differs from examination in that the latter is concerned rather with inquiry, whereas the former is true and certain vision of mind.[1] Now such vision pertains to the intellect, inquiry, on the other hand, to the reason. Hence, on S. Bernard's teaching, the contemplative life will consist not in an act of reason, but in an act of the intellect.

Again, Aristotle holds that *by contemplation we communicate with God.*[2] But we do not do this by reasoning inquiry, so much as by vision of intellect, therefore the contemplative life consists only in an act of the intellect.

3. Again, it seems that every act of the intellect pertains to the contemplative life. For, just as there is a proportion between the active life and things to be done, so there is also a relation between the contemplative life and truths to be known. Now all acts concerning the former pertain to the active life, hence also all acts of the latter pertain to the contemplative life.

Moreover, the contemplative life, according to Aristotle, *consists in the consideration of philosophy.*[3] Now the faculty which contemplates reality, the peculiar province of philosophy, is the intellect, hence contemplation will consist in operations of the intellect.

Moreover, Richard of S. Victor speaks of six kinds of contemplation. The first kind is attained when, reflecting upon the beauty of material things, we wonder at the divine wisdom. When we search into their causes, we have the second kind. The third is found when we arise from visible to invisible things. And when we leave the imagination behind, and occupy ourselves only with pure intelligible truths, we have the fourth kind. We

---

[1] *De Consid.* [2] *Eth. Nic.* 1178, b. 25–7.
[3] *Eth. Nic.* 1177, a. 32.

go a step further, when we meditate on what we know, not from human reason but from divine revelation. The highest stage of contemplation is reached when we consider those greatest truths which seem even to contradict human reason. Now in these kinds of contemplation are included all the acts of our intellect, therefore every act of the latter must pertain to the contemplative life.

Yet against this, Isidore says that *the contemplative life, renouncing the world, delights to live in God alone.*[1] To live only for God requires contemplation of God only. Therefore not every operation of the intellect belongs to the contemplative life.

Again, the contemplative life and contemplative happiness seem to be concerned with the same object. Now contemplative happiness consists only in a consideration of the most noble and intelligible being, that is of God, as Aristotle says.[2]

First solution. I answer to the first question that the life about which we were now speaking, consists in that operation to which man is principally dedicated, for the attainment of which he removes all impediments, and seeks and pursues all things which further its progress. This faculty must be the will, whose function is to accept one course of human action rather than another, whatsoever that action may be. Now since the will is the mover of the other faculties of the soul, it must have a relation to the object and acts of the other faculties, only in so far as they have a goodness of their own, because every proper act of a faculty is its good. And so, the contemplative life consists in an act of the understanding preceded by desire of some kind. But

---

[1] *De Summo Bono.*   [2] *Eth. Nic.* 1177, a. 30.

since an operation is in some way an intermediary between the person acting and the object (as perfection of the knower, and itself perfected by the object which specifies it), so, contemplation can be desired in two ways. In one way, it is desired as a perfection of the knower, thus proceeding from self-love, as was the case in the contemplative life of the philosophers. In the second way, it is desired because attracted by an object, and such a desire of contemplation originates in love of the object, for whither the affections go, thither is the eye turned, *where your treasure is, there is your heart also.*[1] And in this way, the contemplative life of the saints, about which we are talking, makes use of the will.

Yet in spite of this, contemplation essentially consists in an act of the understanding; presupposing charity, however, for the reason just given. And so we find S. Gregory saying that *the contemplative life preserves the love of God, and the love of the neighbour with all our strength, and rests from external activity: so that, now, no longer pleased by external activity, and having despised earthly cares, the soul is consumed with desire to see its Creator's face.*[2]

In answer to the first objection, we reply that the purpose of contemplation, strictly so called, is truth alone. But in so far as contemplation is regarded as a way of life, it becomes something desirable and something good, as was said above.

We answer to the second objection that the will is not only a motive force to the exterior movements which are repugnant to the state of leisure, but also it is a motive force to the internal movements, even to the movement of the intellect itself. Aristotle says *that these are*

---

[1] Matt. vi. 21.　　　　[2] *Hom.* xiv *in Ezech.*

movements equivocally speaking, because they are perfect acts; and therefore, they are more assimilated to something in rest, than to something in motion.[1] Consequently, he who indulges in intellectual pursuits is said to desist from external action, as is clear from the authority we have been using.

In answer to the third objection, we reply that although the habits of the contemplative life are intellectual, yet their actions can be commanded or approved by the will. Thus contemplation consists in them also.

Second solution. To the second question, we must reply that the contemplative life consists in that operation which a man chooses in preference to others. Hence it is a kind of end in respect of other human operations, since they are done for it. Now just as an inquiry of reason proceeds from an intuition of the intellect (since a man proceeds to inquire from the principles which he holds by his intellect), so also it ends with a certitude of the intellect, when the conclusions arrived at are traced back to their principles on which their certainty rests. Therefore, the contemplative life principally consists in an act of the intellect, and this is implied by the very word contemplation, which word signifies vision. The contemplative, however, uses discursive reason in order to arrive at that vision of contemplation which is his principal concern, and it is this reasoning which S. Bernard calls inquiry.

To the first objection, therefore, we reply that just as animals border upon human nature by their instinct-faculty, the highest faculty of the animal world, by which animals act in a way similar to men; in so far as he is a contemplative, man becomes more than a man. The

[1] 3 *De Anima,* 407, a. 32.

reason is that in the operation of the understanding that comes with simple vision, a man borders upon those beings superior to himself which are called angels and pure intelligences.

To the second, we must reply that although visible things are means to the contemplation of divine truths, yet contemplation does not consist principally in this life, but in the life to come.

To the third objection, we answer that Richard of S. Victor does not mean that the contemplative life principally consists in these various movements of the mind, but rather that it moves them as means to end.

Third solution. In reply to the third question, we must say that the contemplative life of holy men presupposes a love of the object contemplated, from which object it takes its rise. Hence, since the contemplative life consists in that operation which is most intended, it must therefore be about the object that is most loved, that is about God. Hence it consists principally in an operation of the intellect about God. So we read in S. Gregory that *the contemplative life longs to see only its Creator, namely God.*[1] Nevertheless, the contemplative also considers all other things in so far as they are ordained to God; for example, he considers creatures, for he admires in such the divine majesty, wisdom, and goodness; and from these reflections, his love of God increases. He also reflects upon his own sins, from which his soul has been purified, in order that he may see God. Hence also, the very word contemplation signifies that principal act whereby a man contemplates God in Himself; whereas speculation rather signifies that act whereby one sees God in created things as in a mirror. In the

[1] *Hom. in Ezech.*

same way also, the happiness of the contemplative which the philosophers speak about consists in the contemplation of God; because, as Aristotle says, *it consists in the act of the highest faculty which is in us, that is the intellect; and in the most noble habit, namely wisdom; and also in the most noble object, which is God.*[1] That is why philosophers kept the latter part of their lives in contemplating divine things; whereas in the time preceding this, they studied the other sciences; so that from speculating on these they might be better qualified to study divine things.

To the first objection it must be said that there is no natural order among the acts of the active life as there is among the acts of the contemplative life; and hence the active life cannot strictly be said principally to consist in any one act. But in regard of an individual man, the active life will consist principally in the act which he more often practises; as some pay more attention to works of justice, others to those of self-restraint, and so on.

We answer to the second objection, that Aristotle, in that context, is speaking of philosophy strictly so called—knowledge of divine truths—which is called by the special name of First Philosophy.

Our answer to the third objection is that although the contemplative occasionally considers those kinds of contemplation which Richard of S. Victor enumerates, yet the contemplative life does not consist principally in them.

3 *In Sent.* xxxv. Q. 1. a. 2.

[1] *Eth. Nic.* 1177, a. 13.

43

THE ACT OF FAITH

REASONS IN SUPPORT

We proceed thus to the Tenth Article.

Objection 1. It would seem that reasons alleged in support of what we believe lessen the merit of faith. For Gregory says that *there is no merit in believing where human reason furnishes experimental proof.*[1] If, therefore, human reason provides sufficient proof, the merit of faith is altogether taken away. Therefore it seems that any kind of human reasoning in support of matters of faith, diminishes the merit of believing.

Obj. 2. Further, whatever lessens the measure of virtue, lessens the amount of merit, since *happiness is the reward of virtue,* as even Aristotle says.[2] Now human reasoning seems to diminish the measure of the virtue of faith, since it is essential to faith to be about the unseen, as stated above.[3] Now the more a thing is supported by reasons the less is it unseen. Therefore human reasons in support of matters of faith diminish the merit of faith.

Obj. 3. Further, contrary things have contrary causes. Now suggestions which are against the faith increase the merit of faith—whether it consist in persecution inflicted by one who endeavours to force a man to renounce his faith, or in an argument persuading him to

Hom. xxvi *in Evang.*   [2] *Eth. Nic.* 1099, b. 16.
[3] Q. i. as. 4, 5.

do so. Therefore reasons in support of faith diminish the merit of faith.

On the contrary, it is written: *Being ready always to satisfy every one that asketh you a reason of that faith* [1] *and hope which is in you.* [2] Now the apostle would not give this advice, if it would imply a diminution in the merit of faith. Therefore reason does not diminish the merit of faith.

I answer that, as stated above,[3] the act of faith can be meritorious, in so far as it is subject to the will, not only in the act of consent, but also in the assent itself. Now human reasoning in support of what we believe, may stand in a twofold relation to the will of the believer. First, as antecedent to the act of the will; as, for instance, when a man either has not the will, or not a prompt will, to believe, unless he be moved by human reasons: and in this way human reasoning diminishes the merit of faith. In this sense it has been said above [4] that, in moral virtues, a *passion antecedent* to choice makes the virtuous act less praiseworthy. For just as a man ought to perform acts of moral virtue, on the judgment of his reason, and not on the impulse of passion, so ought he to believe matters of faith, not on the strength of human reason, but on the divine authority. Secondly, human reasons may be consequent upon the will of the believer. For when a man's will is ready to believe, he loves the truth he believes, he thinks out and adopts whatever reasons he can find in support thereof; and in this way, human reason does not exclude the merit of faith, but is a sign of greater

---

[1] Vulg., *of that hope which is in you.* S. Thomas's reading is apparently taken from Bede.
[2] Pet. iii. 15.　　　[3] A. 9.
[4] 2 I. Q. xxiv. a. 3, *r. obj.* 1; q. lxxvii. a. 6, *r. obj.* 2.

merit. So also in the moral virtues, a *passion consequent*, is the sign of a more prompt will, as stated above.[1] We have an indication of this in the words of the Samaritans to the woman, who is a type of human reason: *We now believe, not for thy saying.*[2]

Reply Obj. 1. Gregory is referring to the case of a man who has no will to believe what is of faith, except for the alleged reasons. But when a man has the will to believe what is of faith, on the authority of God alone, even though he has apodeictic proof for some of them, e.g. of the existence of God, the merit of his faith is not, for that reason, lost or diminished.

Reply Obj. 2. The reasons which are brought forward in support of the authority of faith, are not demonstrations which can bring intellectual vision to the human intellect, wherefore they do not cease to belong to the 'unseen.' But they remove obstacles to faith, by showing that what faith proposes is not impossible; wherefore such reasons do not diminish the merit or the measure of faith. On the other hand, though apodeictic proofs alleged in support of matters of faith [3] (which matters are but the preamble to the articles of faith), diminish the measure of faith, since they make the thing believed to be seen, yet they do not diminish the measure of charity, which makes the will ready to believe them, even if they were unseen; and so the measure of merit is not diminished.

Reply Obj. 3. Whatever is in opposition to faith, whether it consist in the argument of another, or in outward persecution, increases the merit of faith, in so far as the will is shown to be more prompt and firm in

---

[1] 2 I. Q. xxiv. a. 3, *r. obj.* 1.   [2] John iv. 42.
[3] The Leonine edition reads: *in support of matters of faith which are, however, preambles to the articles of faith, diminish*, etc.

believing.   Hence the martyrs had more merit of faith,
through not renouncing the faith on account of persecution; and even learned men have greater merit of faith,
through not renouncing their faith on account of the
reasons brought forward by philosophers or heretics in
opposition to it.   On the other hand, things that are
favourable to faith, do not always diminish the prompt-
ness of the will to believe, and therefore they do not
always diminish the merit of faith.

44

QUESTION: OF CHRIST'S MANNER OF LIFE

(*In Four Articles*)

AFTER the discussion of Christ's origin or entry into the world, the next subject of inquiry is His life therein. We must consider (1) His manner of life; (2) His temptation; (3) His doctrine; (4) His miracles.

Under this head four questions arise: (1) Whether Christ should have led a solitary life, or have associated with men? (2) Whether He should have led an austere life as regards food, drink, and clothing? or should He have conformed Himself to others in these respects? (3) Whether He should have adopted a lowly state of life, or one of wealth and honour? (4) Whether He should have lived in conformity with the Law?

FIRST ARTICLE

WHETHER CHRIST SHOULD HAVE ASSOCIATED WITH MEN OR LED A SOLITARY LIFE?

We proceed thus to the First Article.

Objection 1. It would seem that Christ should not have associated with men, but should have led a solitary life. For it behoved Christ to show by His manner of life not only that He was man, but also that He was God. But it is not becoming that God should associate with men, for it is written: *Except the gods, whose conversation is not with men;* [1] and Aristotle says that he who lives alone *is either a beast*—that is, if his way of life is the expression of savagery—*or a god,* [2] if his motive be the contemplation of truth. Therefore it seems that it was not becoming for Christ to associate with men.

Obj. 2. Further, while He lived in mortal flesh, it behoved Christ to lead the most perfect life. But the most perfect is the contemplative life, as we have stated. [3] Now, solitude is most suitable to the contemplative life: *I will lead her into the wilderness, and I will speak to her heart.* [4] Therefore it seems that Christ should have led a solitary life.

Obj. 3. Further, Christ's manner of life should have been consistent because it should always have given evidence of that which is best. But at times Christ avoided the crowd and sought lonely places: hence Remigius, commenting on Matthew, says: *We read that our Lord had three places of refuge: the ship, the mountain, the desert; to one or other of which He betook Himself whenever He was harassed by the crowd.* [5] Therefore He ought always to have led a solitary life.

On the contrary, it is written: *Afterwards He was seen upon earth and conversed with men.* [6]

I answer that Christ's manner of life was, rightly, determined by the purpose of His Incarnation, by reason of which He came into the world. Now He came into the world, first, that He might proclaim the truth; thus He says Himself: *For this was I born, and for this came I into the world, that I should give testimony to the truth.* [7] Hence it was fitting not that He should hide Himself by leading a solitary life, but that He should appear

---

[1] Dan. ii. 11.   [2] *Polit.* i.   [3] 2 II. Q. clxxxii. a. 1, 2.
[4] Osee (Hosea) ii. 14.   [5] Cf. *Catena Aurea*, Matt. v. 1.
[6] Baruch iii. 38.   [7] John xviii. 37.

openly and preach in public. Wherefore He says to those who wished to stay Him: *To other cities also I must preach the kingdom of God : for therefore am I sent.*[1]

Secondly, He came in order to free men from sin: *Christ Jesus came into this world to save sinners.*[2] And hence, as Chrysostom says, *although Christ might, while staying in the same place, have drawn all men to Himself, to hear His preaching, yet He did not do so ; thus giving us the example to go about and seek those who perish, like the shepherd in his search of the lost sheep, and the physician in his attendance on the sick.*

Thirdly, He came that by Him *we might have access to God,* as it is written.[3] And thus it was fitting that He should give men confidence in approaching Him by associating familiarly with them. Wherefore it is written: *It came to pass as He was sitting . . . in the house, behold, many publicans and sinners came, and sat down with Jesus and His disciples.*[4] On which Jerome comments as follows: *They had seen that the publican, converted from a sinful to a better life, had not been denied the opportunity of repentance,* and *consequently they did not despair of their own salvation.*

Reply Obj. 1. Christ wished to make His Godhead known through His human nature. And therefore, it was by associating with men, which belongs to human nature, that He manifested His Godhead to all, preaching and working miracles, and leading among men a blameless and righteous life.

Reply Obj. 2. As stated,[5] the contemplative life is, absolutely speaking, more perfect than an active life taken up with merely physical activities; yet that form

[1] Luke iv. 42, 43. [2] 1 Tim. i. 15. [3] Rom. v. 2.
[4] Matt. ix. 10. [5] 2 II Q. clxxxii. a. 1; q. clxxxviii. a. 6.

of active life in which a man, by preaching and teaching, delivers to others the fruits of his contemplation, is more perfect than the life that stops at contemplation, because such a life is built on an abundance of contemplation, and consequently such was the life chosen by Christ.

Reply Obj. 3. Christ's action is our instruction. And therefore, in order to teach preachers that they ought not to be for ever before the public, our Lord withdrew Himself sometimes from the crowd. We are told of three reasons for His doing this. First, for the rest of the body: hence it is stated that our Lord said to His disciples: *Come apart into a desert place, and rest a little. For there were many coming and going: and they had not so much as time to eat.*[1] But sometimes it was for the sake of prayer; thus it is written: *It came to pass in those days, that He went out into a mountain to pray; and He passed the whole night in the prayer of God.*[2] On this Ambrose remarks that *by His example He instructs us in the precepts of virtue.* And sometimes He did so in order to teach us to avoid the favour of men. Wherefore Chrysostom, commenting on *Jesus, seeing the multitude, went up into a mountain,* says: *By sitting not in the city and in the market-place, but on a mountain and in a place of solitude, He taught us to do nothing for show, and to withdraw from the crowd, especially when we have to discourse of what is absolutely indispensable.*

[1] Mark vi. 31.   [2] Luke vi. 12.

WHETHER IT WAS BECOMING THAT CHRIST SHOULD LEAD AN AUSTERE LIFE IN THIS WORLD?

We proceed thus to the Second Article.

Objection 1. It would seem that it was becoming that Christ should lead an austere life in this world. For Christ preached the perfection of life much more than John did. But John led an austere life in order that he might persuade men by his example to embrace a perfect life; for it is written that *the same John had his garment of camel's hair and a leathern girdle about his loins: and his meat was locusts and wild honey*;[1] on which Chrysostom comments as follows: *It was a marvellous and strange thing to behold such endurance in a human frame: and it particularly attracted the Jews.*[2] Therefore it seems that an austere life was much more becoming to Christ.

Obj. 2. Further, abstinence is a means to continence, for it is written: *they shall eat and shall not be filled; they have committed fornication, and have not ceased.*[3] But Christ both observed continence in Himself and proposed it as an ideal for others when He said: *There are eunuchs who have made themselves eunuchs for the kingdom of heaven: he that can take it let him take it.*[4] Therefore it seems that Christ should have maintained an austere life Himself and among His disciples.

Obj. 3. Further, it seems absurd for a man to begin a stricter form of life and to return to an easier life: for he seems open to the stricture implied in *This man began*

---

[1] Matt. iii. 4.   [2] *Hom.* x.
[3] Osee (Hosea) iv. 10.   [4] Matt. xix. 12.

to build, and was not able to finish.[1] Now Christ began
a very strict life after His baptism, remaining in the
desert and fasting for *forty days and forty nights.* Therefore it seems unbecoming that, after leading such a strict
life, He should return to the common manner of living.

On the contrary, it is written: *The Son of Man came
eating and drinking.*[2]

I answer that, as stated above,[3] it was in keeping with
the end of the Incarnation that Christ should not lead
a solitary life, but should associate with men. Now it
is most fitting that he who associates with any group
of persons should conform to their manner of living;
according to the words of the apostle: *I became all things
to all men.*[4] And therefore it was most fitting that
Christ should eschew singularity in food and drink.
Hence Augustine says that *John is described as 'neither
eating nor drinking,' because he did not take the same food
as the Jews. Therefore, unless our Lord had taken it,
it would not be said of Him, in contrast, 'eating and
drinking.'* [5]

Reply Obj. 1. In His manner of living our Lord gave
an example of perfection in everything that has an
essential bearing on salvation. Now abstinence in eating and drinking has no essential bearing on salvation:
The kingdom of God is not meat and drink.[6] And Augustine explains *Wisdom is justified by her children,*[7] saying
that this is because the holy apostles *understood that the
kingdom of God does not consist in eating and drinking,
but in resignation to either lot,*[8] for they are neither
elated by abundance, nor distressed by want. Again,
he says that in all such things *it is not the use of them,*

[1] Luke xiv. 30.   [2] Matt. xi. 19.   [3] A. 1.
[4] 1 Cor. ix. 22.   [5] *Contra Faust.* xvi.   [6] Rom. xiv. 17.
[7] Matt. xi. 19.   [8] *De Qu. Evang.* ii. 9, 11.

but the unregulated desire of the user that *is sinful.*[1]
Both these lives are lawful and praiseworthy—namely,
that a man withdraw from the society of other men and
observe abstinence; and that he associate with other
men and live like them.   And therefore our Lord willed
to give men an example of both lives.

As to John, according to Chrysostom, *he gave no sign
beyond his life and righteous conduct . . . but Christ had
the testimony also of miracles.   Leaving, therefore, John
to shine before men by his fasting, He Himself came the
opposite way, both coming unto publicans' tables and eating
and drinking.*[2]

Reply Obj. 2. Just as by abstinence other men acquire
the power of self-restraint, so also Christ, in Himself and
His disciples, subdued the flesh by the power of His
Godhead.   Wherefore, as we read, the Pharisees and the
disciples of John fasted, but not the disciples of Christ.[3]
On which Bede comments, saying that *John drank neither
wine nor strong drink: because abstinence is meritorious
where the nature is weak.   But why should our Lord,
whose right by nature it is to forgive sins, avoid those whom
He could make more pure than such as abstain?*

Reply Obj. 3. As Chrysostom says: *that thou mightest
learn how great a good is fasting, and what sort of a shield
it is against the devil, and that after baptism thou shouldst
give thyself up, not to luxury, but to fasting—for this cause
did He fast, not as needing it Himself, but as teaching
us. . . . And for this did He proceed no further than Moses
and Elias, lest His assumption of our flesh might seem in-
credible.*[4]   The mystical meaning, as Gregory says, is
that by Christ's example the number *forty* is observed

[1] *De Doct. Christ.* iii.   [2] *Hom.* xxxvii *sup. Matt.*
[3] Matt. ix. 14.   [4] *Hom.* xiii *sup. Matt.*

in His fast, because the good life outlined in the *decalogue finds its fulfilment in the four books of the Holy Gospel, since ten multiplied by four amounts to forty. Or, because we live in this mortal body compounded of the four elements, and by its lusts we transgress the commandments of the Lord, which are expressed in the decalogue.*[1] Or, according to Augustine: *To know the Creator and the creature, sums the teaching of wisdom. The Creator is the Trinity, the Father, the Son, and the Holy Ghost. Now, the creature is partly invisible, as the soul, to which the number three may be ascribed, for we are commanded to love God in three ways, 'with our whole heart, our whole soul, and our whole mind'; and partly visible, as the body, which is an instance of the number four in so far as it is compounded of heat, moisture, cold, and dryness. Hence if we multiply ten, which may be referred to the entire moral code, by four (which is the characteristic number of the body) because it is the body that executes the law, the product is the number forty: in which,* consequently, *the time during which we sigh and grieve is shown forth.*[2] And yet there was no inconsistency in Christ's returning to the common manner of living, after fasting and (retiring into the) desert. For it is becoming to that kind of life, which we hold Christ to have embraced, wherein a man delivers to others the fruits of his contemplation, that he devote himself first of all to contemplation, and that he afterwards come down to the publicity of active life by associating with other men. Hence, Bede says, *Christ fasted, that thou mightest not disobey the commandment; He ate with sinners, that thou mightest discern His sanctity and acknowledge His power.*[3]

---

[1] *Hom.* xvi *in Evang.*   [2] *De Qu. Evang.* lxxxiii. Q. 81.
[3] Mark ii. 18.

WHETHER CHRIST SHOULD HAVE LED A LIFE OF POVERTY
IN THIS WORLD?

We proceed thus to the Third Article.

Objection 1. It would seem that Christ should not have
led a life of poverty in this world. Because Christ should
have embraced that form of life which is most worthy
of choice. But the most eligible form of life is that which
is a mean between riches and poverty; for it is written:
*Give me neither beggary nor riches; give me only the neces-
saries of life.*[1] Therefore Christ should have led a life,
not of poverty, but of moderation.

Obj. 2. Further, external wealth is a means to the
satisfaction of the body's need of food and clothing.
But Christ conformed His manner of life to those among
whom He lived, in the matter of food and clothing.
Therefore it seems that He should have observed the
ordinary manner of life as to riches and poverty, and
have avoided extreme poverty.

Obj. 3. Further, Christ specially invited men to imitate
His example of humility: *Learn of Me, because I am meek
and humble of heart.*[2] But humility is most commend-
able in the rich; thus it is written: *Charge the rich of this
world not to be high-minded.*[3] Therefore it seems that
Christ should not have chosen a life of poverty.

On the contrary, it is written: *The Son of Man hath not
where to lay His head;* [4] as though He were to say, as
Jerome observes: *Why desirest thou to follow Me for the
sake of riches and worldly gain; since I am so poor that*

---

[1] Prov. xxx. 8.   [2] Matt. xi. 29.
[3] 1 Tim. vi. 17.   [4] Matt. viii. 20.

*I have not even the smallest dwelling-place, and I am
sheltered by a roof that is not Mine?* And on *that we
may not scandalize them, go to the sea,*[1] Jerome says: *This
incident, taken literally, affords edification to those who
hear it when they are told that our Lord was so poor that
He had not the wherewithal to pay the tax for Himself and
an apostle.*

I answer that it was fitting for Christ to lead a life of
poverty in this world.   First, because this was in keeping
with the duty of preaching, for which purpose He says
that He came: *Let us go into the neighbouring towns and
cities, that I may preach there also: for to this purpose am
I come.*[2]   Now in order that the preachers of God's word
may be able to give all their time to preaching, they must
be wholly free from care of worldly matters: but this
is not possible for the wealthy.   Wherefore the Lord
Himself, when sending the apostles to preach, said to
them: *Do not possess gold or silver.*[3]   And the apostles
say: *It is not reasonable that we should leave the word of
God and serve tables.*[4]

Secondly, because just as He took upon Himself the
death of the body in order to bestow spiritual life on us,
so did He bear bodily poverty, in order to enrich us
spiritually: *You know the grace of our Lord Jesus Christ:
that . . . He became poor for our sakes, that through His
poverty we might be rich.*[5]

Thirdly, lest if He were rich His preaching might be
ascribed to cupidity.   Wherefore Jerome says that if
the disciples had been possessed of wealth, *they had
seemed to preach for gain, not for the salvation of mankind.*[6]
And the same reason applies to Christ.

---

[1] Matt. xvii. 26.   [2] Mark i. 38.   [3] Matt. x. 9.
[4] Acts vi. 2.   [5] 2 Cor. viii. 9.   [6] Matt. x. 9.

Fourthly, that the more lowly He seemed by reason of His poverty, the greater might the power of His Godhead be shown to be.   Hence in a sermon of the Council of Ephesus we read: *He chose all that was poor and common, all that was apparently mean and undistinguished, that it might be recognized that it was His Godhead which had transformed the world.   This was the reason why He chose a poor maid for His mother, a poorer birthplace; for this reason did He live in want.   This is the meaning of the manger.*[1]

Reply Obj. 1. Those who wish to live virtuously need to avoid abundance of riches and beggary, in as far as these are occasions of sin: since abundance of riches is an occasion for being proud; and beggary is an occasion of thieving and lying, or even of perjury.   But forasmuch as Christ was incapable of sin, He had not the same motive as Solomon for avoiding these things. Yet neither is every kind of beggary an occasion of theft and perjury, as Solomon seems to imply;[2] but only the beggar who is a beggar against his will may turn thief and perjurer to escape from his condition.   But voluntary poverty is not open to this danger: and such was the poverty chosen by Christ.

Reply Obj. 2. A man may feed and clothe himself like others, not only by possessing riches, but also by receiving the necessaries of life from those who are rich. This is what happened in regard to Christ: for it is written that certain women followed Christ and *ministered unto Him of their substance.*[3]   For, as Jerome says: *It was a Jewish custom, nor was it thought wrong for women, following the ancient tradition of their nation, out of their*

[1] P. iii. c. ix.

[2] Ibid.   [3] Luke viii. 2, 3.

I 953

private means to provide their instructors with food and clothing. But as this might give scandal to the heathens, Paul says that he gave it up : [1] thus it was possible for them to be fed out of a common fund, but not to possess wealth, without their duty of preaching being hindered by anxiety.

Reply Obj. 3. Humility is not much to be praised in one who is poor of necessity. But in one who, like Christ, is poor willingly, poverty itself is a sign of very great humility.

FOURTH ARTICLE

WHETHER CHRIST CONFORMED HIS CONDUCT TO THE LAW?

We proceed thus to the Fourth Article.

Objection 1. It would seem that Christ did not conform His conduct to the law. For the law forbade any work whatsoever to be done on the Sabbath, since God *rested on the seventh day from all His work which He had done.* But He healed a man on the Sabbath, and commanded him to take up his bed. Therefore it seems that He did not conform His conduct to the law.

Obj. 2. Further, what Christ taught, that He also did: *Jesus began to do and to teach.* [2] But He taught that *not all that which goeth into the mouth defileth a man*: [3] and this is contrary to the precept of the law, which declared that a man was made unclean by eating and touching certain animals, as stated. [4] Therefore it seems that He did not conform His conduct to the law.

Obj. 3. Further, he who consents to anything is of the

---

[1] Matt. xxvii. 55.   [2] Acts i. 1.   [3] Matt. xv. 11.   [4] Lev. xi.

same mind as he who does it: *Not only they that do them,
but they also that consent to them that do them.*[1] But
Christ, by excusing His disciples, consented to their
breaking the law by plucking the ears of corn on the
Sabbath; as is related.[2] Therefore it seems that Christ
did not conform His conduct to the law.

On the contrary, it is written: *Do not think that I come
to destroy the law or the prophets.*[3] Commenting on these
words, Chrysostom says: *He 'fulfilled' the law, . . . in
one way, by transgressing none of the precepts of the law;
secondly, by justifying us through faith, where the law,
through the letter, did not avail.*

I answer that Christ conformed His conduct in all
things to the precepts of the law. In token of this He
wished even to be circumcised; for the circumcision
implies the solemn recognition of one's subjection to the
law: *I testify to every man circumcising himself, that he
is a debtor to do the whole law.*[4]

And Christ, indeed, wished to conform His conduct to
the law, first, to show His approval of the old law.
Secondly, that the law might be seen to derive its meaning and value from Him in whom it reached its consummation and its end. Thirdly, to deprive the Jews
of an excuse for slandering Him. Fourthly, in order to
deliver men from subjection to the law: *God sent His Son
. . . made under the law, that He might redeem them who
were under the law.*[5]

Reply Obj. 1. Our Lord excuses Himself from any
transgression of the law in this matter, for three reasons.
First, the precept of the hallowing of the Sabbath for-
bids not divine work, but human work: for though God

---

[1] Rom. i. 32.   [2] Matt. xii. 1–8.   [3] Matt. v. 17.
[4] Gal. v. 3.   [5] Gal. iv. 4, 5.

ceased on the seventh day from the creation of new creatures, yet He ever works by keeping and governing His creatures. Now Christ's miracles were divine works, hence, He says: *My Father worketh until now; and I work.*[1]

Secondly, He excuses Himself on the ground that this precept does not forbid works which are necessary for our physical welfare. Wherefore He says: *Doth not every one of you on the Sabbath-day loose his ox or his ass from the manger, and lead them to water?*[2] And farther on: *Which of you shall have an ass or an ox fall into a pit, and will not immediately draw him out on the Sabbath-day?*[3] Now it is manifest that the miraculous works done by Christ concerned men's corporal and spiritual welfare.

Thirdly, because this precept does not forbid works pertaining to the worship of God. Wherefore He says: *Have ye not read in the law that on the Sabbath-days the priests in the temple break the Sabbath, and are without blame?*[4] And it is written that a man receives circumcision on the Sabbath-day.[5] Now when Christ commanded the paralytic to carry his bed on the Sabbath-day, this pertained to the worship of God—i.e. to the praise of God's power. And thus it is clear that He did not break the Sabbath: although the Jews threw this false accusation in His face, saying: *This man is not of God, who keepeth not the Sabbath.*[6]

Reply Obj. 2. By those words Christ wished to show that man is made unclean as to his soul, by the use of any sort of foods considered not in their nature, but only in virtue of some significance attached to them. And when certain foods are in the law called 'unclean,' this

---

[1] John v. 17.   [2] Luke xiii. 15.   [3] Luke xiv. 5.
[4] Matt. xii. 5.   [5] John vii. 23.   [6] John ix. 16.

is by a kind of symbolism; when Augustine says: *If a question be raised about swine and lambs, both are clean by nature, since 'all God's creatures are good'; but symbolically speaking lambs are clean and swine unclean.*[1]

Reply Obj. 3. The disciples also, when, being hungry, they plucked the ears of corn on the Sabbath, are to be excused from transgressing the law, since they were pressed by hunger: just as David did not transgress the law when, through being compelled by hunger, he ate the loaves which it was not lawful for him to eat.

III. Q. xl.

[1] *Contra Faust.* vi.

45

QUESTION: OF THE PRIESTHOOD OF CHRIST

(*In Six Articles*)

WE have now to consider the priesthood of Christ; and under this head there are six points of inquiry: (1) Whether it is fitting that Christ should be a priest? (2) Of the victim offered by this priest. (3) Of the effect of this priesthood. (4) Whether the effect of His priesthood pertains to Himself, or only to others? (5) Of the eternal duration of His priesthood. (6) Whether He should be called *a priest according to the order of Melchisedech?*

FIRST ARTICLE

WHETHER IT IS FITTING THAT CHRIST SHOULD BE A PRIEST?

We proceed thus to the First Article.

Objection 1. It would seem unfitting that Christ should be a priest. For a priest is less than an angel; whence it is written: *The Lord showed me the high-priest standing before the angel of the Lord.*[1] But Christ is greater than the angels, *being made so much better than the angels, as He hath inherited a more excellent name than they.*[2] Therefore it is unfitting that Christ should be a priest.

Obj. 2. Further, the events narrated in the Old Testament were figures of Christ, *which are a shadow of things*

[1] Zach. iii. 1.   [2] Heb. i. 4.

to come, but the body is Christ's.[1] But Christ was not descended from the priests of the old law, for the apostle says: *It is evident that our Lord sprang out of Juda, in which tribe Moses spoke nothing concerning priests.*[2] Therefore it is not fitting that Christ should be a priest.

Obj. 3. Further, in the old law, which is a foreshadowing of Christ, the lawgivers and the priests were distinct: wherefore the Lord said to Moses the lawgiver: *Take unto thee Aaron, thy brother, . . . that he may minister to Me in the priest's office.*[3] But Christ is the giver of the new law: *I will give My law in their bowels.*[4] Therefore it is unfitting that Christ should be a priest.

On the contrary, it is written: *We have therefore a great high-priest that hath passed into the heavens, Jesus, the Son of God.*[5]

I answer that the office proper to a priest is to be a mediator between God and the people: to wit, inasmuch as he bestows divine things on the people, wherefore *sacerdos* (priest) means a giver of sacred things (*sacra dans*): *They shall seek the law at his*—i.e. the priest's— *mouth*;[6] and again, forasmuch as he offers up the people's prayers to God, and, in a manner, makes satisfaction to God for their sins; wherefore the apostle says: *Every high priest taken from among men is ordained for men in the things that appertain to God, that he may offer up gifts and sacrifices for sins.*[7] Now this is most befitting to Christ. For through Him are gifts bestowed on men, *by whom* (i.e. by Christ) *He hath given us most great and precious promises, that by these you may be made partakers of the divine nature.*[8] Moreover, He reconciled

[1] Col. ii. 17.
[2] Heb. vii. 14.
[3] Exod. xxviii. 1.
[4] Jer. xxxi. 33.
[5] Heb. iv. 14.
[6] Mal. ii. 7.
[7] Heb. v. 1.
[8] 2 Pet. i. 4.

the human race to God: *In Him* (i.e. Christ) *it hath well pleased* (*the Father*) *that all fulness should dwell, and through Him to reconcile all things unto Himself.*[1]   Therefore it is most fitting that Christ should be a priest.

Reply Obj. 1. Priestly power appertains to the angels, inasmuch as they are also midway between God and man, as Dionysius explains,[2] so that the priest himself, as being between God and man, is called an angel, *He is the angel of the Lord of hosts.*[3]   Now Christ was greater than the angels, not only in His godhead, but also in His humanity, as having the fullness of grace and glory. Wherefore also He had the hierarchical or priestly power in a higher degree than the angels, so that even the angels were ministers of His priesthood: *Angels came and ministered unto Him.*[4]   But in His suffering humanity He *was made a little lower than the angels*, as the apostle says,[5] and thus He was conformed to those men upon earth who are ordained to the priesthood.

Reply Obj. 2. As Damascene says: *What is like in every particular must be, of course, identical, and not a copy.*[6]   Since, therefore, the priesthood of the old law was a foreshadowing of the priesthood of Christ, He did not wish to be born of the stock of the priests who prefigured Him, that it might be made clear that His priesthood is not quite the same as theirs, but different, as reality differs from type.

Reply Obj. 3. As stated above,[7] individual men have their individual graces: but Christ, as being the Head of all, has the perfection of all graces. Wherefore, as to others, one is a lawgiver, another is a priest, another is

[1] Col. i. 19, 20.   [2] *Cael. Hier.* ix.
[3] Mal. ii. 7.   [4] Matt. iv. 11.
[5] Heb. ii. 9.   [6] *De Fide Orth.* iii. 26.
[7] Q. vii. a. 7, *r. obj.* 1.

a king; but all these powers are found together in Christ, Who is the source of all grace. Hence it is written: *The Lord is our Judge, the Lord is our Lawgiver, the Lord is our King: He will come and save us.*[1]

SECOND ARTICLE

Whether Christ Himself was both Priest and Victim?

We proceed thus to the Second Article.

Objection 1. It would seem that Christ Himself was not both priest and victim at the same time. For it is the duty of the priest to slay the victim. But Christ did not kill Himself. Therefore He was not both priest and victim.

Obj. 2. Further, the priesthood of Christ has a greater similarity to the Jewish priesthood, instituted by God, than to the priesthood of the Gentiles, by which the demons were worshipped. Now in the old law man was never offered up in sacrifice; whereas this was very much to be reprehended in the sacrifices of the Gentiles, that *they shed innocent blood; the blood of their sons and of their daughters, which they sacrificed to the idols of Canaan.*[2] Therefore in Christ's priesthood the Man Christ should not have been the victim.

Obj. 3. Further, every victim, through being offered to God, is consecrated to God. But the humanity of Christ was from the beginning consecrated and united to God. Therefore it cannot be said fittingly that Christ as man was a victim.

On the contrary, the apostle says: *Christ hath loved us,*

---

[1] Isa. xxxiii. 22.   [2] Ps. cv. 38.

and hath delivered Himself for us, an oblation and a victim to God for an odour of sweetness.[1]

I answer that, as Augustine says: *Every visible sacrifice is a sacrament,* i.e. *a sacred sign of an invisible sacrifice.*[2] Now the sacrifice by which a man offers his soul to God is an invisible sacrifice: *A sacrifice to God is an afflicted spirit.*[3] Wherefore, whatever is offered to God in order to raise man's spirit to Him, may be called a sacrifice.

Now man requires to offer sacrifice for three reasons. First, for the remission of sin, as a result of which he is estranged from God. Hence the apostle says that it appertains to the priest *to offer gifts and sacrifices for sins.*[4] Secondly, that man may be preserved in a state of grace, by ever clinging to God, wherein his peace and salvation consist. Wherefore under the old law there was a sacrifice of peace-offerings offered up for the salvation of the offerers, as is prescribed in the third chapter of Leviticus. Thirdly, in order that the spirit of man be perfectly united to God: which will be most perfectly realized in heaven. Hence, under the old law, the holocaust was offered, so called because the victim was wholly burnt, as we read in the first chapter of Leviticus.

Now these benefits came to us by the humanity of Christ. For, in the first place, our sins were blotted out: *Who was delivered up for our sins.*[5] Secondly, through Him we received the grace of salvation: *He became to all that obey Him the cause of eternal salvation.*[6] Thirdly, through Him we have acquired the perfection of glory, *we have a confidence in the entering into the Holies* (i.e. the

[1] Eph. v. 2.   [2] *De Civ. Dei*, x. 5.   [3] Ps. l. 19.
[4] Heb. v. 1.   [5] Rom. iv. 25.   [6] Heb. v. 9.

heavenly glory) *through His blood*.[1] Therefore Christ Himself, as man, was not only priest, but also a perfect victim, being at the same time victim for sin, victim for a peace-offering, and a holocaust.

Reply Obj. 1. Christ did not slay Himself, but of His own free will He exposed Himself to death: *He was offered because it was His own will*.[2] Thus He is said to have offered Himself.

Reply Obj. 2. The slaying of the Man Christ may be referred to a twofold will. First, to the will of those who slew Him: and in this respect He was not a victim: for the slayers of Christ are not accounted as offering a sacrifice to God, but as guilty of a great crime. (The nefarious rites of the pagans in which they sacrificed men to idols bear some likeness to this sin.) Secondly, the slaying of Christ may be considered in reference to the will of the sufferer, who freely offered Himself to suffering. In this respect He is a victim, and in this He differs from the sacrifices of the Gentiles.

(*The reply to the third objection is wanting in the original manuscripts, but it may be gathered from the above.*—ED.) [3]

---

[1] Heb. x. 19.   [2] Is. liii. 7.

[3] Some editions, however, give the following reply: '*Reply Obj.* 3. The fact that Christ's manhood was holy from its beginning does not prevent that same manhood, when it was offered to God in the Passion, being sanctified in a new way—namely, as a victim actually offered then. For it acquired then the actual holiness of a victim, from the charity which it had from the beginning, and from the grace of union sanctifying it absolutely.'

WHETHER THE EFFECT OF CHRIST'S PRIESTHOOD IS THE
EXPIATION OF SINS?

We·proceed thus to the Third Article.

Objection 1. It would seem that the effect of Christ's
priesthood is not the expiation of sins. For it belongs
to God alone to blot out sins: *I am He that blots out thy
iniquities for My own sake.*[1] But Christ is priest, not as
God, but as man. Therefore the priesthood of Christ
does not expiate sins.

Obj. 2. Further, the apostle says that the victims of
the Old Testament could not *make their worshippers
perfect: for then they would have ceased to be offered; because the worshippers once cleansed should have no
conscience of sin any longer; but in them there is made a
commemoration of sins every year.*[2] But in like manner
now in the time of priesthood of Christ a commemoration
of sins is made in the words: *Forgive us our trespasses.*[3]
Moreover, sacrifice is offered continuously in the Church;
wherefore again we say: *Give us this day our daily bread.*
Therefore sins are not expiated by the priesthood of
Christ.

Obj. 3. Further, in the sin-offerings of the old law, a
he-goat was mostly offered for the sin of a prince, a she-
goat for the sin of some private individual, a calf for
the sin of a priest, as we gather from Leviticus.[4] But
Christ is compared to none of these, but to the lamb:
I was as a meek lamb, that is carried to be a victim.[5]

[1] Is. xliii. 25.   [2] Heb. x. 1–3.   [3] Matt. vi. 12.
[4] iv. 3, 23, 28.   [5] Jer. xi. 19.

Therefore it seems that His priesthood does not expiate sins.

On the contrary, the apostle says: *The blood of Christ, who by the Holy Ghost offered Himself unspotted unto God, shall cleanse our conscience from dead works, to serve the living God.*[1] But dead works denote sins. Therefore the priesthood of Christ has the power to cleanse from sins.

I answer that two things are required for the perfect cleansing from sins, corresponding to the two things comprised in sin—namely, the stain of sin and the debt of punishment. The stain of sin is, indeed, blotted out by grace, by which the sinner's heart is turned to God: whereas the debt of punishment is entirely removed by the satisfaction that man offers to God. Now the priesthood of Christ produces both these effects. For by its virtue grace is given to us, by which our hearts are turned to God, *being justified freely by His grace, through the redemption that is in Christ Jesus, whom God hath proposed to be a propitiation, through faith in His blood.*[2] Christ also made satisfaction for us fully, inasmuch as *He hath borne our infirmities and carried our sorrows.*[3] Wherefore it is clear that the priesthood of Christ has full power to expiate sins.

Reply Obj. 1. Although Christ was a priest, not as God, but as man, yet one and the same was both priest and God. Wherefore in the Council of Ephesus we read: *If any one say that it was not the very Word of God who became our high-priest and apostle, but perchance one other than this very man born of woman, let him be anathema.*[4] Hence in so far as His human nature operated

---

[1] Heb. ix. 14.   [2] Rom. iii. 24, 25.
[3] Isa. liii. 4.   [4] III. i. anath. 10.

by virtue of the divine, that sacrifice was most efficacious for the blotting out of sins.   For this reason Augustine says: *So that, since four things are to be observed in every sacrifice—to whom it is offered, by whom it is offered, what is offered, for whom it is offered; the same one true Mediator reconciling us to God by the sacrifice of peace, was one with Him to whom it was offered, united in Himself those for whom He offered it, at the same time offered it Himself, and was Himself that which He offered.*[1]

Reply Obj. 2. Sins are commemorated in the new law, not on account of the inefficacy of the priesthood of Christ, as though sins were not sufficiently expiated by Him: but in regard to those who either are not willing to be participators in His sacrifice, such as unbelievers, for whom we pray that they may turn from their sins; or who, after taking part in this sacrifice, fall away from it by whatsoever kind of sin.   The sacrifice which is offered every day in the Church is not distinct from that which Christ Himself offered, but is a commemoration thereof.   Wherefore Augustine says: *Christ Himself both is the priest who offers it and the victim; and of this He wished the daily sacrifice of the Church to be a sacred sign.*[2]

Reply Obj. 3. As Origen says,[3] though various animals were offered up under the old law, yet the daily sacrifice, which was offered up morning and evening, was a lamb, as appears from Numbers.[4]   By which it was signified that the offering up of the true lamb—i.e. Christ— was the culminating sacrifice of all.   Hence it is said: *Behold the Lamb of God, behold Him Who taketh away the sins of the world.*[5]

[1] *De Trin.* iv. 14.
[3] *In Ioan.* i. 29.
[6] John i. 29.
[2] *De Civ. Dei*, x. 20.
[4] xxxviii. 3, 4.

FOURTH ARTICLE

WHETHER THE EFFECT OF THE PRIESTHOOD OF CHRIST
  PERTAINED NOT ONLY TO OTHERS, BUT ALSO TO
  HIMSELF?

We proceed thus to the Fourth Article.

Objection 1. It would seem that the effect of the priesthood of Christ pertained not only to others, but also to
Himself. For it belongs to the priest's office to pray for
the people: *The priests made prayer while the sacrifice was
consuming.*[1] Now Christ prayed not only for others,
but also for Himself, as we have said above,[2] and as is
expressly stated: *In the days of His flesh, with a strong
cry and tears, He offered*[3] *up prayers and supplications
to Him that was able to save Him from death.*[4] Therefore
the priesthood of Christ had an effect not only in others,
but also in Himself.

Obj. 2. Further, in His passion Christ offered Himself
as a sacrifice. But by His passion He merited, not
only for others, but also for Himself, as stated above.[5]
Therefore the priesthood of Christ had an effect not only
in others, but also in Himself.

Obj. 3. Further, the priesthood of the old law was a
figure of the priesthood of Christ. But the priest of the
old law offered sacrifice not only for others, but also for
himself: for it is written *that the high-priest goeth into the
sanctuary to pray for himself and his house, and for the
whole congregation of Israel.*[6] Therefore the priesthood
of Christ also had an effect not merely in others, but also
in Himself.

[1] 2 Mach. i. 23.   [2] Q xxi. a. 3.   [3] Vulg., *offering*.
[4] Heb. v. 7.   [5] Q. xix. as. 3, 4.   [6] Lev. xvi. 17.

On the contrary, we read in the acts of the Council of Ephesus: *If any one say that Christ offered sacrifice for Himself, and not rather for us alone (for He who knew not sin needed no sacrifice), let him be anathema.*[1] But the priest's office consists principally in offering sacrifice. Therefore the priesthood of Christ had no effect in Himself.

I answer that, as stated above,[2] a priest is set midway between God and the people. Now he needs someone between himself and God, who of himself cannot approach to God; and such a one is subject to the priesthood by sharing in the effect thereof. But this cannot be said of Christ; for the apostle says: *Coming of Himself to God, always living to make intercession for us.*[3] And therefore it is not fitting for Christ to be the recipient of the effect of His priesthood, but rather to communicate it to others. For the influence of the first agent in every genus is such that it receives nothing in that genus: thus the sun gives but does not receive light; fire gives but does not receive heat. Now Christ is the fountain-head of the entire priesthood: for the priest of the old law was a figure of Him; while the priest of the new law works in His person: *For what I have pardoned, if I have pardoned anything, for your sakes have I done it in the person of Christ.*[4] Therefore it is not fitting that Christ should receive the effect of His priesthood.

Reply Obj. 1. Although prayer is befitting to priests, it is not their proper office, for it is befitting to every one to pray both for himself and for others: *Pray for one another that you may be saved.*[5] And so we may say that the prayer by which Christ prayed for Himself was not

---

[1] III. i. anath. 10.   [2] A. 1.   [3] Heb. vii. 25.
[4] 2 Cor. ii. 10.   [5] Jas. v. 16.

an action of His priesthood. But this answer seems to be precluded by the apostle, who, after saying: *Thou art a priest for ever according to the order of Melchisedech*, adds, *Who in the days of His flesh offering up prayers*,[1] etc., as quoted above;[2] so that it seems that the prayer which Christ offered pertained to His priesthood. We must therefore say that other priests partake in the effect of their priesthood, not as priests, but as sinners, as we shall state farther on.[3] But Christ had, simply speaking, no sin; though He had the *likeness of sin in the flesh*, as is written.[4] And, consequently, we must not say literally that He shared in the effect of His priesthood, but that He shared in it in this sense, that His passible human nature shared therein. Wherefore he adds pointedly, *that was able to save Him from death*.

Reply Obj. 2. Two things may be considered in the offering of a sacrifice by any priest—namely, the sacrifice itself which is offered, and the devotion of the offerer. Now the proper effect of priesthood is that which results from the sacrifice itself. But Christ obtained a result from His passion, not as by virtue of the sacrifice, which is offered by way of satisfaction, but by the very devotion with which out of charity He humbly endured the passion.

Reply Obj. 3. A figure cannot equal the reality, wherefore the symbolical priest of the old law could not attain to such perfection as not to need a sacrifice of satisfaction. But Christ did not stand in need of this. Consequently, the reason alleged does not apply equally to both, and this is what the apostle says: *The law maketh men priests, who have infirmity; but the word of the oath, which was since the law, the Son who is perfected for ever more*.[5]

---

[1] Heb. v. 6. [2] *Obj.* 1. [3] *R. obj.* 3.
[4] Rom. viii. 3. [5] Heb. vii. 28.

WHETHER THE PRIESTHOOD OF CHRIST ENDURES FOR
EVER?

We proceed thus to the Fifth Article.

Objection 1. It would seem that the priesthood of
Christ does not endure for ever. For as stated above,[1]
those alone need the effect of the priesthood who have the
weakness of sin, which can be expiated by the priest's
sacrifice. But this will not be for ever. For in the
saints there will be no weakness: *Thy people shall be all
just,*[2] while no expiation will be possible for the weakness of sin, since *there is no redemption in hell.*[3]   Therefore the priesthood of Christ endures not for ever.

Obj. 2. Further, the priesthood of Christ was made
manifest most of all in His passion and death, when
by His own blood He entered into the Holies.[4]   But the
passion and death of Christ will not endure for ever, as
stated : *Christ rising again from the dead, dieth now no
more.*[5]   Therefore the priesthood of Christ will not endure
for ever.

Obj. 3. Further, Christ is a priest, not as God, but as
man. But at one time Christ was not man, namely
during the three days He lay dead. Therefore the
priesthood of Christ endures not for ever.

On the contrary, it is written: *Thou art a priest for ever.*[6]

I answer that in the priestly office, we may consider two
things: first, the offering of the sacrifice; secondly, the
consummation of the sacrifice, consisting in this, that
those for whom the sacrifice is offered, obtain the end

[1] A. 4, *r. obj.* 1, 3.   [2] Isa. lx. 21.
[3] *Office of the Dead*, resp. vii.   [4] Heb. ix. 12.
[5] Rom. vi. 9.   [6] Ps. cix. 4.

of the sacrifice. Now the end of the sacrifice which Christ offered consisted not in temporal but in eternal good, which we obtain through His death: *Christ is a high-priest of the good things to come;* [1] for which reason the priesthood of Christ is said to be eternal. Now this consummation of Christ's sacrifice was foreshadowed in this, that the high-priest of the old law, once a year, entered into the Holy of Holies with the blood of a he-goat and a calf, as laid down, [2] and yet he offered up the he-goat and calf not within the Holy of Holies, but without. In like manner Christ entered into the Holy of Holies—that is, into heaven—and prepared the way for us, that we might enter by the virtue of His blood, which He shed for us on earth.

Reply Obj. 1. The saints who will be in heaven will not need any further expiation by the priesthood of Christ, but having expiated, they will need consummation through Christ Himself, on Whom their glory depends, as is written: *The glory of God hath enlightened it,* that is, the city of the saints—*and the Lamb is the lamp thereof.* [3]

Reply Obj. 2. Although Christ's passion and death are not to be repeated, yet the virtue of that victim endures for ever, for, as it is written, *by one oblation He hath perfected for ever them that are sanctified.* [4]

Wherefore the reply to the third objection is clear.

As to the unity of this sacrifice, it was foreshadowed in the law in that, once a year, the high-priest of the law entered into the holies, with a solemn oblation of blood, as set down. [5] But the figure fell short of the reality in this, that the victim had not an everlasting virtue, for which reason those sacrifices were renewed every year.

---

[1] Heb. ix. 11.   [2] Lev. xvi. 11.   [3] Apoc. xxi. 23.
[4] Heb. x. 14.   [5] Lev. xvi. 11.

SIXTH ARTICLE

WHETHER THE PRIESTHOOD OF CHRIST WAS ACCORDING TO THE ORDER OF MELCHISEDECH?

We proceed thus to the Sixth Article.

Objection 1. It would seem that Christ's priesthood was not according to the order of Melchisedech. For Christ is the fountain-head of the entire priesthood, as being the principal priest. Now that which is principal is not secondary in regard to others, but others are secondary in its regard. Therefore Christ should not be called a priest according to the order of Melchisedech.

Obj. 2. Further, the priesthood of the old law was more akin to Christ's priesthood than was the priesthood that existed before the law. But the nearer these sacred signs were to Christ, the more clearly they signified Him; as is clear from what we have said.[1] Therefore the priesthood of Christ should be named after the priesthood of the law, rather than after the order of Melchisedech, which was before the law.

Obj. 3. Further, it is written: *That is 'king of peace,' without father, without mother, without genealogy; having neither beginning of days nor ending of life,*[2] which can be referred only to the Son of God. Therefore, Christ should not be called a priest according to the order of Melchisedech, i.e. after someone else, but according to His own order.

On the contrary, it is written: *Thou art a priest for ever according to the order of Melchisedech.*[3]

I answer that, as above stated,[4] the priesthood of the law was a figure of the priesthood of Christ, not as

[1] 2 II. Q. ii. a. 7.   [2] Heb. vii. 2, 3.
[3] Ps. cix. 4.   [4] A. 4, *r. obj.* 3.

adequately representing the reality, but as falling far short thereof: both because the priest of the law did not wash away sins, and because it was not eternal, as the priesthood of Christ. Now the excellence of Christ's over the Levitical priesthood was foreshadowed in the priesthood of Melchisedech, who received tithes from Abraham, in whose loins the priesthood of the law was tithed. Consequently the priesthood of Christ is said to be *according to the order of Melchisedech*, on account of the excellence of the true priesthood over the symbolical priesthood of the law.

Reply Obj. 1. Christ is said to be according to the order of Melchisedech not as though the latter were a more excellent priest, but because he foreshadowed the excellence of Christ's priesthood over the Levitical.

Reply Obj. 2. Two things may be considered in Christ's priesthood: namely, the offering made by Christ, and (our) partaking thereof. As to the actual offering, the priesthood of Christ was more distinctly foreshadowed by the priesthood of the law, by reason of the shedding of blood, than by the priesthood of Melchisedech in which there was no blood-shedding. But if we consider the participation of this sacrifice and the effect thereof, wherein the excellence of Christ's priesthood over the priesthood of the law principally consists, then the former was more distinctly foreshadowed by the priesthood of Melchisedech, who offered bread and wine, signifying, as Augustine says,[1] the unity of the Church, which is established by our taking part in the sacrifice of Christ.[2] Wherefore also in the new law the true sacrifice of Christ is presented to the faithful under the form of bread and wine.

[1] *In Ioan.* 26.   [2] Cf. Q. lxxix. a. 1.

Reply Obj. 3. Melchisedech is described as *without father, without mother, without genealogy,* and as *having neither beginning of days nor ending of life,* not as though he had not these things, but because these details in his regard are not supplied by Holy Scripture. And in this it is that, as the apostle says in the same passage, he is *likened unto the Son of God,* Who had no earthly father, no heavenly mother, and no genealogy: *Who shall declare His generation?*[1] and Who in His Godhead has neither beginning nor end of days.

III. Q. xxii.

[1] Isa. liii. 8.

46

QUESTION: OF THE OTHER EFFECT OF THE SACRAMENTS, WHICH IS A CHARACTER

(*In Six Articles*)

WE have to now consider the other effect of the sacraments, which is a character: and concerning this there are six points of inquiry: (1) Whether by the sacraments a character is produced in the soul? (2) What is this character? (3) Of whom is this character? (4) In what does it reside? (5) Is it indelible? (6) Whether every sacrament imprints a character?

FIRST ARTICLE

WHETHER A SACRAMENT IMPRINTS A CHARACTER ON THE SOUL?

We proceed thus to the First Article.

Objection 1. It seems that a sacrament does not imprint a character on the soul. For the word *character* seems to signify some kind of distinctive sign. But Christ's members are distinguished from other men by eternal predestination, which does not imply anything in the predestined, but only in God who predestinates, as we have stated.[1] For it is written: *The sure foundation of God standeth firm, having this seal: The Lord knoweth who are His.*[2] Therefore the sacraments do not imprint a character on the soul.

[1] 1. Q. xxii. a. 2.   [2] 2 Tim. ii. 19.

Obj. 2. Further, a character is a distinctive sign. Now a sign, as Augustine says, *is that which conveys something else to the mind, besides the species which it impresses on the senses.*[1] But nothing in the soul can impress a species on the senses. Therefore it seems that no character is imprinted on the soul by the sacraments.

Obj. 3. Further, just as the believer is distinguished from the unbeliever by the sacraments of the new law, so was it under the old law. But the sacraments of the old law did not imprint a character; whence they are called *justices of the flesh* [2] by the apostle. Therefore neither seemingly do the sacraments of the new law.

On the contrary, the apostle says: *He . . . that hath anointed us is God; Who also hath sealed us, and given the pledge of the spirit in our hearts.*[3] But a character means nothing else than a kind of sealing. Therefore it seems that by the sacraments God imprints His character on us.

I answer that as is clear from what has been already stated,[4] the sacraments of the new law are ordained for a twofold purpose; namely, for a remedy against sins; and for the perfecting of the soul in things pertaining to the divine worship according to the rite of the Christian life. Now whenever any one is deputed to some definite purpose he is wont to receive some outward sign thereof; thus in olden times soldiers who enlisted in the ranks used to be marked with certain characters on the body because they were being set aside for a bodily service. Since, therefore, by the sacraments men are deputed to a spiritual service pertaining to the worship of God, it follows that by their means the faithful receive a certain

[1] *De Doct. Christ.* ii.   [2] Heb. ix. 10.
[3] 2 Cor. i. 21, 22.   [4] Q. lxii. a. 5.

spiritual character. Wherefore Augustine says: *If a deserter from the battle, through dread of the mark of enlistment on his body, throws himself on the emperor's clemency, and having besought and received mercy, return to the fight; is that character renewed, when the man has been set free and reprimanded? is it not rather acknowledged and approved? Are the Christian sacraments, by any chance, of a nature less lasting than this bodily mark?* [1]

Reply Obj. 1. The faithful of Christ are destined to the reward of the glory that is to come, by the seal of divine predestination. But they are deputed to acts becoming the Church militant by a certain spiritual seal that is set on them, and is called a character.

Reply Obj. 2. The character imprinted on the soul is a kind of sign in so far as it is imprinted by a sensible sacrament: since we know that a certain one has received the baptismal character from the fact that he has been cleansed by the sensible water. Nevertheless by a certain likeness, anything that assimilates one thing to another, or discriminates one thing from another, even though it be not sensible, can be called a character or a seal; thus the apostle calls Christ *the figure* or χαρακτήρ *of the substance* of the Father. [2]

Reply Obj. 3. As stated above, [3] the sacraments of the old law had not in themselves any spiritual power of producing a spiritual effect. Consequently in those sacraments there was no need of a spiritual character, and bodily circumcision sufficed, which the apostle calls *a seal.* [4]

---

[1] *Contra Parmen.* ·11.
[2] Heb. i. 3.
[3] Q. lxii. a. 6.
[4] Rom. iv. 11.

WHETHER A CHARACTER IS A SPIRITUAL POWER?

We proceed thus to the Second Article.

Objection 1. It seems that a character is not a spiritual power. For *character* seems to be the same thing as *figure*; hence, where we read *figure of His substance* [1] for *figure* the Greek has χαρακτήρ. Now *figure* is in the fourth species of quality, and thus differs from *power* which is in the second species. Therefore character is not a spiritual power.

Obj. 2. Further, Dionysius says: *The divine Beatitude admits him that seeks happiness to a share in Itself, and grants this share to him by conferring on him Its light as a kind of seal.* [2] Consequently, it seems that a character is a kind of light. Now light belongs rather to the third species of quality. Therefore a character is not a power, since this seems to belong to the second species.

Obj. 3. Further, character is defined by some thus: *A character is a holy sign of the communion of faith and of the holy ordination, conferred by a hierarch.* Now a sign is in the genus of *relation*, not of *power*. Therefore a character is not a spiritual power.

Obj. 4. Further, a power is in the nature of a cause and principle. [3] But a *sign* which is included in the definition of a character is rather in the nature of an effect. Therefore a character is not a spiritual power.

On the contrary, Aristotle says: *There are three things in the soul, power, habit, and passion.* [4] Now a character is not a passion: since a passion passes quickly, whereas

---

[1] Heb. i. 3.   [2] *Eccl. Hier.* ii.
[3] *Metaph.* v.   [4] *Eth. Nic.* ii.

a character is indelible, as will be made clear further on.[1] In like manner it is not a habit: because no habit is indifferent to acting well or ill: whereas a character is indifferent to either, since some use it well, some ill. Now this cannot occur with a habit: because no one abuses a habit of virtue, or uses well an evil habit. It remains, therefore, that a character is a power.

I answer that, as stated above,[2] the sacraments of the new law produce a character, in so far as by them we are deputed to the worship of God according to the rite of the Christian religion. Wherefore Dionysius, after saying that God *by a kind of sign grants a share of Himself to those that approach Him*, adds *by making them Godlike and communicators of divine gifts*.[3] Now the worship of God consists either in receiving divine gifts, or in bestowing them on others. And for both these purposes some power is needed; for to bestow something on others, active power is necessary; and in order to receive, we need a passive power. Consequently, a character signifies a certain spiritual power ordained unto things pertaining to the divine worship.

But it must be observed that this spiritual power is instrumental, as we have stated above,[4] of the virtue which is in the sacraments. For to have a sacramental character belongs to God's ministers: and a minister is a kind of instrument, as Aristotle says.[5] Consequently, just as the virtue which is in the sacraments is not of itself in a genus, but is reducible to a genus, for the reason that it is of a transitory and incomplete nature: so also a character is not properly in a genus or species, but is reducible to the second species of quality.

---

[1] A. 5.   [2] A. 1.   [3] *Eccl. Hier.* ii.
[4] Q. lxii. a. 4.   [5] *Polit.* i.

Reply Obj. 1. Configuration is a certain termination of quantity. Wherefore, properly speaking, it is only in corporeal things; and of spiritual things is predicated metaphorically. Now that which decides the genus or species of a thing must needs be predicated of it properly. Consequently, a character cannot be in the fourth species of quality, although some have held this to be the case.

Reply Obj. 2. The third species of quality contains only sensible passions or sensible qualities. Now character is not a sensible light. Consequently, it is not in the third species of quality as some have maintained.

Reply Obj. 3. The relation signified by the word *sign* must have some basis in reality. Now the relation signified by this sign which is a character, cannot be founded immediately on the essence of the soul: because then it would belong to every soul naturally. Consequently, there must be something in the soul on which such a relation is founded. And it is in this that a character essentially consists. Therefore it need not be in the genus *relation* as some have held.

Reply Obj. 4. A character is in the nature of a sign in comparison to the sensible sacrament by which it is imprinted. But considered in itself, it is in the nature of a principle, in the way already explained.

THIRD ARTICLE

WHETHER THE SACRAMENTAL CHARACTER IS THE CHARACTER OF CHRIST?

We proceed thus to the Third Article.

Objection 1. It seems that the sacramental character is not the character of Christ. For it is written: *Grieve not the Holy Spirit of God, whereby you are sealed.*[1] But a character essentially involves this act of being sealed. Therefore the sacramental character should be attributed to the Holy Ghost rather than to Christ.

Obj. 2. Further, a character has the nature of a sign. And it is a sign of the grace that is conferred by the sacrament. Now grace is poured forth into the soul by the whole Trinity; wherefore it is written: *The Lord will give grace and glory.*[2] Therefore it seems that the sacramental character should not be attributed specially to Christ.

Obj. 3. Further, a man is marked with a character that he may be distinguishable from others. But the saints are distinguishable from others by charity, which, as Augustine says, *alone separates the children of the Kingdom from the children of perdition:*[3] wherefore also the children of perdition are said to have *the character of the beast.*[4] But charity is not attributed to Christ, but rather to the Holy Ghost: *The charity of God is poured forth in our hearts, by the Holy Ghost, who is given to us;*[5] or even to the Father, *The grace of our Lord Jesus Christ and the charity of God.*[6] Therefore it seems that the sacramental character should not be attributed to Christ.

On the contrary, some define character thus: *A character is a distinctive mark printed in a man's rational soul by the eternal Character, whereby the created trinity is sealed with the likeness of the creating and recreating Trinity, and distinguishing him from those who are not so enlikened, according to the state of faith.* But the eternal Character is Christ Himself: *Who being the brightness of His glory*

---

[1] Eph. iv. 30. [2] Ps. lxxxiii. 12. [3] *De Trin.* xv.
[4] Apoc. xiii. 16, 17. [5] Rom. v. 5. [6] 2 Cor. xiii. 13.

and the figure, or character, *of His substance.*[1] It seems, therefore, that the character should properly be attributed to Christ.

I answer that, as has been made clear above,[2] a character is properly a kind of seal, whereby something is marked, as being ordained to some particular end: thus a coin is marked for use in exchange of goods, and soldiers are marked with a character as being deputed to military service. Now the faithful are deputed to a twofold end. First and principally to the enjoyment of glory. And for this purpose they are marked with the seal of grace: *Mark thou upon the foreheads of the men that sigh and mourn;*[3] and, *Hurt not the earth, nor the sea, nor the trees, till we sign the servants of our God in their foreheads.*[4]

Secondly, each of the faithful is deputed to receive, or to bestow on others, things pertaining to the worship of God. And this, properly speaking, is the purpose of the sacramental character. Now the whole rite of the Christian religion is derived from Christ's priesthood. Consequently, it is clear that the sacramental character is specially the character of Christ, to Whose priesthood the faithful are likened by reason of the sacramental characters, which are nothing else than certain participations of Christ's priesthood, flowing from Christ Himself.

Reply Obj. 1. The apostle speaks there of that sealing by which a man is assigned to future glory, and which is effected by grace. Now grace is attributed to the Holy Ghost, inasmuch as it is through love that God gives us something gratis, which is the very nature of grace: while the Holy Ghost is love. Wherefore it is written: *There are diversities of graces, but the same spirit.*[5]

---

[1] Heb. i. 3.   [2] A. 1.   [3] Ezech. ix. 4.
[4] Apoc. vii. 3.   [5] 1 Cor. xii. 4.

Reply Obj. 2. The sacramental character is a thing as regards the exterior sacrament, and a sacrament in regard to the ultimate effect. Consequently, something can be attributed to a character in two ways. First, if the character be considered as a sacrament: and thus it is a sign of the invisible grace which is conferred in the sacrament. Secondly, if it be considered as a character. And thus it is a sign conferring on a man a likeness to some principal person in whom is vested the authority over that to which he is assigned: thus soldiers who are assigned to military service, are marked with their leader's sign, by which they are, in a fashion, likened to him. And in this way those who are deputed to the Christian worship, of which Christ is the author, receive a character by which they are likened to Christ. Consequently, properly speaking, this is Christ's character.

Reply Obj. 3. A character distinguishes one from another, in relation to some particular end, to which he, who receives the character, is ordained: as has been stated concerning the military character [1] by which a soldier of the king is distinguished from the enemy's soldier in relation to the battle. In like manner the character of the faithful is that by which the faithful of Christ are distinguished from the servants of the devil, either in relation to eternal life, or in relation to the worship of the Church that now is. Of these the former is the result of charity and grace, as the objection runs; while the latter results from the sacramental character. Wherefore the *character of the beast* may be understood by opposition, to mean either the obstinate malice for which some are assigned to eternal punishment, or the profession of an unlawful form of worship.

[1] A. 1.

FOURTH ARTICLE

WHETHER THE CHARACTER RESIDES IN POWERS OF THE SOUL?

We proceed thus to the Fourth Article.

Objection 1. It seems that the character does not reside in the powers of the soul. For a character is said to be a disposition to grace. But grace resides in the essence of the soul as we have stated.[1] Therefore it seems that the character is in the essence of the soul and not in the powers.

Obj. 2. Further, a power of the soul does not seem to be the subject of anything save habit and disposition. But a character, as stated above,[2] is neither habit nor disposition, but rather a power: the subject of which is nothing else than the essence of the soul. Therefore it seems that the character does not reside in a power of the soul, but rather in its essence.

Obj. 3. Further, the powers of the soul are divided into those of knowledge and those of appetite. But it cannot be said that a character is only in a cognitive power, nor, again, only in an appetitive power: since it is neither ordained to knowledge only, nor to desire only. Nor can it be said to be in both, because the same accident cannot be in several subjects. Therefore it seems that a character does not reside in a power of the soul, but rather in the essence.

On the contrary, a character, according to its definition given above,[3] is imprinted in the rational soul *by way of an image.* But the image of the Trinity in the soul is

---

[1] 2 I. Q. cx. a. 4.   [2] A. 2.   [3] A. 3.

seen in the powers. Therefore a character is in the powers of the soul.

I answer that, as stated above,[1] a character is a kind of seal by which the soul is marked, so that it may receive, or bestow on others, things pertaining to divine worship. Now the divine worship consists in certain actions: and the powers of the soul are properly ordained to actions, just as the essence is ordained to existence. Therefore a character does not reside in the essence of the soul, but in its power.

Reply Obj. 1. The subject is ascribed to an accident in respect of that to which the accident disposes it proximately, but not in respect of that to which it disposes it remotely or indirectly. Now a character disposes the soul directly and proximately to the fulfilling of things pertaining to divine worship: and because such cannot be accomplished suitably without the help of grace, since *they that adore* God *must adore Him in spirit and in truth*,[2] it follows that the divine bounty bestows grace on those who receive the character, so that they may accomplish worthily the service to which they are deputed. Therefore the subject should be ascribed to a character in respect of those actions that pertain to the divine worship, rather than in respect of grace.

Reply Obj. 2. The essence of the soul is the subject of the natural power, which flows from the principles of the essence. Now a character is not a power of this kind; but a spiritual power coming from without. Wherefore, just as the essence of the soul, from which man has his natural life, is perfected by grace from which the soul derives spiritual life; so the natural power of the soul is perfected by a spiritual power, which is a

---

[1] Ibid.   [2] John iv. 24.

character. For habit and disposition belong to a power of the soul, since they are ordained to actions of which the powers are the principles. And in like manner whatever is ordained to action, should be attributed to a power.

Reply Obj. 3. As stated above, a character is ordained unto things pertaining to the divine worship; which is a protestation of faith expressed by exterior signs. Consequently, a character needs to be in the soul's cognitive power, where also is faith.

FIFTH ARTICLE

WHETHER A CHARACTER CAN BE BLOTTED OUT FROM THE SOUL?

We proceed thus to the Fifth Article.

Objection 1. It seems that a character can be blotted out from the soul. Because the more perfect an accident is, the more firmly does it adhere to its subject. But grace is more perfect than a character; because a character is ordained unto grace as to a further end. Now grace is lost through sin. Much more, therefore, is a character so lost.

Obj. 2. Further, by a character a man is deputed to the divine worship, as stated above.[1] But some pass from the worship of God to a contrary worship by apostasy from the faith. It seems, therefore, that such lose the sacramental character.

Obj. 3. Further, when the end ceases, the means to the end should cease also: thus after the resurrection there will be no marriage, because begetting will cease, which is the purpose of marriage. Now the exterior worship to which a character is ordained, will not endure in heaven,

---

[1] As. 3, 4.

where there will be no shadows, but all will be truth without a veil. Therefore the sacramental character does not last in the soul for ever: and consequently it can be blotted out.

On the contrary, Augustine says: *The Christian sacraments are not less lasting than the bodily mark* [1] of military service. But the character of military service is not repeated, but is *recognized and approved* in the man who obtains the emperor's forgiveness after offending him. Therefore neither can the sacramental character be blotted out.

I answer that, as stated above,[2] in a sacramental character Christ's faithful have a share in His priesthood; in the sense that as Christ has the full power of a spiritual priesthood, so His faithful are likened to Him by sharing a certain spiritual power with regard to the sacraments and to things pertaining to the divine worship. For this reason it is unbecoming that Christ should have a character: but His priesthood is compared to a character, as that which is complete and perfect is compared to some participation of itself. Now Christ's priesthood is eternal: *Thou art a priest for ever, according to the order of Melchisedech.*[3] Consequently, every sanctification wrought by His priesthood, is perpetual, enduring as long as the thing sanctified endures. This is clear even in inanimate things; for the consecration of a church or an altar lasts for ever unless they be destroyed. Since, therefore, a character is stamped on the intellective part of the soul, where faith resides as stated above; [4] it is clear that, the intellect being perpetual and incorruptible, a character cannot be blotted out from the soul.

---

[1] *Contra Parmen.* ii.
[3] Ps. cix. 4.
[2] A. 3.
[4] A. 4, *r. obj.* 3.

Reply Obj. 1. Both grace and character are in the soul, but in different ways. For grace is in the soul, as a form having complete existence therein: whereas a character is in the soul, as an instrumental power, as stated above.[1] Now a complete form is in its subject according to the condition of the subject. And since the soul as long as it is a wayfarer is changeable in respect of the free will, it results that grace is in the soul in a changeable manner. But an instrumental power follows rather the condition of the principal agent: and consequently a character exists in the soul in an indelible manner, not from any perfection of its own, but from the perfection of Christ's priesthood, from which the character flows like an instrumental power.

Reply Obj. 2. As Augustine says, *even apostates are not deprived of their baptism, for when they repent and return to the fold they do not receive it again; whence we conclude that it cannot be lost.*[2] The reason of this is that a character is an instrumental power, as stated above,[3] and the nature of an instrument as such is to be moved by another, but not to move itself; this belongs to the will. Consequently, however much the will be moved in the contrary direction, the character is not removed, by reason of the immobility of the principal mover.

Reply Obj. 3. Although external worship does not last after this life, yet its end remains. Consequently, after this life the character remains, both in the good as adding to their glory, and in the wicked as increasing their shame: just as the character of the military service remains in the soldiers after the victory, as the boast of the conquerors, and the disgrace of the conquered.

[1] A. 2.   [2] *Contr. Parmen.* ii.   [3] *R. obj.* 1.

SIXTH ARTICLE

WHETHER A CHARACTER IS IMPRINTED BY EACH SACRAMENT OF THE NEW LAW?

We proceed thus to the Sixth Article.

Objection 1. It seems that a character is imprinted by all the sacraments of the new law: because each sacrament of the new law makes man a participator in Christ's priesthood. But the sacramental character is nothing but a participation in Christ's priesthood, as already stated.[1] Therefore it seems that a character is imprinted by each sacrament of the new law.

Obj. 2. Further, a character may be compared to the soul in which it is, as a consecration to that which is consecrated. But by each sacrament of the new law man becomes the recipient of sanctifying grace, as stated above.[2] Therefore it seems that a character is imprinted by each sacrament of the new law.

Obj. 3. Further, a character is both a reality and a sacrament. But in each sacrament of the new law, there is something which is only a reality, and something which is only a sacrament, and something which is both reality and sacrament. Therefore a character is imprinted by each sacrament of the new law.

On the contrary, those sacraments in which a character is imprinted, are not reiterated, because a character is indelible, as stated above:[3] whereas some sacraments are repeated, for instance, penance, and matrimony. Therefore not all the sacraments imprint a character.

I answer that, as stated above,[4] the sacraments of the new law are ordained for a twofold purpose, namely,

---

[1] As. 3, 5.   [2] Q. lxii. a. 1.   [3] A. 5.   [4] Q. lxii. as. 1, 5.

as a remedy for sin, and for the divine worship. Now all the sacraments, from the fact that they confer grace, have this in common, that they afford a remedy against sin: whereas not all the sacraments are directly ordained to the divine worship. Thus it is clear that penance, whereby man is delivered from sin, does not afford man any advance in the divine worship, but restores him to his former state.

Now a sacrament may belong to the divine worship in three ways: first, in regard to the action itself; secondly, in regard to the agent; thirdly, in regard to the recipient. In regard to the thing done, the Eucharist belongs to the divine worship, for the divine worship consists principally therein, so far as it is the sacrifice of the Church. And by this same sacrament a character is not imprinted on man; because it does not ordain man to any further sacramental action or benefit received, since rather is it *the end and consummation of all the sacraments*, as Dionysius says.[1] But it contains within itself Christ, in Whom there is not the character, but the very plenitude of the priesthood.

But it is the sacrament of order that pertains to the sacramental agents: for it is by this sacrament that men are deputed to confer sacraments on others: while the sacrament of baptism pertains to the recipients, since it confers on man the power to receive the other sacraments of the Church; whence it is called the *door of the sacraments*. In a way confirmation also is ordained for the same purpose, as we shall explain in its proper place.[2] Consequently, these three sacraments imprint a character namely baptism, confirmation, and order.

Reply Obj. 1. Every sacrament makes man a sharer

---

[1] *Eccl. Hier.* iii.　　　[2] Q. lxv. a. 3.

in Christ's priesthood, from the fact that it confers on him some effect thereof. But every sacrament does not depute a man to do or receive something pertaining to the worship of the priesthood of Christ: while it is just this that is required for a sacrament to imprint a character.

Reply Obj. 2. Man is sanctified by each of the sacraments, since sanctity means immunity from sin, which is the effect of grace. But in a special way some sacraments, which imprint a character, bestow on man a certain consecration, thus deputing him to the divine worship: just as inanimate things are said to be consecrated forasmuch as they are deputed to divine worship.

Reply Obj. 3. Although a character is a reality and a sacrament, it does not follow that whatever is a reality and a sacrament, is also a character. With regard to the other sacraments we shall explain further on what is the reality and what is the sacrament.

III. Q. lxiii.

47

QUESTION: OF THE EFFECTS OF LOVE

(*In Six Articles*)

WE now have to consider the effects of love: under which head there are six points of inquiry: (1) Whether union is an effect of love? (2) Whether mutual indwelling is an effect of love? (3) Whether ecstasy is an effect of love? (4) Whether zeal is an effect of love? (5) Whether love is a passion that is hurtful to the lover? (6) Whether love is cause of all that the lover does?

WHETHER UNION IS AN EFFECT OF LOVE?

We proceed thus to the First Article.

Objection 1. It would seem that union is not an effect of love. For absence is incompatible with union. But love is compatible with absence; for the apostle says: *Be zealous for that which is good in a good thing always* (speaking of himself, according to a gloss), *and not only when I am present with you.*[1] Therefore union is not an effect of love.

Obj. 2. Further, every union is either according to essence—thus form is united to matter, accident to subject, and a part to the whole, or to another part in order to make up the whole: or according to likeness, in genus, species, or accident. But love does not cause union of essence; else love could not be between things essentially distinct. On the other hand, love does not cause union of likeness, but rather is caused by it, as stated above.[2] Therefore union is not an effect of love.

Obj. 3. Further, the sense in act is the sensible in act, and the intellect in act is the thing actually understood. But the lover in act is not the beloved in act. Therefore, union is the effect of knowledge rather than of love.

On the contrary, Dionysius says that every love is a *unitive force.*[3]

I answer that the union of lover and beloved is twofold. The first is real union; for instance, when the beloved is present with the lover. The second is union of affection: and this union must be considered in relation to the preceding apprehension; since movement of the appetite

---

[1] Gal. iv. 18.   [2] Q. xxvii. a. 3.   [3] *Div. Nom.* iv.

follows apprehension. Now love being twofold, viz. love of concupiscence, and love of friendship; each of these arises from a kind of apprehension of the oneness of the thing loved with the lover. For when we love a thing, by desiring it, we apprehend it as belonging to our well-being. In like manner when a man loves another with the love of friendship, he wills good to him, just as he wills good to himself: wherefore he apprehends him as his other self, in so far, to wit, as he wills good to him as to himself. Hence a friend is called a man's *other self*,[1] and Augustine says: *Well did one say to his friend: Thou half of my soul.*[2]

The first of these unions is caused *effectively* by love; because love moves man to desire and seek the presence of the beloved, as of something suitable and belonging to him. The second union is caused *formally* by love; because love itself is this union or bond. In this sense Augustine says that *love is a vital principle uniting, or seeking to unite, two together, the lover, to wit, and the beloved.*[3] For in describing it as *uniting* he refers to the union of affection, without which there is no love: and in saying that *it seeks to unite*, he refers to real union.

Reply Obj. 1. This argument is true of real union. That is necessary to pleasure as being its cause; desire implies the real absence of the beloved: but love remains whether the beloved be absent or present.

Reply Obj. 2. Union has a threefold relation to love. There is a union which causes love; and this is substantial union, as regards the love with which one loves oneself; while as regards the love wherewith one loves other things, it is the union of likeness, as stated above.[4]

[1] *Ethic.* ix. 4.   [2] *Conf.* iv. 6.
[3] *De Trin.* viii. 10.   [4] Q. xxvii. a. 3.

There is also a union which is essentially love itself. This union is according to a bond of affection, and is likened to substantial union, inasmuch as the lover stands to the object of his love, as to himself, if it be love of friendship; as to something belonging to himself, if it be love of concupiscence. Again there is a union, which is the effect of love. This is real union, which the lover seeks with the object of his love. Moreover this union is in keeping with the demands of love, for as Aristotle relates, *Aristophanes states that lovers would wish to be united both into one*, but since *this would result in either one or both being destroyed*,[1] they seek a suitable and becoming union—to live together, speak together, and be united in other like things.

Reply Obj. 3. Knowledge is perfected by the thing known being united, through its likeness, to the knower. But the effect of love is that the thing itself which is loved, is, in a way, united to the lover, as stated above. Consequently the union caused by love is closer than that which is caused by knowledge.

SECOND ARTICLE

WHETHER MUTUAL INDWELLING IS AN EFFECT OF LOVE?

We proceed thus to the Second Article.

Objection 1. It would seem that love does not cause mutual indwelling, so that the lover be in the beloved and vice versa. For that which is in another is contained in it. But the same cannot be container and contents. Therefore love cannot cause mutual indwelling, so that the lover be in the beloved and vice versa.

[1] *Polit.* ii. 1.

Obj. 2. Further, nothing can penetrate within a whole, except by means of a division of the whole. But it is the function of the reason, not of the appetite where love resides, to divide things that are really united. Therefore mutual indwelling is not an effect of love.

Obj. 3. Further, if love involves the lover being in the beloved and vice versa, it follows that the beloved is united to the lover, in the same way as the lover is united to the beloved. But the union itself is love, as stated above.[1] Therefore it follows that the lover is always loved by the object of his love; which is evidently false. Therefore mutual indwelling is not an effect of love.

On the contrary, it is written: *He that abideth in charity abideth in God, and God in him.*[2] Now charity is the love of God. Therefore, for the same reason, every love makes the beloved to be in the lover, and vice versa.

I answer that this effect of mutual indwelling may be understood as referring both to the apprehensive and to the appetitive power. Because, as to the apprehensive power, the beloved is said to be in the lover, inasmuch as the beloved abides in the apprehension of the lover, *for that I have you in my heart*:[3] while the lover is said to be in the beloved, according to apprehension, inasmuch as the lover is not satisfied with a superficial apprehension of the beloved, but strives to gain an intimate knowledge of everything pertaining to the beloved, so as to penetrate into his very soul. Thus it is written concerning the Holy Ghost, Who is God's love, that He *searcheth all things, yea the deep things of God.*[4]

As to the appetitive power, the object loved is said to

[1] A. 1.　　[2] 1 John iv. 16.　　[3] Phil. i. 7.　　[4] 1 Cor. ii. 10.

be in the lover, inasmuch as it is in his affections, by a
kind of complacency: causing him either to take pleasure
in it, or in its good, when present; or, in the absence of
the object loved, by his longing, to tend towards it with
the love of concupiscence, or towards the good that he
wills to the beloved, with the love of friendship: not
indeed from any extrinsic cause (as when we desire one
thing on account of another, or wish good to another
on account of something else), but because the complacency in the beloved is rooted in the lover's heart.
For this reason we speak of love as being *intimate*; and
of *the bowels of charity*. On the other hand, the lover is
in the beloved, by the love of concupiscence and by the
love of friendship, but not in the same way. For the
love of concupiscence is not satisfied with any external
or superficial possession or enjoyment of the beloved;
but seeks to possess the beloved perfectly, by penetrat-
ing into his heart, as it were. Whereas, in the love of
friendship, the lover is in the beloved, inasmuch as he
reckons what is good or evil to his friend, as being so to
himself; and his friend's will as his own, so that it seems
as though he felt the good or suffered the evil in the person of his friend. Hence it is proper to friends *to desire
the same things, and to grieve and rejoice at the same*,
as Aristotle says.[1] Consequently in so far as he reckons
what affects his friend as affecting himself, the lover
seems to be in the beloved, as though he were become
one with him: but in so far as, on the other hand, he
wills and acts for his friend's sake as for his own sake,
looking on his friend as identified with himself, thus the
beloved is in the lover.

In yet a third way, mutual indwelling in the love of

Ethic. ix. 3 and *Rhet.* ii. 4.

friendship can be understood in regard to reciprocal love: inasmuch as friends return love for love, and both desire and do good things for one another.

Reply Obj. 1. The beloved is contained in the lover, by being impressed on his heart and thus becoming the object of his complacency. On the other hand, the lover is contained in the beloved, inasmuch as the lover penetrates, so to speak, into the beloved. For nothing hinders a thing from being both container and contents in different ways: just as a genus is contained in its species, and vice versa.

Reply Obj. 2. The apprehension of the reason precedes the movement of love. Consequently, just as the reason divides, so does the movement of love penetrate into the beloved, as was explained above.

Reply Obj. 3. This argument is true of the third kind of mutual indwelling, which is not to be found in every kind of love.

THIRD ARTICLE

WHETHER ECSTASY IS AN EFFECT OF LOVE?

We proceed thus to the Third Article.

Objection 1. It would seem that ecstasy is not an effect of love. For ecstasy seems to imply loss of reason. But love does not always result in loss of reason: for lovers are masters of themselves at times. Therefore love does not cause ecstasy.

Obj. 2. Further, the lover desires the beloved to be united to him. Therefore he draws the beloved to himself, rather than betakes himself into the beloved, going forth out from himself as it were.

Obj. 3. Further, love unites the beloved to the lover,

as stated above.[1]   If, therefore, the lover goes out from himself, in order to betake himself into the beloved, it follows that the lover always loves the beloved more than himself: which is evidently false.   Therefore ecstasy is not an effect of love.

On the contrary, Dionysius says that *the divine love produces ecstasy*, and that *God Himself suffered ecstasy through love*.[2]   Since, therefore, according to the same author,[3] every love is a participated likeness of the divine love, it seems that every love causes ecstasy.

I answer that to suffer ecstasy means to be placed outside oneself.   This happens as to the apprehensive power and as to the appetitive power.   As to the apprehensive power, a man is said to be placed outside himself, when he is placed outside the knowledge proper to him.   This may be due to his being raised to a higher knowledge; thus, a man is said to suffer ecstasy, inasmuch as he is placed outside the connatural apprehension of his sense and reason, when he is raised up so as to comprehend things that surpass sense and reason: or it may be due to his being cast down into a state of debasement; thus a man may be said to suffer ecstasy, when he is overcome by violent passion or madness.   As to the appetitive power, a man is said to suffer ecstasy, when that power is borne towards something else, so that it goes forth out from itself, as it were.

The first of these ecstasies is caused by love dispositively, in so far, namely, as love makes the lover dwell on the beloved, as stated above,[4] and to dwell intently on one thing draws the mind from other things. The second ecstasy is caused by love directly; by love of friendship, simply; by love of concupiscence, not

[1] A. 1.   [2] *De Div. Nom.* iv.   [3] Ibid.   [4] A. 2.

simply but in a restricted sense. Because in love of concupiscence, the lover is carried out of himself, in a certain sense; in so far, namely, as not being satisfied with enjoying the good that he has, he seeks to enjoy something outside himself. But since he seeks to have this extrinsic good for himself, he does not go out from himself simply, and this movement remains finally within him. On the other hand, in the love of friendship, a man's affection goes out from itself simply; because he wishes and does good to his friend, by caring and providing for him, for his sake.

Reply Obj. 1. This argument is true of the first kind of ecstasy.

Reply Obj. 2. This argument applies to love of concupiscence, which, as stated above, does not cause ecstasy simply.

Reply Obj. 3. He who loves goes out from himself, in so far as he wills the good of his friend and works for it. Yet he does not will the good of his friend more than his own good: and so it does not follow that he loves another more than himself.

II. Q. xxviii, as. 1–3.

MADE AT THE
TEMPLE PRESS
LETCHWORTH

GREAT BRITAIN

EVERYMAN'S
LIBRARY

EDITED BY ERNEST RHYS

A CLASSIFIED LIST
OF THE FIRST 942 VOLUMES

In Cloth Binding
In Special Library Binding
Also Selected Volumes in Leather

EVERYMAN'S LIBRARY

CLASSIFIED LIST *of* 942 VOLS. *in* 13 SECTIONS

In each section of this list the volumes are arranged, as a general rule, alphabetically under the authors' names. Where authors appear in more than one section, a reference is given, viz.: (See also FICTION). The number at the end of each item is the number of the volume in the series.

Volumes obtainable in Leather are marked L

BIOGRAPHY

Audubon the Naturalist, Life and Adventures of. By R. Buchanan. 601

Baxter (Richard), Autobiography of. Edited by Rev. J. M. Lloyd Thomas. 868

Beaconsfield (Lord), Life of. By J. A. Froude. 666

Berlioz (Hector), Life of. Translated by Katherine F. Boult. 602

Blackwell (Dr Elizabeth): Pioneer Work for Women. With an Introduction by Mrs Fawcett. 667

L Boswell's Life of Johnson. 2 vols. 1–2
  (See also TRAVEL)

Browning (Robert), Life of. By E. Dowden. 701

Buxton (Sir Thomas Fowell), Memoirs of. Edited by Charles Buxton. Introduction by Lord Buxton. 773

L Byron's Letters. Introduction by André Maurois. 931

Carey (William), Life of: Shoemaker and Missionary. 395

Carlyle's Letters, and Speeches of Cromwell. 3 vols. 266–8

  „ Reminiscences. 875
  (See also ESSAYS *and* HISTORY)

L Cellini's (Benvenuto) Autobiography. 51

Cibber's (Colley) An Apology for his Life. 668

Constable (John), Memoirs of. By C. R. Leslie, R.A. 563

Cowper (William), Selected Letters of. Intro. by W. Hadley, M.A. 774
  (See also POETRY *and* DRAMA)

De Quincey's Reminiscences of the Lake Poets. Intro. by E. Rhys. 163
  (See also ESSAYS)

De Retz (Cardinal): Memoirs. By Himself. 2 vols. 735–6

Evelyn's Diary. 2 vols. Introduction by G. W. E. Russell. 220–1

Forster's Life of Dickens. Intro. by G. K. Chesterton. 2 vols. 781–2
  (See also FICTION)

Fox (George), Journal of. Text revised by Norman Penney, F.S.A. Introduction by Rufus M. Jones, LL.D. 754

Franklin's (Benjamin) Autobiography. 316

Froude's Life of Benjamin Disraeli, Earl of Beaconsfield. 666

L Gaskell's (Mrs) Life of Charlotte Brontë. Intro. by May Sinclair. **318**

Gibbon (Edward), Autobiography of. Intro. by Oliphant Smeaton. **511**
  (See also HISTORY)

Gladstone, Life of. By G. W. E. Russell ('Onlooker'). 661

Hastings (Warren), Life of. By Capt. L. J. Trotter. 452

Helps' (Sir Arthur) Life of Columbus. 332

Hodson, of Hodson's Horse. By Capt. L. J. Trotter. 401

Holmes' Life of Mozart. Introduction by Ernest Newman. 564

Houghton's Life and Letters of Keats. Introduction by Robert Lynd. 801

Hutchinson (Col.) Memoirs of. Intro. Monograph by F. P. G. Guizot. 317

Irving's Life of Mahomet. Introduction by Professor E. V. Arnold. 513

Johnson's Lives of the Poets. Intro. by Mrs Archer-Hind, M.A. 770–1

Lamb (Charles), Letters of. 2 vols. 342–3
  (See also ESSAYS *and* FOR YOUNG PEOPLE)

Lewes' Life of Goethe. Introduction by Havelock Ellis. 269

Lincoln (Abraham), Life of. By Henry Bryan Binns. 783
  (See also ORATORY)

Lockhart's Life of Robert Burns. Introduction by E. Rhys. 156

L „ Life of Napoleon. 3

  „ Life of Sir Walter Scott (abridged). 55

Mazzini, Life of. By Bolton King, M.A. 562   [Newcastle. 722

Newcastle (First Duke of), Life of, and other writings by the Duchess of

Outram (Sir J.), The Bayard of India. By Capt. L. J. Trotter. 396

BIOGRAPHY—continued

CLASSICAL

ESSAYS AND BELLES-LETTRES

FICTION—*continued*

FICTION—continued

FICTION—*continued*

HISTORY

POETRY AND DRAMA—*continued*

REFERENCE

ROMANCE

SCIENCE

SCIENCE—continued

TRAVEL AND TOPOGRAPHY

FOR YOUNG PEOPLE

FOR YOUNG PEOPLE—*continued*

PUBLISHERS:

J. M. DENT & SONS LTD
ALDINE HOUSE · BEDFORD STREET
LONDON W.C.2

E. P. DUTTON & COMPANY INC.
286–302 FOURTH AVENUE
NEW YORK

Made in Great Britain at The Temple Press, Letchworth, Herts   (L 347)

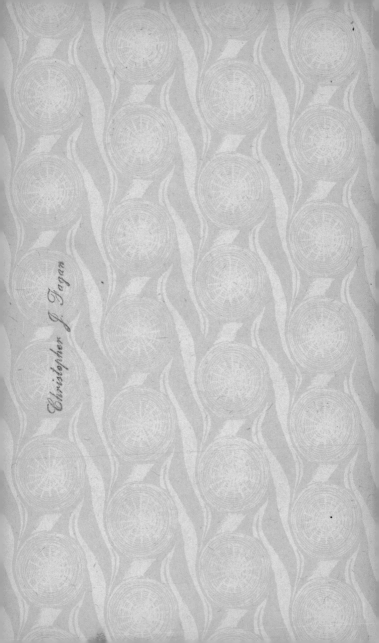